SHARON
AN ISRAELI CAESAR

SHARON

AN ISRAELI CAESAR

by Uzi Benziman

ADAMA BOOKS
NEW YORK

Translated by Louis Rousso

Copyright © 1985
Adam Publishers (1985) Ltd., Tel Aviv

Computerized typography, including automatic pagination, by M. Rachlin Printing

Library of Congress Cataloging-in-Publication Data
Benziman, Uzi, 1941–
Sharon, an Israeli caesar
1. Sharon, Ariel. 2. Israel – History, Military. 3. Israel – Politics and government. 4. Generals – Israel – Biography. 5. Israel – Armed forces – Biography. 6. Cabinet, Officers – Israel – Biography. I. Title.
DS119.2.B48 1985   965.94'05'0924   85–13461
ISBN 0–915361–23–X

Adama Books, 306 West 38 street, New York, NY 10018

Printed in Israel

To my children
Naama, Yotam, Reuma and Yuval

PREFACE

This book was written without the cooperation of its hero. For reasons best known to him, Ariel Sharon refused to have anything to do with it. Still, I believe I have done my best to portray him fairly, on the basis of the thousands of facts and details amassed and sifted in the course of three years. But Sharon wasn't the only one to refuse to cooperate: many of the people who worked in close proximity with him over the years rejected my overtures. While Sharon's reticence is, perhaps, understandable – he may be at work on an autobiography or wary of my approach – that of the others is suspect. Most left me with the impression that they were, in some way, afraid. Strange as this may sound, it happens to be true: Arik Sharon intimidates people. This pervasive fear, then, is a fact in itself.

Many, indeed, refused to help, but not all. One hundred and twelve people lent me documents, shared with me recollections and offered written and oral testimony to the stormy career and stormy character of our protagonist. For the most, they asked to remain anonymous. I would like to thank them for their cooperation, perhaps even for their courage.

The idea for the book came from my editor, Yehuda Melzer. The first draft was ready in the spring of 1982 and did not include Chapter 14, on the war in Lebanon, although, to be sure, shades of the future are foreshadowed in an assessment made, at the end of Chapter 13, on his likely behavior as Minister of Defense. Circumstances took me to the United States for two years from July 1982 to July 1984 (a sabbatical and an assignment from my paper, *Ha'aretz*), during which time, two research assistants, Yehoshua (Shuki) Yashuv and Michael (Mike) Levin, gathered more material for me on Arik. I would like to to take this opportunity to express my gratitude to them for their diligence and dedication. I would also like to thank Yehudit Shargal who completed the research at the beginning of 1985. And last but certainly not least, I am most grateful to Yehuda Melzer for his unlimited patience and his unswerving faith in the book.

Daniel Defoe once said something to the effect that the writer should provide pleasure and a public service to his readers. When the writer is a journalist and he is writing an unauthorized biography, the order should be reversed: he should provide a public service and please his readers. That at least is my modest intention.

Uzi Benziman
Jerusalem, October 1985

CHAPTER 1

The sounds outside her cabin were unmistakable, and Vera Scheinerman acted quickly. With one hand she grabbed her young daughter, Dita, and with the other she rummaged through the blankets in the crib and pulled out her infant son, Arik. Clutching the children, she kicked open the door and fled into the cold night, dashing to a small barn in the center of the village. She laid her young charges on a mound of hay and huddled beside them. Soon there were makeshift beds all around her. Kfar Malal was preparing to defend itself against attack by Bedouins of the Abu Kishak tribe assisted by Arabs from the surrounding communities of Kalkilya and Tul Karem. Outside the barns, in the center of the village, the men patrolled with rifles, and on the outer perimeter of the village the guards waited in tense silence for the coming attack. Safe for the time being in their sanctuaries, the women listened in fear for the first sounds of the attack.

The attack of the Abu Kishak was part of what became known as "the riots" or "the disturbances of 1929." In August of that year, Arab gangs, living in close proximity to their Jewish neighbors, attacked Jewish settlements, killing a relatively large number of people. The pretext for the disturbances was the Moslem-Arab claim that Jewish prayer at the Wailing Wall was an infringement of Moslem religious interests. Moslem tradition holds that the Prophet Mohammed ascended to heaven on a horse from the Temple Mount, and the site is considered the third most sacred place for Islam. Jewish prayer so close by was construed as a defilement.

But that was a pretext and nothing more. From the turn of the twentieth century, with the beginning of Zionist settlement in Palestine, national frictions grew between the Jews and the Palestinian Arabs. At first, the conflict took the form of criminal assaults on Jews and on Jewish property by Arab marauders. But with the growth and expansion of immigration and Jewish settlement, it acquired the characteristics of a national conflict.

By the end of the First World War, Britain received a mandate over Palestine, replacing previous Ottoman rule, and by promising "to view with favor" the establishment of a Jewish National Home in Palestine brought about an intensification of Arab restiveness. In 1920 there were Arab riots against the Jews in Jerusalem and in the Galilee. The Jews had no defense force except for a watchmen's association which had been organized ten years before, and which was incapable of responding adequately to Arab assaults. There were some Jewish units within the British army, but they were prohibited from assisting the settlers. The 1920 riots were repeated in 1921, and at that point the Jewish community in Palestine resolved to organize a country-wide defense force, whether the British approved or not.

The decision was only partially implemented, for two reasons. First of all, the following years were fairly tranquil; secondly, the British High Commissioner, Sir Herbert Samuel, was sympathetic to the Zionist idea and did his best to appease the Arabs, as did his successor, Lord Plumer. But this relative quiet was breached in August 1929, just a few months after John Chancellor became high commissioner. The disturbances began in Jerusalem and spread to all parts of the country. Only a few hundred members of the Jewish defense organization stood between the Jewish settlers and the thousands of Arab assailants. The members of Kfar Malal organized their own defense in preparation for the attack of the Abu Kishak.

For years Vera Scheinerman carried the bitter memory of the

events of that August night in 1929, an almost palpable memory of the prickly hay, the pungent odor of the cows and their sour fodder, and the fear and innocence on the faces of the children. That dark night was inextricably tied to another memory, one she carried with her for seven years after landing in Israel: .a very tall Arab was standing in the small boat used to carry passengers to shore. As she later recalled, two thick arms reached out from that huge boatman. His hands circled her hips and lifted her high in the air as he took her down from the ship to his waiting dinghy. Vera screamed in panic to her husband Samuel, who stood indifferently in line waiting his turn to leave the ship. Vera could not overcome the fear Arabs seemed to instill in her. Through her stories and recollections, this feeling remained a part of her legacy to her children.

That fateful night in August 1929 passed quietly. The residents of Kfar Malal were fortunate that the violent events, which so marred the period, by-passed them. But the tension and fear remained.

Seven years earlier, in February 1922, Vera and Samuel had boarded the ship that was to take them to Israel at the Russian port of Baku on the Black Sea, near the Turkish border. They were fleeing the Soviet security forces who were rampaging through the Georgian capitol of Tiflis. For Samuel, this was the beginning of a long period of adjustment, a period of misgiving and misery.

Vera Shneirov had not been a Zionist. Born to a wealthy family in Mohilev in White Russia (Byelorussia), she understood the whole concept of the "Land of Israel" as some abstract religious vision. Vera had gone to Tiflis to study medicine and was in her fourth year of studies when she met Samuel Scheinerman. This overly serious young man won her with his inner strength and overpowering self-confidence. Samuel Scheinerman was definitely a Zionist and, in fact, was very active in the Zionist movement. He had arrived in Tiflis from Brest-Litovsk and was studying agronomy to prepare himself for his expected occupation in Israel. At the beginning of the century, when he was only a child, Samuel's family had emigrated to Israel. His father, Mordecai Scheinerman, a

Hebrew teacher in Brest-Litovsk, had settled the family in the town of Rehovot, where he made every effort to put down roots and establish the family in their new home. He was unsuccessful, though, as the young children and his wife could not stand up to the hardships of their existence in a hot and difficult land. The family returned to Russia, but Samuel knew that someday he would settle in Israel.

Samuel had fled to Tiflis from the turbulence surrounding Brest-Litovsk during the First World War. In Tiflis he became one of the leaders of the Zionist movement and led the "Workers of Zion" (Poalei Zion) party, maintaining the tradition of his father, who had been a delegate to the World Zionist Congress in Switzerland. His Zionist activities actually forced him to emigrate to Israel. Communist activists at the time were particularly virulent in their opposition to "separatist" student organizations, of which the most prominent was the Zionist. One day, in February 1922, the activists surrounded the Zionist club in Tiflis where Samuel taught Hebrew. All the Jewish students were arrested and exiled to Siberia, but, by chance, Samuel was late for class that day. When he found out what had happened, he fled with his wife to the port of Baku, where they waited for the first ship to Israel. Vera and Samuel arrived at the port of Jaffa with very little in the way of personal belongings, but with a Caucasian knife and a violin.

Samuel hoped to put down roots in Israel. Vera dreamed of returning to Russia. When it became apparent that his training in agronomy would have little relevance in Israel, Samuel did not hesitate to enroll at the agricultural school at Mikveh Israel. Vera was unhappy. She longed for her family and her life in Russia. Many years later, Vera recalled that Samuel had converted her to Zionism by force.

Samuel wanted to become an active part of the renewal of the Land of Israel by working and living from the land. After completing his studies at the agricultural school, he turned down all offers to join a kibbutz, with its collective social and economic organization, and opted instead to join a young moshav. Here he hoped to preserve something of his private life, while working the land. Samuel and Vera selected Moshav Ein

Hai, south of the town of Petah Tikvah. Vera, in particular, liked this choice because it held out the hope of allowing her to reconstruct something of the life she had led in Russia. The moshav was not too far from Tel Aviv, and Vera hoped that this proximity would allow her and Samuel to savor, on occasion, some of the special pleasures of city life that they had regularly enjoyed in Russia.

But the exigencies of their existence on the moshav were stronger, and Vera bent to the overpowering will of her husband and his chosen way of life. Farming the land on the moshav, which soon changed its name to Kfar Malal, demanded an almost complete enslavement to the needs of agriculture. There were few options. Vera and Samuel committed themselves fully to the land. Their hopes of recreating the life of culture they had led in Russia gradually faded. Despite this, Vera and Samuel continued to see themselves as people of education and culture who could still delight in the pleasures of art and literature. It was this perception of themselves which, in large measure, shaped their relationship to the other members of the moshav, the very people with whom they were to spend the rest of their lives.

The plot of land given them was criss-crossed with mounds and trenches, vestiges of the First World War. Despite the fact that the land had been purchased from a local Arab some time ago, a group of Bedouins from a local tribe were camped on this small plot. In the center stood a dilapidated tent surrounded by a thick growth of weeds and brambles. Vera and Samuel required the assistance of the authorities to remove the Bedouins and secure possession of the land. They were provided with a small budget to build a home, but Samuel, never very handy, built a cabin whose defects were all too obvious. Samuel was no more successful in agriculture during his first years on the moshav. The Russian agronomist refused to follow the accepted agricultural practices of planting crops with a high probability of success. Instead, he chose to conduct various agricultural experiments, none of which proved successful. It was not long before Samuel Scheinerman had developed a reputation as a failure.

The loose boards on the Scheinerman cottage and Samuel's eccentricities as a farmer provided further cause for their basic alienation from the other members of the moshav. Samuel referred to himself as "Agronomist Scheinerman" and expected others to address him that way. The residents of Kfar Malal, simple farmers toughened by their way of life, refused this request. As they saw it, the moshav denoted a society of equality and fraternity that did not allow for such distinctions among its members. Scheinerman's notions were foreign to this society. They viewed this agronomist from Russia as arrogant and vain, attempting to introduce unacceptable standards of behavior. The refusal to address Samuel as Agronomist Scheinerman was only the external manifestation of the deepening gap that existed between Samuel and Vera and the other members of the moshav.

If Samuel could not impose his way of life on Kfar Malal, he was at least determined to preserve it within the confines of his own home. This tall, husky man zealously guarded his privacy and pursued his own goals with a fierce tenacity. He certainly raised his family and his crops with a flare for the unique. He planted avocado, cotton and tangerines and refused to consider planting the more traditional crops like alfalfa or other grains. He also refused to market his produce through the normal marketing channels of the moshav. He became further entangled with the moshav when an insurance case came up before the courts between a hired agricultural worker and the moshav's insurance company. When pressured by the moshav not to testify on behalf of the worker, he once again declined to accept collective authority. He was the first member to build a fence around his home, and even planted a grove of trees between his home and the main road, in order to insulate himself even further. However, ultimately the main reason for the tension between the Scheinermans and their neighbors was the result of a serious difference of opinion regarding the relationship between the freedom of the individual and his obligations to the community. In Israel at the time, there was a deep sense of communal solidarity and a clear and unquestioned willingness on the part of the individual to make personal sacrifices for the common good. Samuel and Vera, who supported her husband in every respect, maintained that their membership in the moshav did not obligate them to forego their criticism, or to overlook the wrongs and blunders of the public establishment. It most certainly did not obligate them to accept, quietly and resignedly, decisions which clearly infringed on their own rights. Samuel and Vera found themselves, on a number of occasions, in a very small minority on the moshav, as they fought to maintain their individuality.

Vera identified completely with her husband and, in her own way, worked to realize his views, even if it meant breaking the law. Every moshav member had been granted a plot of about twenty acres for their farming; however, various national organizations responsible for the new settlements had been appropriating portions of these plots, and parts of the land originally allotted to Kfar Malal were now being transferred to other new settlements being established in the same general area. In a vote among the members on the issue, they all supported the national authorities – all except Vera and Samuel.

One night, while Samuel was away in Tel Aviv, Vera went out to the family vineyard with a rifle and shears. A few days earlier a fence had been erected in the center of this section to mark its transferral to the newly created neighboring settlement, Ramot Hashavim. Dressed warmly and wearing heavy boots, she ran out to the vineyard from her cottage and, with the shears, she cut the fence all over and ran back home. The following morning, the members of both Kfar Malal and Ramot Hashavim discovered the damage and immediately suspected an Arab from the Abu Kishak tribe of the vandalism. He was turned over to the British police, the ruling authority in Israel at the time. When Samuel returned home, Vera told him what had happened; he reacted in anger, making it clear to her that she could go to prison for her crime. Vera responded self-righteously, claiming that she was justified because the moshav had no right to appropriate the land, even if the decision was made by a majority. She was perfectly willing to go to prison for her action. They confided the truth to the contractor who had originally constructed the fence and admonished him to rebuild it, but without including their vineyard in the portion to be transferred to Ramot Hashavim. The contractor complied with their request, but he also informed the leaders of Kfar Malal of the conversation and of Vera's confession. The leaders decided not to report Vera to the authorities, but their aversion to the Scheinermans became an irrevocable fact.

Ariel (Arik) was born in 1928 into a family (his parents Vera and Samuel and his two-year-old sister, Yehudit) that lived in isolation and alienation. At the age of three, Arik fell while playing and gashed open his chin. His mother lifted him up and ran over two miles to the office of a Russian doctor in the town of Kfar Sava, preferring the distant Russian to the doctor in Kfar Malal. Many years later, Arik could still remember the picture of his mother in her blood-stained dress, holding her son so that the doctor could stitch his chin. His mother's concern and exhaustion after the long run became irrefutable evidence to Arik of the antagonism of the members of Kfar Malal for his family.

As he grew up, this feeling intensified. He learned that his parents took turns guarding their agricultural produce against the possible vandalism of their neighbors. Even at night his parents would keep watch on the fruit trees they had planted. He came to understand that there was an interminable dispute between his family and the rest of the moshav on the basic questions of the economic foundation of the moshav and its social framework. He, too, personally, felt this enmity, as the hostility of the parents was transmitted to their children.

Arik came to realize that the children of the moshav were afraid of his father and avoided him, for Samuel had developed a reputation as a bitter, irascible man. The children had heard about his ill-temper and sharp tongue, and they were warned to keep clear of his violent outbursts of rage. Arik was only six years old when his father armed him with a club and ordered him to search for the youngsters who had dared to pick fruit from Samuel's garden. From then on, Arik went around with an oversized club, either to protect himself from the jackals that roamed the area, or to give himself a sense of security in the face of intimidation by the other children.

Arik did not play a central role in the life of the community; in fact, he barely had a part in any aspect of the social life of the youth. He sought their companionship and would go out to the clearing in the woods where they would gather daily to play ball, but he was always among the last to be chosen. He was no more successful in the other games and activities. Arik grew up in the shadow of his father.

Samuel Scheinerman was a strict father who demanded absolute obedience. The young Arik received an almost tyrannical education at home: one of prohibitions, orders and corporal punishment, but it taught him to honor and obey the will of his father. He learned to respect and protect the family property, to be satisfied with very little and to believe in his parents' perspective in their quarrels with the moshav. Samuel was often away from the moshav, seeking employment as an agricultural instructor, and Arik relished these brief respites from the rigors of discipline. The family was poor and Arik had to learn to manage with what there was. Vera prepared their meals from whatever they raised on their land, and for extended periods of time, Arik would eat only dishes prepared from peanuts and yams. It was this meager diet which apparently played a role in developing his appetite for large quantities of rich food, the effects of which are very apparent in the portly gourmand of today. Even as a child, despite the poor diet, Arik was chubby, and his broad hips and large thighs were the subject of much ridicule among the children. His friends nicknamed him "bull," and even he would often make jokes about his own girth.

Samuel was not just a demanding father, but also a man of faith and intellectual bearing who strove to impart to his two children the principles that formed such a vital part of his life. At a young age, Arik heard his father speaking and reading Latin. He was privy to the unending fights and arguments between his parents and the moshav, but he was also aware of his parents' overwhelming concern for the education of their children. In complete contrast to the practice of the moshav, Samuel hired a private tutor for his son. The boy was an average student who had no particular difficulty with his studies, but

Samuel wanted to provide him with every possible advantage in
pursuing a university education. Arik knew his father to be a
foulmouthed disputer with anyone who displeased him, as well
as a man who sent him to the well-known violinist, Borochov, to
study violin. And just as he was witness, on more than one
occasion, to beatings given by his father to children who stole
fruit, he was also witness to his father contemplating a picture in
their home which depicted a pogrom, beseeching his son, "this
must never be allowed to happen again." Samuel was irritable
and often even frightening, but he was also a man of vision and
principles who forged his own way of life. His intransigence, his
haughtiness, his ridicule of his neighbors and his narrow-minded
belief that everyone else was wrong in their conflicts with him,
did not diminish his very real originality, his determination, and
his pioneering approach to agriculture. He raised peanuts,
avocado and cotton well before they became important crops in
Israel. Arik held his father in awe, but also in the highest
esteem.

Arik Scheinerman's world was created in his parents' home.
His mother's memory of the Arab boatman in Jaffa and of the
perils that hung over Kfar Malal during the rioting of 1929
merged with Arik's own childhood experiences and were fused
by the abiding threat to the moshav from its Arab neighbors.
The children of Kfar Malal, as those of the other moshavim and
kibbutzim, were born into a world of persistent danger of attack
by the Arabs, where every person had to be ready to defend
himself. Arms were found in every home. From his earliest
years, Arik imbibed a yearning for national independence, for
the redemption of the land from the foreigners who then
controlled it. The need to be prepared at all times to meet any
outside threat complemented the comprehensive credo that
Samuel passed on to his son. Its imperatives were
resourcefulness, steadfastness, frugality in times of hardship and
mastering the secret of survival.

Arik saw that his father was indifferent to either the means or
the price required to achieve his goals. He quarrelled with his
entire community, even resorting to violence if necessary; he
was willing to lower his standard of living and suffer the

attendant hardships; and he would abandon his fields if he felt the crops would not be successful and go, instead, to seek employment in other villages, even if this meant going as far as Turkey, from where he would send money back to support Vera and their two children.

From his father Arik learned the virtues of persistence and the benefits of perseverance. For years, Samuel was the object of ridicule on the moshav because of his adventurous ideas on agriculture. But the man persisted, and in the end enjoyed the fruits of the new and often original crops he had cultivated. Arik obeyed his father and followed his orders and, unlike his friends, he devoted most of his free time to work on the family farm. Arik also noted the efficacy of force. The family plot was the largest in Kfar Malal because his mother was willing to resort to force in setting its boundaries. He must also have discerned the advantages of intimidation. The dogs and fences which surrounded the Scheinerman property, like Samuel's contentiousness, may have justly earned the enmity and estrangement of their neighbors, but they certainly served the family well in protecting their property. He grew up convinced of the injustice of the moshav to his family and of the need to fight for their rights. Arik's identification with his parents was complete.

Samuel's influence was just as strong on the other members of the family. Vera completely subordinated her own will to that of her husband, and his opinions became hers. Arik's older sister, Dita, also grew up in the shadow of her father's dominating personality. She was a shy, introverted girl whose whole life was spent in the home. She even deferred to her parents in her selection of a husband.

At the age of ten, Arik joined the Labor Youth Movement. The group leader, Yoske Golobov, was surprised to discover that Arik attended the group's activities holding a club. Arik hit the other children over the head to make them quiet and orderly, believing that this was what the leader wanted. Golobov understood that Arik was only trying to befriend him. Still, he ordered him never to use the club at the meetings. Arik obeyed the leader's orders, but he still carried the club.

There was no improvement in Arik's social standing in grammar school. He continued to be regarded as a lackluster child, and was excluded from most social activities. The parents and children ostracized him for being the Scheinerman's son, while his own parents continued to make special demands of him. Arik and his sister were set apart from the others in many ways. For instance, most of the children worked on their family farms, and after grade school they assumed even larger full-time responsibilities. Very few continued their studies, even in agricultural programs. But Arik was registered in an academic high school in Tel Aviv. He acquiesced to his parents' decision and adjusted his life accordingly. Every morning he began his day at dawn. First he tended to his chores on the family farm, and then took the bus to Tel Aviv, walking a full hour from the bus stop to school. At the end of the day, he did his evening chores and then his homework. Samuel was willing to bear the financial burden of sending his son to the high school. He didn't care about his son's social isolation.

Arik's military career started in the Gadna, a para-military high-school organization. After completing a course for instructors at kibbutz Ruhama in the Negev, Arik became a Gadna instructor at the Mossinsohn Agricultural School.

The Gadna provided Arik with his first real taste of the military, though this was preceded by his formal enlistment in the Haganah, the mainstream underground organization in pre-Independence Israel and the precursor of the IDF (Israel Defense Forces, the official name of the Israeli armed forces). In their mid-teens, the youths of Kfar Malal were summoned one by one and, in the middle of the night, stole their way to the cottage of Bella Altbach, which served as the local headquarters of the Haganah. They went there by roundabout routes, entering the house under the cover of darkness and, placing their hands on a pistol, they swore their allegiance to the Haganah and vowed to obey all commands.

By this time the Haganah was a first-rate country-wide military organization, with units in all of the Jewish settlements in town and country. During that same period, when Arik joined the Haganah, it was clear to the country's leaders that they had to prepare for a major war: the Arab countries would never agree to the emergence of the Jewish state.

Later, Arik recalled that his father made him promise never to participate in any action designed to turn over other Jews to the British Mandate authorities. Nevertheless, Arik, together with other Haganah members, clashed with members of the dissident underground groups, Etzel (also known as the Irgun, the underground of the Revisionist Movement) and Lehi (also known as the Stern Gang, an extreme splinter group).

Arik's talents for fighting quickly became apparent in the course for Gadna instructors. He is remembered as being particularly vicious in the hand-to-hand combat which was part of the training. His isolation continued to attract attention; he remained a loner and rarely took part in the social events. Yet, during the course, his special skills, unrecognized until then, began to become apparent. Micah Almog, the commander of the course, recalls that Arik never used the prepared lessons, preferring to teach the material his own way. Arik also had a natural talent for navigation, especially during the nighttime field maneuvers. Just as there were those who shied away from him because of his excessive violence during their exercises with ersatz bayonets, the trainees tried to join him during the patrols and field exercises.

At one point during the course, Almog asked Arik to transfer pistols from one settlement to another. At the time, possession of weapons was deemed a very serious crime by the British authorities, and Arik refused, claiming the risk of discovery by the British police was too high. Almog did not press the issue and gave the assignment, instead, to another instructor. He felt instructors should not be forced to complete this type of assignment. He was certain that Arik's response had nothing to do with cowardice or even fear, but was, rather, the result of the particular mood he was in at the time. Arik was very much a loner given to drastically varying moods, like his father's. After Gadna, Arik joined the Supernumerary Police (he'd finished high school by then). This entailed taking an oath of loyalty to the British government.

Shortly thereafter, the UN General Assembly passed a

resolution partitioning Israel into a Jewish state and an Arab state. A wave of exultation swept over the entire Jewish community of Israel, and Kfar Malal was no exception. But of all the revelers on the moshav that evening, it was Arik Scheinerman who stood out. He burst into the home of his friend, Oded Zalmanson, and threw in a detonator to rouse him from his sleep when he didn't come out fast enough. He marched along the central road of the moshav, cheering and carousing, singing and firing into the air. To his neighbors' surprise, Arik appeared happy and good-natured, taking part in all the celebrations.

At his father's request, Arik registered at the Hebrew University's extension in Rehovot, to study agriculture, but the mounting tension as the British Mandate drew to a close foiled Samuel Scheinerman's plans for his son. Arik turned to the infantry in the Haganah and abandoned his role as an instructor in the Gadna. He was placed in charge of a squad assigned to lay traps for the Bedouins of the Abu Kishak tribe. Squad members noted his natural sense of orientation in the field and his composure and self-control in the toughest situations. They accepted his leadership without question. The War of Independence put an end to Samuel's dream of having his son follow in his footsteps. When the Haganah rallied its members to enlist, Arik joined the Alexandroni Brigade.

CHAPTER 2

The actual outbreak of the War of Independence brought little change to either Kfar Malal or to Arik Scheinerman. The tension remained high and was strained even further by each report that bands of Arabs were planning to attack the moshav and surrounding communities. Reprisals and preemptive strikes were initiated by the Haganah to disrupt the Arab attackers. Defense preparations continued apace, and fortifications were constructed in all the Jewish settlements. Arik Scheinerman's activities continued: laying ambushes for Arab vehicles, stalking Arabs suspected of planning attacks, and defending Jewish settlements in the Sharon coastal plain. The major difference between the period prior to the war and the months immediately following its outbreak was organizational. The military infrastructure organized by the Haganah in the Sharon plain during the latter part of the British mandate had become a brigade within the framework of the newly formed army of the State of Israel. The Haganah unit commanded by Arik Scheinerman was reconstituted as a platoon in the Alexandroni Brigade of the Israel Defense Forces (IDF).

It quickly became apparent, both to his soldiers and to his commanding officers, that beneath the severe countenance and bashful reticence, Arik Scheinerman was an extremely daring and courageous soldier. The son of Samuel Scheinerman bore a striking resemblance to his father. He too was irascible and belligerent, haughty and remote. Indeed, much as Samuel's jarring manner hid a different nature, one of vision, resolution, erudition and love of country, Arik, too, hid his true personality behind a sullen demeanor. Arik Scheinerman was a true fighter. The battlefield was the primary arena of his creativity and it was here that his personality developed.

This taciturn young man behaved strangely, with odd quirks and changing moods, but he radiated a positive sense of leadership. Though aggressive and sometimes even violent during training, he nevertheless instilled confidence, especially during the night exercises. Soldiers liked to serve with him during the raids and ambushes. He combined daring with complete control, seeking direct contact with the enemy with tactics and leadership that brought him the respect of all his soldiers. These small raids and ambushes, undertaken in the Sharon valley during 1947, earned him the reputation of a soldier who put fear into the Arabs.

This reputation continued to grow with the outbreak of the War of Independence. The patrols and raids conducted by Arik's platoon were all successful. Moshe Lancet, a fellow platoon commander in the same brigade, describes the events of the night he came to understand Scheinerman's skill. Lancet set out with his platoon to intercept a group of Arab infiltrators who were hiding by a well near Kfar Sava. Arik volunteered to join Lancet's platoon. As they approached the well, Lancet began to deploy his forces in textbook fashion. He split his platoon into three groups: one was deployed in the breach, the second on the flank, while the third was held back as reinforcement. The platoon was spotted by the Arabs who opened fire. Lancet hesitated, considering what action to take in the face of this unexpected development, but Arik did not let him consider very long.

"Moshik, what the hell are you waiting for? Attack!"

"But how?"

"Simple. Take your soldiers and charge!"

Lancet took this advice and the mission was successful. Arik's response was instinctive and typified his style of command, showing Lancet the source of Arik's charisma and success as a commander.

Scheinerman had a natural talent for reading the battle quickly and accurately and for exploiting the terrain to maximize his advantage. In contrast with the complicated and overly cautious tactics of the older commanders, Arik preferred the bold frontal attack. His decisive action in combat earned him the respect of his soldiers and motivated them to follow him faithfully. He molded his troops into a highly disciplined unit. Arik's skills and the discipline of his platoon quickly attracted the attention of the senior officers of the Alexandroni Brigade, and the number of raids assigned to him and his platoon increased rapidly.

Arik had turned to a military career after completing high school, not as someone fulfilling some long-held ambition, but rather to meet his unquestioned obligation. He was in this respect a typical Israeli youth, raised to seek the independence of his people and, if necessary, to fight for it. The events encompassing the end of the British Mandate and the Declaration of Independence fixed his path to the military.

Arik's involvement in military life, in the pre-army Gadna youth corps as well as in the Alexandroni Brigade, had kindled a spark that had been stifled until then. The aggression that had been seething within him since childhood could be legitimately released on the battlefield. He probably harbored a secret dream of being a hero admired by those around him. He undoubtedly entered the battlefield with a sense of loneliness and alienation, with a feeling of incessant threat and relentless grievance, but with strict discipline and a stubbornness that had been his birthright.

The military proved to be his natural milieu. In the years to come his talents as a soldier developed. Ultimately these early years in the army became the dominant experience of his life. The military was not only an occupation for him, but an entire way of life, where he could give expression to all his skills, drives and desires. The military provided Arik Scheinerman a framework for shaping his entire personality. He himself once said that his personality was a reflection of inherited traits and childhood memories. Indeed, the self-righteousness, determination, patriotism and the belief in the use of force to achieve justified ends – all part of the prevailing climate during Arik's childhood – left their mark on Arik and found renewed expression during his early years on the battlefield.

When the Alexandroni Brigade was called on to participate in "Operation Bin-Nun" to capture Latroun police headquarters from the Jordanian Legion, it was only natural that Arik would play a key role. And so, when Arik returned from his briefing at brigade staff, he proudly and happily informed his troops, "We're going to be the point platoon for the company!"

The capture of Latroun had very high priority for the prime minister, David Ben Gurion, and for the General Staff, who were anxious to maintain open channels of communication with Jerusalem. The city had been under siege since the beginning of hostilities and had to be given every possible assistance in order to hold out and assure its remaining an integral part of the Jewish state. Ben Gurion realized that if Jerusalem fell or were even cut off from the rest of the country, the effects would be disastrous: loss of the capital would symbolize Israel's vulnerability, perhaps even its transience. He pressed the general staff to capture the police station at Latroun which would then give them control over the road to Jerusalem.

The news was well-received. The soldiers knew they were being given a major role in one of the most important missions of the war: breaking through to the Jerusalem road and liberating the city from the Jordanian siege. Their young commander, with a stubborn cowlick and his left arm in a cast as a result of an earlier accident, inspired them. They had camped near Kibbutz Hulda, and all around them impressive preparations were being made. Buses arrived discharging hundreds of soldiers, armored units drove back and forth, and the field mortar units bustled with activity. To the soldiers of Arik's unit, the First Platoon, it was obvious that they were going to take part in a major battle, well supported in logistics and ordinance. As they boarded the buses for the trip from Hulda to the front, spirits were high.

Only a few hours later, the picture was completely reversed.

Dawn of May 24, 1948 found Arik on a rocky hillside opposite Latroun, while around him lay his men. Many were wounded. Arik understood that the attack had been upset and, in fact, that the turning point had been at the very beginning of the action. Arik's unit had led the entire force – one brigade reinforced by an additional company – in its advance from Kibbutz Nahshon to the foot of the rise dominated by the Latroun police station. As they cautiously moved forward, a flare went off, lighting up the hillside. Arik instinctively hit the ground, followed by the rest of the force. They apparently had already been spotted. After a brief pause, the Israeli units continued to move forward until they had crossed the main road to Jerusalem and began to deploy around the rise of the police station. As they started taking up their positions, a hail of deadly accurate fire descended on them. The point platoon sustained the brunt of this attack, as confusion set in and the rest of the force scattered in search of cover. The advance had been halted before it began, as the first light of dawn hung on the horizon.

Blocked by the thick wall of fire directed at them by the Jordanian Legion, Asher Levi, commander of the battalion for Arik's platoon, decided to change his line of attack. He redirected his battalion to a nearby hill to evade Jordanian fire and to regroup to attack the police station from a different direction. Arik's platoon was assigned to cover the other two platoons as they made their way to the new positions. It was Levi's intention that these two units would, in their turn, provide covering fire for Arik's platoon as soon as they were out of the line of fire.

The rising sun illuminated the plight of the Israeli forces in all its grimness. The force had been shattered into small groups, each fighting for itself, as the Jordanian fire wreaked havoc among them. Its splintered remnants struggled to flee the deathly battleground. The reinforced brigade which had set out to capture Latroun had not succeeded in fighting as a cohesive unit.

On the morning of May 24, as Arik lay on the rocky hillside, he could see only a small sector of the battlefield. With a handful of men scattered over the valley, Arik covered the advance of the rest of the battalion to the adjacent hill. Not all of his men kept up with him; some were trapped, exposed to fire on the slopes of the hill. Arik directed the platoon machine gunner, behind a rock overlooking the valley, by shouting his orders. By 7:00 a.m., the First Platoon had already lost eight men, communications were cut, and attempts to maintain them by using runners had to be abandoned under the onslaught of the Jordanian fire. Advancing slowly, Levi and a part of his troops gained the adjacent hill after a fierce exchange of fire. In the course of their advance, however, a portion of the force had been cut off and the wounded were left behind. Levi had assumed that reinforcements would arrive shortly and that the wounded could then be collected and treated. Now it was the First Platoon's turn to evacuate. But it was too late. The First Platoon was completely surrounded and all attempts at providing covering fire proved futile.

Pinned down in the valley, Arik and his troops struggled to stay alive. The heat was oppressive, stoked by the fires that had been ignited by the shooting in the adjoining grain fields. Water and ammunition were running out. The wounded cried in agony for water and in desperation some were even reduced to licking grease off their guns. As the hours passed, they were enveloped by a numbing apathy. But Arik clung to his hope that the setback was only temporary. From his vantage point, he could not read the entire battle. He could not know that the brigade which his company had reinforced had been assembled only a few days prior to the battle, or that most of the soldiers were new immigrants with no combat experience or military training. Nor could he know that the promised artillery support would be so pitifully inadequate. He placed his trust in his commanding officers. On the strength of this trust, Arik continued to encourage his men.

"You'll see. We'll get out of this. We've been in tight spots before and we'll get out of this one too. Our counterattack will soon begin. Help is on the way."

He maintained his control by shouting out orders and passing on instructions to his soldiers, but as the hours passed their faith in their commander was shaken. They saw before them a bold and attractive officer who had, in the past, led them successfully through a series of raids and ambushes. But the harsh reality of the battlefield was overwhelming. Not only was his arm in a cast, he was also bloody from a bullet wound that had gouged his thigh and his stomach. He reminded them of their successful missions together and exhorted them to trust in his judgement again. But what they felt was the heat and the thirst – enemy fire and mosquitoes were winning the fight. And, as time passed, Arik's efforts weakened, sapped by the despondency and exhaustion.

The afternoon turned quiet, and suddenly Arik seemed to spring back to life. He assumed that the coveted reinforcements had finally arrived and that the attack on Latroun would finally begin. He suddenly began to shout, "The fields are crawling with Arabs! Every man for himself! Get out of the wadi! Get out of the wadi!"

Arik did not know that Levi had been ordered to evacuate the field. He did not know that as the Israelis withdrew they were being pursued by the Legionnaires, who took prisoners and left many dead behind. All he could see from his position was a narrow sector of the field where the fighting subsided. Within moments, however, he grasped that he and his men were completely surrounded by hundreds of Legionnaires, covering the field in search of the wounded and their booty.

The remains of the First Platoon began to crawl westward in a frantic attempt to escape the blazing fields around Latroun. It was not an orderly retreat. Seven men were cut off from the main body of the platoon and others collapsed and entreated their comrades to leave them behind. Arik gave the order to abandon the wounded. He feared they would all be doomed if they delayed. Much later, he revealed that this was the most difficult decision of his life. It led him to formulate a cardinal rule, which became an army rule: "Never leave the wounded behind." As the platoon fled, they met stragglers from other units groping their way back over the lines. The soldiers of the First Platoon were routed; it was now every man for himself.

Yaacov Bugin was one of these men, crawling his way along a path through a burning wheat field. He had joined the First

Platoon barely three days before, and his first encounter with Arik had left him with a feeling of veneration. He felt a special need to excel in the eyes of his commander, but almost as soon as the battle began, he was wounded in the face and couldn't function. He found cover near Arik and waited for the tide of battle to turn. Bugin had been terrified that afternoon, when he heard Arik enjoining his men to run for their lives. He now found himself scrambling through the field in the direction of Hulda, when he came across the platoon machine gunner.

"Simcha, leave everything and come with us," he urged.

"Shut up and get out of here!" The machine gunner snapped back in reply.

"But the Arabs are very close by and..."

"Stop talking and get away," were the machine gunner's final words.

Yaacov Bugin continued his crawl away and as he turned to look at the machine gunner, he noticed that he was severely wounded in both legs and could not move.

All around him the field was full of Arab Legionnaires in search of booty. As he crawled forward, he came upon Arik's submachine gun, abandoned on the path. He dragged it along, thinking how pleased his commander would be with him for having retrieved the weapon. But a few minutes later he, too, abandoned the gun, too weak from his wounds to carry it any further. Continuing his retreat he heard moans just ahead of him, and as he approached he saw a wounded man sprawled across the path, bleeding profusely from the stomach. It was Arik. Bugin crawled closer and tried to encourage him, but Arik was in a stupor and just mumbled to leave him alone.

"Arik, your gun is only a few meters back," Bugin informed him somewhat proudly.

"Leave me alone! Let me be," Arik groaned. "Get out of here and save yourself!"

Bugin disregarded the order and helped Arik to his feet, and, supporting him on his shoulder, began to move forward slowly. They could hear the clamor of hundreds of Legionnaires not thirty meters from the path, but their progress remained agonizingly slow. Both were wounded and weak, and Bugin had to shift Arik from shoulder to shoulder to bear the strain. The Arabs did not notice these two feeble, bleeding men stumbling along. Time and again Arik insisted that Bugin leave him and continue alone, but the young soldier refused. Almost overcome by the torpor of their exhaustion, they foundered, but managed to steer clear of the fighting, while Arik pointed out the general direction of retreat. At times they would pause and Arik would study the area through the binoculars strung around his neck. Every fold in the terrain, every bump in the path, required an immense and painful effort. Much later Bugin recounted that neither man believed there was any chance to escape.

Further along the path of their retreat, Moshe Lancet, deputy commander of the battalion came upon them, and Arik asked him to help. As Lancet recalls, he tried to help Bugin support Arik, but Arik finally cried out, "I can't go on! Carry me."

Lancet hoisted Arik on to his back and they started off again in the direction of the evacuation point, but after a few minutes, Lancet collapsed, fainting in exhaustion. When he recovered, he went on to the evacuation point alone, promising to send them assistance. Shortly thereafter, they were picked up by an armored car. Arik asked only for water.

As he lay in Hadassah Hospital in Tel Aviv, recuperating from his wounds, Arik began to mull over the battle of Latroun and its consequences. He attests that, as he lay opposite the beds of his wounded soldiers, he began to relive the sense of helplessness that had engulfed him in the burning field, his guilt over the abandonment of the wounded, and the consuming feeling of despair as death loomed closer. His reflections, however, were subordinated by the anger and the frustration that overcame him: anger at the army's poor planning; resentment at the inadequate organization of the fighting force; indignation at the lack of intelligence about the enemy forces; frustration at the dismal defeatism of some of the soldiers. Arik felt that he and his platoon had fallen victim to mistaken judgements and blunders. The sights and sounds of that battle haunted him in the hospital and, as he put it, convinced him that the IDF must prepare itself to win every single battle against the Arab enemy.

Arik shared these sentiments with Zvi Guerman, the company commander, who visited him in the hospital. Operation Bin-Nun was indeed the IDF's most egregious failure in the War of Independence: a reinforced brigade had even failed to attack a significantly weaker Jordanian force. Instead of opening up the battle, attacking, and taking the Latroun hill, most of the fighting was devoted to rescuing the forces caught in the Jordanian gunfire. The brigade had not been properly briefed; many of the soldiers had never even held a gun; much of their equipment was defective; intelligence on the enemy forces was inaccurate; and there was a decisive delay in the start of the fighting, exposing the movement of the Israeli forces toward Latroun. The Israeli defeat was no accident. It was the direct result of dubious planning and inferior organization.

Arik recovered rapidly from his wounds and soon rejoined his company, this time in a patrol unit. Again, he witnessed another army failure: the attempted capture of the Egyptian Army stronghold at Faloujah in the Negev Dessert. On December 28, 1948 the Alexandroni Brigade was sent on a mission to break through to the Egyptian position at the fortress "Iraq El-Manshiya," but the brigade once again failed in its mission: one of the units assigned to set up a blockade completely failed, and part of one of the battalions assigned to attack the Egyptian stronghold was wiped out. Although Arik's unit played only a secondary role, it was sufficient to exacerbate his sense of anger and frustration.

With the War of Independence finally over, Arik stopped to contemplate his future. His father was once again pressing him to resume his studies, but Arik had been captivated by the army. He was now a man of twenty, and parental authority, however much respected, was not enough to move him from his path. His military record had built up his confidence in his own abilities as a fighter and as a commander. He savored the thrill of command in battle and luxuriated in the esteem of his soldiers, especially in his reputation as an uncompromising fighter. He was certain, too, of his ability to improve his own unit and contribute in a meaningful way to the IDF. He agreed to remain in the army at the entreaty of Ben-Zion Friedan, commander of the

Alexandroni Brigade. Friedan argued that it was time to reorganize the brigade, to institute an orderly training regimen, to analyze and draw conclusions from the lessons of the war, and to develop new techniques of combat. These arguments spoke directly to Arik's own experience and understanding of the war, for the bitter memories of the battles at Latroun and Faloujah aroused his ambition to contribute to the IDF and ensure that such defeats would not be repeated. His motives for remaining in uniform were not entirely altruistic. The military satisfied his deepest desires and emotional needs, bringing out his own natural abilities and enabling him to secure a position of prestige and recognition.

One of his first assignments was as commander of a battalion of new immigrants. He had been granted the rank of battalion commander, without having completed the requisite course, in testimony to the high regard his superiors had for him. Managing the cultural conflicts and disciplinary problems of the new immigrants was a difficult challenge, for these soldiers lacked the military consciousness and educational background of the young Israelis recruited at the same time. The insubordination of the new immigrants reached the point where one soldier physically threatened him. Arik could not let this affront to his leadership stand unattended. As he understood the situation, he would either have to confront the soldier directly and overcome him, or be forced to resign. He took on the recalcitrant soldier and won the fight. This installed fear and grudging respect in the other soldiers in the battalion. To tighten his control over the men, he dismissed them for weekend leave, saying that on their return, the battalion would go on a long, one-day march. He knew that a large number of them would return late to miss the march. And so, on Sunday, Arik mustered the few men who had returned on time and set out on the planned march. At the conclusion of the exercise, he dismissed the men for the night, and they rushed off for a well earned rest. At around midnight, after confirming that all the laggards had finally arrived, Arik called out the entire battalion for roll call. Those soldiers who had arrived on time and participated in the day's exercises were dismissed, while those

soldiers who had missed the march boarded a truck that had
been waiting nearby. The soldiers, bundled up in heavy winter
coats against the chill night, stared in disbelief as Arik joined
them in shorts and a t-shirt. The truck took them to a point
about ten miles from the base, where they began a tortuous run
back. Four hours later, they finally got to sleep, only to be
awakened an hour later. The combination of the gruelling
night-run and the exhaustion from lack of sleep taught the
soldiers of his battalion a lesson: Arik was not a commander to
be disobeyed.

Arik's next commission was as commander of the
reconnaissance battalion in the Alexandroni Brigade. He taught
his soldiers how to move, both in daylight and at night, and tried
to instill the confidence necessary to function properly when
alone in the field. Once again Arik was conscious of the aura of
admiration and respect surrounding him. The soldiers liked to be
near him, absorbing what they could of his knowledge and
understanding.

Organizational changes were taking place rapidly in the young
IDF and when the Alexandroni Brigade was converted to a
reserve unit, Arik took command of the reconnaissance unit of
the Golani Brigade, a brigade whose soldiers were considered
troublemakers. Arik distinguished himself here as well, not only
as a commander, but also as an officer who did not restrain from
arguing with his superiors. The brigade commander, Avraham
Yoffe, and the commander of the northern sector, Major-
General Yosef Avidar, both respected his skills and were
repeatedly willing to overlook his cantankerousness. Avidar, in
fact, apparently had such great respect for Arik's abilities and
his promise as a future military leader that he intervened
personally on at least one occasion to extricate him from a
court-martial.

In one instance, Arik was charged with disobeying a military
policeman. He had been speeding in a military jeep and ignored
the order of an MP to stop. The commander of the military
police was incensed and, together with the commander of the
manpower branch of the army, decided to press charges in a
court-martial before Major-General Avidar. Avidar was in a

dilemma. Arik was clearly guilty, and if convicted before a major-general would be sentenced to thirty days in the brig. Avidar was convinced that Arik would leave the army, a loss the IDF could not afford. He declined to preside at the court-martial, so Arik was brought to trial before lower ranking officers who did not have the authority to impose prison sentences.

Not long after, Zvi Guerman, Arik's former battalion commander in the Alexandroni Brigade, was promoted to chief of staff for the central sector and secured Arik's transfer from the northern sector, appointing him information officer. Arik immediately set about building an information network which justly earned him the praise of his superior officers. Arik joked that although he knew all the secrets of the Jordanian king's palace, he had no idea what was going on in the IDF. He left a very strong impression on all his superiors as a very ambitious, well-disciplined and highly skilled officer. He diligently fostered a strong personal relationship with the senior officers of the Central Command and visited the chief of staff at his home on a regular basis. Arik received new and challenging assignments. Any assignment given him would be well performed.

In the summer of 1950, Arik was sent to a course for battalion commanders under the direction of Yitzhak Rabin. He completed the course with honors and was assigned as information officer for the northern sector. He rapidly grew bored with the job. From his perspective, the serious weakness in the IDF was in its inability to respond adequately to the provocations of the Arab infiltrators, a feebleness that was in part, at least, the result of combat weakness. He yearned for real action, but there was little of this in the IDF at the time. He was witness to the frequent cancellations of activities planned against the Arab units that had attacked Jewish settlements; he noted the near paralysis of the units sent out to attack; and he marked the lack of fighting spirit among many of the officers. Moshe Dayan's appointment as commander of the northern sector roused his hope for change, and, indeed, Dayan's initiatives and inventiveness soon shook the entire sector out of its apathy.

On one occasion Dayan approached Arik and asked, "Do you think it would be possible to kidnap two Jordanian Legionnaires?"

"I'll check, sir." Arik responded crisply.

Arik was surprised by Dayan's interest. He knew that only a few days earlier two soldiers from the Yardeni Brigade had been kidnapped by Jordanian Legionnaires, but he never expected the government or the general staff to approve a retaliatory strike. Arik had long maintained that the only way to combat the Arab provocations was to respond with counterattacks and reprisals; however, he was aware of the government's aversion to this type of response, as well as of the IDF's limited ability to carry it out. Arik, therefore, naturally assumed that once again the government would opt to apply to the Israel-Jordan Cease-Fire Commission or to the United Nations to secure the release of the two soldiers. Was Dayan now indicating that there had been a change of policy?

That very night Arik set out together with Shlomo Gruber, one of his officers, to the Sheik Hussein Bridge on the Jordan River. Their approach to the Jordanian guardhouse was carefully planned and after learning that there were no other soldiers around, they fell upon the two sentries, easily overcoming them. At gunpoint they led the Jordanians back to the van they had left on the Israeli side of the border, and set out for their base. By dawn they had arrived at the nothern sector headquarters, and their prisoners were placed under guard. Arik waited for Dayan at his office, and when he arrived Arik reported with obvious satisfaction:

"The two Jordanian soldiers are now under guard in the brig."

Dayan did not try to conceal his surprise. Less than twenty-four hours later, his suggestion had become fact. Dayan was not accustomed to such alacrity. He praised Arik and made a mental note of the young officer's daring. Arik was overjoyed: not only had he demonstrated his own personal capability, but he had earned the public commendation of his commanding officer. He had clearly demonstrated that it was possible to operate effectively in a manner very different from what was accepted in the IDF.

Life in the northern sector, however, soon became routine again, especially after Dayan was posted to the general staff in Tel Aviv, where he was appointed commander of the operations branch of the army. Arik's disappointment and frustration with the general ability of the army deepened. He felt trammelled, unable to influence events around him, forced to submit to a defeatism completely alien to him, and to obey incorrect orders.

Arik's unease with government policy finally prompted him to take a leave of absence from the army and resume his studies. In 1952 he registered at the Hebrew University in Jerusalem, to major in history and Near Eastern studies. His plan was to complete his education and then decide whether to return to the army. Circumstances and his own temperament obviated this decision.

CHAPTER 3

Arik settled down with his young wife, Margalit, in a small apartment in the Beit Hakerem quarter of Jerusalem. The romance had been going on since they first met, while Arik was a Gadna instructor in Magdiel. Margalit was from Barshov, Transylvania. She was only 15 when they met. Her poverty-stricken family, plucking chickens for a living, stayed in Hungary. She spent her first months in Israel at a detention camp, where the British held immigrants caught stealing into the country. After her release, Margalit went to agricultural school near Kfar Malal. There, the love affair blossomed between the attractive teenager and the Gadna instructor. The affair caught everyone's attention, because romances between schoolgirls and military instructors were unusual. But everyone agreed that the two were meant for each other. He was unapproachable, ambitious, a loner who often withdrew to his own inner world and thoughts. She was an interesting, proud, intelligent, and introverted girl. The relationship between them grew increasingly serious during and immediately after the War of Independence, when she went to study nursing and he worked his way up the ranks in the army. Both were possessed of a consuming desire to succeed in their professions; both were endowed with uncommon determination. Margalit won Arik's heart because she was sensitive and yet enterprising, and able to make her own way in life. Arik won her over because he was an officer with an excellent reputation. He was a strong and forceful sabra. A liaison with him was a concrete sign of her success in adjusting to her new homeland.

At the start of the academic year in 1952, it seemed that Arik was about to settle into a contented life. He attended his classes regularly and kept very orderly notes. In the evenings he ate delicious, Hungarian meals. They were a perfect culinary match: Margalit loved to cook and Arik loved to eat. Margalit was an attractive, neat, curly-haired woman, very serious about her work as a psychiatric nurse. Arik was a diligent 25-year-old student who loved to play with his closest friend's son. He visited his parents in Kfar Malal regularly. This comfortable routine did not satisfy him though. His real skills required the battlefield, and he was drawn back to the army.

Arik derived some satisfaction from his position as a battalion commander in the Jerusalem Brigade. He arrived at the battalion with a reputation as an irregular commander, but his soldiers, including veterans of the Palmah, accepted his authority without question. Despite his very youthful appearance, he had no difficulty in imposing his leadership on the soldiers.

During regular training exercises, Arik informed his staff officers that, according to army procedures, a battalion commander was empowered to use mortars, without getting prior approval from his superior officers, in the event that he found himself in a skirmish calling for artillery support. A few days later he called his officers together to inform them that the women of the Arab village of Katama, on the way to the well for water, crossed the border in violation of Israel's territorial sovereignty. He claimed that the border was not clear and that the village residents were taking advantage of this and intentionally trespassing. To correct this situation, Arik ordered that an ambush be set up to fire on the women. The battalion's mortar unit was ordered to be ready, should Jordanian units fire. Arik ordered his officers to keep quiet about these preparations.

Events proceeded just as he anticipated. Four officers set up an ambush at night and killed two women. The Jordanian response was not long in coming, as they shelled nearby Israeli settlements. Arik had his provocation and immediately responded by having his battalion mortars shell the Jordanian units. The incident was finally settled, but only after the intervention of the UN observers responsible for overseeing the cease-fire between Jordan and Israel. In his summary of the incident for his officers, Arik emphasized the crucial difference between firing at a stationary target and exchanging fire with the enemy while moving.

As a number of these officers recall, the whole experience left them with a bitter taste for many years. They felt that they had become merely tools in the hands of their commander who, for no justifiable reason, chose to fight. Arik's initiative in attacking the village women and in using the mortars had nothing to do with security, but was a result of his desire for adventure and excitement.

Arik was as successful in impressing Michael Shaham, the brigade commander, as he was in impressing most of his fellow soldiers. They both anguished over the IDF's weakness and the government's excessive caution. Shaham saw in Arik an outstanding officer who was also willing to undertake the most difficult assignments. He was particularly impressed by the speed with which Arik organized his battalion for a retaliatory raid in the area of Wadi Foukin. This initiative never reached fruition because of the opposition of the General Staff. Shaham and Arik often exchanged ideas on the overall military and political situation and discovered that they were almost in complete agreement. Arik did not try to hide his criticism of government policy or his reservations regarding the overall level of the senior commanders in the army. These conversations were not limited to the brigade staff; Arik had many similar discussions at his home, with army friends from the War of Independence and with fellow students. They all agreed that the country was in grave condition, that its management was in the hands of incompetents, that the IDF was improperly organized, and that if only they had the opportunity and the authority, they would reshape the army and pursue a much more effective defense policy. The focus of their criticism was on the outgoing Chief of

Staff, Yigal Yadin, and on Major General Haim Laskov, for modelling the IDF after the British army. The responsibility for the inauspicious political situation, as Arik and his coterie of friends saw it, rested with Foreign Minister Moshe Sharett, whom they saw as weak and incapable of contending with Arab aggression. Arik's friends accepted his assessment that the army formed after the War of Independence was not flexible enough; that it functioned in a routine, predictable fashion, inappropriate to the country's needs; and that it lacked initiative and fighting spirit. As a result of government policy and the army's weakness, the public was becoming resigned to harassment by the Arabs.

There was justice in these claims, for the IDF demonstrated little resourcefulness in coping with the minings, the infiltration of saboteurs, or any of the other violations of the armistice agreements between Israel and its neighbors. The few reprisal raids conducted by the IDF were either unsuccessful, or were aborted before they could fail because of the low morale, the poor command and the insufficient training. There was a reciprocal effect between the level of the IDF's combat ability and the government's political and defense policy, which resulted in a general mood of resignation in the public. People began talking of the infiltrators as a passing phenomenon, a temporary expression of the difficulty the Arabs were having in accepting the existence of the State of Israel and its victory in the 1948 war. Arik's diagnosis was much more extreme. He did not believe that the exercise of restraint would, in any way, influence the Arab states to follow suit and curb the activities of the infiltrators and terrorists. His previous experience and the lessons of his childhood had taught him that the Arabs construed Israel's moderation and reserve as the clearest signs of weakness. Israel's insipid posture was a result of an enervating sense of defeatism, whose source was in the fundamental weakness of the IDF.

Arik's criticisms were not aired in drawing-room language. On the contrary, his dissatisfaction with the heads of the state and the army was expressed in vulgar terms and punctuated with ugly epithets. But he got an unmistakable message across to his listeners: had he the power to do so, he would considerably alter and enhance the IDF's ability to respond to Arab provocations. He sincerely believed that this was the way he could best serve his country. But his desire to return to the military and assume a responsible combat role reflected a deep inner need as well. Arik needed the military for his own sense of self-fulfillment, as an outlet for his energy, and as a forum for the expression of his talents. Circumstances were to provide him with just such an opportunity.

In June, 1953, Michael Shaham received the approval of the General Staff to undertake a reprisal raid against the Arab village of Nebi Samuil, the home of Mustafa Samuili, a well-known Arab gang leader. Shaham tried to convince the commanders of the Givati Brigade and of the paratroopers to undertake the mission, but both of them turned him down. He feared that any delay in implementation of the plan would jeopardize it because of the highly fluid political situation. He therefore turned to Arik.

Shaham had long argued in favor of the establishment of a special forces unit that would operate behind the armistice lines in reprisal and preemptive strikes against the Arabs. Shaham had raised this proposition with Moshe Dayan, Chief Operations Officer at the General Staff, but was turned down with the explanation that the paratroopers already constituted such a unit and that the most pressing issue of the day was the upgrading of the entire infantry. When Arik heard Shaham's idea to set up a special forces unit composed of the most daring soldiers, he immediately and unequivocally declared his willingness to lead this unit. Shaham was particularly sensitive to the question of Arab terrorism. As commander of the Jerusalem Brigade, he noted the growing number of raids being conducted against settlements which were nominally within his responsibility. If at first these raids were sporadic and often aimed only at property, incidents of sabotage and murder were increasing in frequency and were terrorizing the civilian population. He also understood that the actions of the Arab infiltrators were coordinated and sanctioned by the regular armies of the neighboring Arab states.

Arik responded quickly when asked to an urgent meeting at

the Schneler base by Shaham. Shaham asked him to put together a small squad of fighters and go out on the mission to attack the home of Mustafa Samuili. Shaham urged him to do this as quickly as possible and, if possible, to carry it out by the next night. If successful, he was convinced that they would get approval for the permanent establishment of just such a special forces unit. Arik did not hesitate. He took a car from the base and went out to recruit seven men, five of whom had served with him during the War of Independence. Two others he knew from the university. The eight of them were hastily briefed, equipped and sent on their way. Together with Shaham, Arik decided not to attack the village itself, but rather the small community less than one mile to the east of it, avoiding any direct contact with the Jordanian Legion artillery battery encamped within the village. Although the four buildings in the adjacent community were generally empty overnight, as the residents slept in the village, still they decided to act quickly.

Arik and his seven fighters made their way slowly up the steep slope leading to the small community at the top of the hill. Out of breath and panting, they arrived unnoticed. Still, their mission failed: the explosives caused only minor damage to the building, while the noise aroused the Jordanian units. They were forced to flee, though they did blow up one small building along the way. Meanwhile, Shaham waited impatiently all night; Arik and his men did not return before morning. A heavy fog forced them to spend the night in Jordanian territory. Shaham greeted them warmly and had a special meal waiting. His assessment of the action was positive: they reached their goal unnoticed, set off two explosions, and returned with no losses. In comparison with the level of performance of the regular army units, Shaham asserted that he was definitely justified in viewing this operation as successful. Arik was less sanguine. He believed that this mission clearly demonstrated the need for intensive training. The relative failure only reinforced his belief in the necessity of setting up a specially trained commando unit, similar to the Palmah shock troops of the Haganah, that had been so successful during the War of Independence.

The next morning, Nehemia Argov, Prime Minister Ben

Gurion's chief military advisor, asked Shaham for a report on the action at Nebi Samuil. Shaham gave Argov a detailed account, emphasizing that Arik's squad operated against empty buildings. At the end of the debriefing, Argov asked, "What do you think should be done in this area?"

Shaham answered confidently, "We must set up a permanent and well-trained commando unit."

"Put your ideas in writing and send one copy to the Prime Minister, one copy to the Chief of the General Staff," Argov encouraged.

Shaham worked all night to prepare his proposal. The next morning he sent out copies to David Ben Gurion and to the Chief of the General Staff, Mordecai Maklef. Ben Gurion was impressed with the report and ordered Maklef to call a meeting of the General Staff to review and approve Shaham's proposal. The Chief Operations Officer of the General Staff, Moshe Dayan, who had in the past opposed the formation of a special unit, happened to be on vacation at the time. He made no effort to participate, claiming that the subject was not sufficiently important to shorten his vacation. In his absence, the General Staff approved the formation of a special unit to wage battle against Arab terrorists. Later, Dayan was informed of this, but voiced no opposition. He appointed Shaham to form the unit, with the Jerusalem Brigade serving as its administrative headquarters. Dayan asked Shaham who could command this unit, and Shaham proposed Ariel Scheinerman. Dayan agreed. From Dayan's headquarters, Shaham called his office and asked that Arik be invited to a meeting that same day.

Before leaving, Dayan asked Shaham, "Do you think that Arik will be willing to give up his studies?"

Shaham was confident. Not much later, when Arik heard the news from Shaham, his response was, "I have an exam coming up in history."

"Why study history? Go out and make history yourself!" said Shaham. That same day Arik collected the first soldiers of his new unit, the seven men who raided Nebi Samuil.

Arik was given a free hand to recruit men from anywhere in the army. For two months about 30 young men, dissatisfied with the military framework in which they were currently serving, trickled into a small army camp outside Abu Ghosh, near Jerusalem, where the new unit took shape. Arik received them all for an informal talk, usually over a meal. He explained the unit's aims and means of operation. His demeanor captivated them. Unlike their former commanders, sticklers for spit and polish, in Arik they met a 25-year-old major who allowed them to train in any outfit. In contrast to the regimen of blind and automatic obedience that permeated their old units, Arik and his small group of officers encouraged initiative and fostered original military thinking. Arik gave his men a sense of being a special, daring group of fighters, a chosen elite. He even found a suitable, and mysterious, name: "The 101st Unit."

Throughout the IDF, in all the camps and bases, a rumor made the rounds about a special group of soldiers with a very unusual lifestyle, somewhere in the Jerusalem area. This aura of mystery also brought a few dozen more volunteers. It was a strange mixture of fighters: some were adventurers; others had simply failed to adapt to the rules and regulations of the regular army; still others were aware of the need to create a unit capable of providing a suitable response to the Arab guerrilla actions. Among the latter were a number of ex-members of the Palmah whom Arik had assiduously courted to ensure a reasonably balanced social composition. At its peak, the unit never numbered more than 50 men. It was marked by a high turnover. Men were ousted for failing to keep up with the level of training, and others left by choice. Throughout its history, however, it maintained a nucleus of fighters who set a standard for the level of combat and purposefulness required. Although small, and operationally active for no more than five months, the 101st left a deep impression on the IDF and the relations between Israel and the Arab states.

In his small room at Camp Staph, the new base for the 101st, Arik sat planning each day's training. He ordered Shlomo Baum, his deputy commander, to divide the men into squads, drill them in shooting, train them in fieldcraft, and improve their level of physical fitness. He personally inculcated three unbending rules: the mission must be executed at all costs;

loyalty must be given to fellow soldiers; and accurate and precise reporting of the battle must occur.

Camp Staph resembled a boom town in an American Western. The unit's 30 or 40 men sported a motley variety of outfits, from khaki uniforms to Arab head scarves. They carried an assortment of weapons: Tommy guns, rifles, Molotov cocktails and commando knives. Explosions were heard in the camp all day long. At Arik's insistence, the IDF supplied him with unlimited quantities of arms and ammunition. The fighters of the 101st were voracious consumers of ammunition. They constantly improvised new targets to improve their aim: flying cans, luckless pigeons, the corners of buildings. Every day brought new tests of courage and skill, such as tossing a grenade onto the roof of a building while standing at the foot of the same building, or shooting from the hip while charging up the steep slope of a rugged hill. In the evenings they would sit down to analyze military problems: how to respond in unexpected situations; how to develop new means of cover; how to move in hostile territory.

The training was supplemented by Arik's psychological and ideological indoctrination. He imbued his men with a sense of mission, making them feel that the fate of the country rested with them. He taught that Jews must not remain passive targets, and that Arab aggression must be returned tenfold. He convinced them that they were the true military elite of the IDF. He introduced tension by dividing them into small squads with an officer at the head of each. He pitted them against one another to create relentless competition.

Within two months, the 40 men had been turned into a group of soldiers that craved battle. Gradually, Arik began sending small groups on reconnaissance missions and ambushes over the border. Before going out on these operations, the squad commanders would discuss their plan of action and propose their own ideas; however, once the specific method of execution was determined by Arik, he insisted that they were to follow it. He also made it clear that should circumstances dictate a change in the original plan, they were expected to exhibit the initiative and resourcefulness necessary to meet the obligations of the mission.

These forays across the border were effected in civilian clothing, without radios, doctors, or even a rescue plan. Arik would wait for his men (most of them 18- and 19-year-olds) to return from their missions and greet them with a lamb stew and other delicacies. He would debrief them, insisting on absolutely truthful reports. The penalty for failing to report the details accurately was severe, and included dismissal.

While training his men, Arik also tried to get the General Staff to approve their use in raids across the border. At first he communicated with the High Command through Michael Shaham, but soon he was to be seen haunting the corridors of the General Staff on his own, courting a series of senior officers, imploring them to launch his unit. He always had a number of operational plans ready for raids against any of a number of Arab targets, so that he could propose them whenever Arab infiltrators attacked an Israeli target. He spent nights, in his room at Camp Staph, pouring over maps and planning operations along the entire length of the Jordanian and Egyptian borders.

But the General Staff did not respond readily to Arik's appeals, although his requests for permission to operate over the border were studied with great care. The need to keep his men under rein was frustrating, and he often burst out in anger in the presence of his men. The men of the 101st would gather around Arik's room at Camp Staph, eavesdropping on their commander's conversations. They could overhear Arik addressing his superiors with an impudence bordering on insubordination. And when he slammed down the receiver, as he often did, he would erupt in a flood of curses and insults aimed at the leaders of the IDF and the government. This became commonplace. Arik regularly referred to the senior commanders of the IDF and the more well-known members of the government as "dumb shits" or "assholes," adding vivid descriptions of the sex life that he assumed they must lead.

This behavior only endeared him more to his men. His ridicule of the Foreign Minister or the Speaker of the Knesset or of the members of the General Staff made the men feel as if they were privy to an important secret. It was as if he had released

them from the binds of awe toward the leaders of the country
and exposed their true faces. Arik's contempt for his superiors
heightened the feeling among his men that he was one of them,
that they shared with him the same beliefs, assessments and
aspirations. Behind the flood of reproaches there was also a
message which the men of the 101st picked up clearly: their unit
was different, they were men of quality, and ultimately their
justice would be proven and their glory achieved. This message
also necessarily implied that their own commander was superior
to the others, a conclusion they readily accepted. His derision
toward his commanders raised the morale of the unit and
sharpened the consciousness of its men of their ability to change
the security situation and of their obligation to prove effective.

Arik's criticism was sincere. He truly regarded most of the
members of the government and many of the military officers as
incompetents. Since the battle at Latroun, he bore an acute
bitterness toward the leaders of the army and the government
and their feckless blunders. His dissatisfaction had prompted
him to leave the army and go to the university, and this lack of
confidence in the leaders of the country accompanied him even
after he took up the position as commander of the 101st. He
became convinced that he was indeed superior to the current
leadership, a feeling that was further reinforced by the response
of his men.

In September, 1953, all of Arik's pleading was finally
successful, and the General Staff presented the 101st with its
first assignment. Their task was to remove the Bedouin tribe of
Azazma from the Negev Desert. The Bedouins had come from
the Sinai peninsula and had settled in a region between Kibbutz
Revivim and Nizana, and all attempts to remove them peacefully
and return them to Egypt were unsuccessful. Arik and his men
went south to the Negev to prepare for their mission. His plan
was simple. The men burst into the Bedouin camp in the middle
of the day, firing in all directions. Frightened, the Bedouins fled.
The 101st then scoured the camp in search of guns and other
weapons and burned a number of tents. Chasing the Bedouins,
they unexpectedly found themselves in the demilitarized zone
between Israel and Egypt. Egyptian policemen circled the Israeli

vehicles and ordered them to march to the station. But Arik suddenly yelled in English, "Get out of our way at once, or we'll do to you what we did in 1948!"

To make this more convincing, he ordered his men to draw the weapons hidden beneath their blankets. The men of the 101st aimed their weapons at the startled Egyptian policemen. Arik continued:

"We're now going to leave this area, but I warn you. If you fire on us we will return and wipe you out."

The Egyptians obeyed and the men made their way back to Israel. Safely home, they praised Arik's quick thinking and composure. For the next few days, the 101st continued to harass the Bedouins until the last of them left the Negev. Later, a few of the men voiced their reservations about using a top army unit to fight off a group of defenseless civilians. Arik responded patiently and quietly to these arguments and explained:

"By removing the Bedouins, the country is preserving its sovereignty. The Bedouins were growing accustomed to seeing our land in the desert as their own, and had we not acted now, it would have been very difficult in the future to build new settlements, or a road."

The success in removing the Bedouins only served to increase Arik's pressure on the General Staff to authorize raids. Arik objected to the restraint being shown in the face of the terrorist infiltrations from the Gaza Strip and the Sinai Desert. Instead of preempting and possibly preventing these strikes, the IDF waited defensively. He believed that the best defense was to attack forcefully, with no sign of weakness. Finally, the 101st was authorized to organize and carry out a raid against the Palestinian refugee camp El-Burj in the Gaza Strip. Arik's plan was to trap Arab refugees in a crossfire between two groups of soldiers, killing a large number of them. One member of the 101st, Shmuel Falah, objected.

As they sat around the fire discussing the operational plans for the raid, Falah announced, "I'm not going to take part in this kind of raid. We should be attacking military targets within Egypt and not civilian targets. After we're successful on this mission, the Egyptians and the guerrillas will only intensify their activities agaist our own civilian population. Our new-immigrant, temporary encampments are almost totally defenseless."

Arik did not respond directly to Falah. Instead he offered him a smaller role, to blow up the home of the Egyptian commander who lived near the refugee camp. Falah, together with two other soldiers, accepted this assignment, while the others set out to complete the main part of Arik's plan.

The results were lethal. Fifteen residents of the camp were killed, including a number of women and children. At the summary of the mission, a number of men voiced their reservations: "Are a few hundred miserable refugees, including women and children, our real enemy?" they asked incredulously.

Arik replied, "The women are the whores of the Arab infiltrators who have been attacking our civilians. If we don't act forcefully against the refugee camps they will turn into comfortable nests for murderers!"

The results of this excursion were beginning to raise questions in other quarters as well, and the Chief of the General Staff, Mordecai Maklef, called Michael Shaham and demanded a detailed account of the mission and why it was necessary to kill so many civilians. Shaham summoned Arik and asked for an explanation. Arik very convincingly explained that the extent of the killing was dictated by an accident with one of the groups. They had come upon a sentry, and rather than kill him, they tied him up. He must have gotten free, however, because as they approached the camp, his screams and shouts alerted everyone in the camp, so the element of surprise was destroyed. The men of the 101st immediately shifted to their contingency plan by splitting into two groups, firing in all directions, and making their way quickly through the camp. Despite their regret at the extent of the action, the General Staff gradually began to understand that the IDF now had a unit which was clearly willing and able to operate against any Arab target.

Arik's increasing involvement in military operations, and in particular his activities with the 101st, were frightening Margalit. On the one hand, she worried about Arik's safety and well-being, but, on the other, she was very proud of him as a soldier and an officer. She talked to Arik about these fears and her unhappiness with the amount of time he was spending in training his unit at Camp Staph. Whenever he was about to leave on a mission, their discussions turned into arguments. She felt guilty, so she welcomed him back from these missions in a spirit of appeasement and extreme tenderness. Arik accepted this with patience and understanding, knowing that Margalit was really very proud of him and shared his military aspirations. In fact, as Arik's involvement increased, so did Margalit's. The officers and soldiers with whom Arik worked became guests in his home. There, Margalit shared their experiences and thoughts while feeding them.

On the night of October 13, 1953, Suzanne Kenias and her two children – Shoshana, three, and Reuven, one and a half – were murdered as they slept. They were the 122nd, 123rd and 124th victims of Arab infiltrators, and their deaths brought to new heights the sense of rage and fear aroused by the terrorists. The following morning, the IDF high command happened to be together in the north, observing a major military exercise. As they stood alongside a jeep, they discussed a response. Defense Minister Pinhas Lavon, the Chief of the General Staff, Mordecai Maklef, and the Chief Operations Officer, Moshe Dayan were joined by David Ben Gurion, vacationing in the area. The four of them agreed that Israel should respond in the firmest possible manner to the murders.

Moshe Dayan returned to Tel Aviv to prepare for the reprisal raid, and the target selected was the Jordanian town of Kibya. It was a town of about 2,000 residents, divided into old and new sections. A Jordanian army outpost was in the town, and about twenty of its residents were members of the Jordanian National Guard. Kibya was chosen because it was a well-known sanctuary for terrorists. Dayan envisioned a broad action against Kibya, with diversionary attacks on two nearby villages, Shukba and Nihilin. A General Staff officer, Meir Amit, carried Dayan's operational order to the Central Sector command to be translated into action.

Sensing that the IDF might respond forcefully to the murder

in Yehud, the Jordanian government turned to Israel through the auspices of the Joint Armistice Committee, urging it to refrain from a reprisal action and promising to find and punish the murderers. But Amman's appeal was never even brought to the attention of the full cabinet, nor was the plan of operation against Kibya. Even Acting Prime Minister Moshe Sharett had only a vague idea of the evolving action. No one had bothered to inform him about what it would entail or listen to his reservations about any kind of military action. The four men who met around the jeep had decided.

Moshe Dayan intended to assign the mission to the only paratroop battalion in the army, supported by the 101st, which would be responsible for the diversionary action in Shukba and Nihilin. But when the operational plan was presented at Central Sector's headquarters, the deputy commander of the paratroop battalion balked at accepting the assignment, claiming that his unit was not ready. Arik Scheinerman, the lowest ranking officer at the meeting, promptly volunteered to assume command of the entire operation and lead both the unprepared paratroop unit and the 101st into battle. To reinforce his own declaration, he proceeded to detail a daring and ambitious plan before the surprised officers. The mission was assigned to Arik and he left for the General Staff to settle the details with Dayan.

At general headquarters Arik was presented with two alternatives. The first aimed at the temporary occupation of the village, blowing up a few houses, shooting at the villagers and forcing them to flee the village. The second aimed at the total destruction of the village and maximum harm to the villagers, again forcing them to flee. The first plan was drawn up by the Operational Division, and its main targets were the public buildings of the village. The second was formulated by the Central Command and allowed for greater latitude in blowing up houses and shooting villagers. Dayan told Arik that if difficulties arose, he should limit himself to the first plan. No explicit orders were given regarding women and children. It was simply assumed that, as usual, the men would conduct themselves according to the accepted standards of behavior of the IDF – not to cause intentional injury to civilians, especially not to women and children. No one at headquarters expected the action to be exceptional in any way.

Arik, however, had different ideas. He was resolved to carry out the second plan, that of the Central Command. And when he gave orders to load 1300 pounds of explosives onto the vehicles, it was clear to his men that he had no intention of demolishing only a few public buildings.

One hundred and three men took part: the paratroop battalion together with twenty men from the 101st. Arik briefed the men in detail, making clear his expectation that the mission would be completed in full. He was convinced that if the Kibya expedition were successful, it would boost the standing of the 101st and speed his own advancement. He believed the deaths of over one hundred Israeli civilians killed in terrorist actions had to be avenged, and that the time had come to teach the enemy a lesson. Arik pronounced that no one was to return unless the mission was executed. Aharon Davidi, the paratroop battalion commander, read harrowing descriptions of the events surrounding the murder of the Kenias family to the soldiers.

Sixty-nine people were killed in Kibya, about half of them women and children. Arik's soldiers blew up over 45 houses. The raid became the subject of a heated controversy throughout the country. Arik and his men contended that they had checked every house before laying the explosives, while critics countered that insufficient attention had been given to the possibility that people might still be hiding in those houses.

After taking control of Kibya and the roads leading to it, Arik and his men had assumed that most of the residents had fled. They proceeded to lay the explosives on the ground floor of all the buildings that had been marked off, key public buildings and the homes of the wealthy. The check for civilians had been superficial: a soldier entered a building, shot, and called out. If no one answered, it was assumed that the building was empty. The soldiers and officers claimed that it would have been impossible to check the buildings thoroughly if they were to complete their mission and return before dawn. They all insisted that they were completely surprised at the number of casualties, because they had been convinced that the buildings were empty.

At his debriefing, Sharon reported to Dayan that he estimated that 10 to 12 Jordanians had been killed, most of them during the fighting that took place for control of the village. By his own testimony, he was taken aback by the Jordanian government's report that 69 people were killed. The operation's critics maintained that Arik took advantage of the fact that he had not been given a clear order to avoid harming the civilians and therefore conducted only perfunctory checks of the houses.

The repercussions of the raid on Kibya were enormous, and at a cabinet meeting Interior Minister Moshe Shapira attacked, "Did the Acting Prime Minister know about the plan of action?!"

Moshe Sharett answered defensively, "The day after the murder of the Kenias family, I knew of the existence of a planned reprisal and saw no reason to oppose it; however, a day later I notified the Defense Minister of my objections. He responded that he would consider them."

Pinhas Lavon, the Defense Minister, answered Shapira directly, "There is a cabinet decision authorizing the Defense Minister to decide about reprisals. It is irrelevant whether others knew about the plan or not. I stand by the authority granted me by a decision of the government."

David Ben Gurion added, "I was on vacation at the time, and no one was obligated to ask for my approval. But if I would have been asked, I would have said to proceed."

Despite the determination with which he ended that discussion, Ben Gurion was upset with the results of the action. He asked his military liaison, Nehemia Argov, to arrange for a meeting with Arik so that he could see for himself who led the battle. Arik was summoned to the Prime Minister through Michael Shaham, who questioned Argov about the purpose of the meeting. Argov explained that Ben Gurion suspected that the 101st was comprised of a bevy of veterans of Etzel and Lehi, because only they would attack enemy civilians. Shaham assured Argov that Ben Gurion was in store for a surprise when he found out who the soldiers of the 101st were.

Shaham brought Arik to Ben Gurion's office, but Ben Gurion wanted a private meeting. Alone with Arik in his office for almost an hour, Ben Gurion grilled him about his past and his education. He was surprised to find out that Arik was raised on a moshav, nominally within the Labor movement, and that he had been a member of the Haganah. He was surprised that many of the members of the 101st were members of kibbutzim and moshavim, and that none had been members of the dissident underground movements. Ben Gurion felt he had no choice but to come out in support of Arik. On the 19th of October he issued a communiqué announcing that no unit of the IDF was away from its base on the night of the Kibya attack, and that the action in Kibya was apparently taken by people from the settlements around Jerusalem, "refugees from Arab countries and survivors of the Nazi concentration camps, who had suffered terribly at the hands of their tormentors and had shown great restraint until now."

If the Kibya action was a source of embarrassment for the government, it was, from Arik's standpoint, a cause for celebration. He won a place in the IDF's gallery of heroes. He was credited with the overall success of the mission and with his willingness to volunteer for it; with the fact that there were no casualties to the attacking force (except for one slightly wounded); and with careful planning and uncompromising execution. Kibya also marked a turning point in the way Israel responded to terrorist actions. For the first time, after three years of failures, the IDF showed it was capable of avenging the murders by the Arab terrorists.

One consequence of this action was to restore a measure of confidence to the General Staff in the ability of the IDF to act effectively against the Arab guerrillas. A few years later Arik recalled that on the eve of the raid he felt the need to prove that any mission was possible if one believed in its urgency. He also added that he had tried to train his men in hand-to-hand combat and direct confrontation with the enemy. Kibya proved that Arik was capable of commanding much larger forces. He and his followers were more convinced than ever that he was possessed of unique military prowess, that he was a natural leader, and that he had the ability to fashion a new military order. After Kibya, Arik's men called him a "military genius," "far-sighted," "bold" and "resolute." They also acclaimed his readiness for a broad interpretation of orders issued by the General Staff. At general headquarters, however, a different conclusion was reached: It was necessary to give explicit instructions in the operational orders, so that civilians would not to be harmed.

At Camp Staph, Arik continued to prepare new plans for attacking Arab targets. He sent out teams deep into enemy territory on patrols and raids. His soldiers were not bothered by the fact that they were generally attacking civilian targets because they had come to accept the Arabs, as a whole, as enemies. Four men from the 101st reached the center of Hebron on a snowy night, covering over thirty miles in each direction on foot, and killed four locals, while successfully evading the gunfire of the residents who came after them. The audacious nature of these raids seemed to endanger the men unnecessarily. A number of staff officers contended that Arik's actions were too wild and uncontrolled and should be curbed. But Arik believed that these attacks undermined the confidence of the enemy and demonstrated the ability of the 101st and the IDF to respond forcefully to Arab terrorism.

The fighters at Camp Staph vied for the opportunity to participate in the raids and patrols. They were proud of their status and believed that they could get away with anything, relying fully on Arik and the support he gave, as long as they proved themselves. They enjoyed working with him: his air of informality, his love for singing with them, and his encouragement of initiative. They treasured the way he shared his values and opinions about the politics and the military. Very few of them tried to understand his other self: his violent temper, his gluttonous appetite, his willingness to expel men from his unit for minor infractions. Nor did they reconcile the contradiction between his love for animals and his total disregard for the enemy's humanity.

They saw many examples of his contradictions. They witnessed him laughing as a junior officer tormented an old Arab and then shot him at close range; they noted his composure as he planned operations designed to kill as many civilians as possible; they carried out his intricate plan to trap a peaceful Bedouin boy shepherding his flock. Still, he would save a wounded falcon, treating it with the same kindness usually reserved for babies. They accepted him as he was, the way members of religious sects worship their leaders.

The 101st provided Arik with the support and encouragement he craved. Only a couple of the older soldiers had any reservations about his extreme behavior, yet they, too, chose to be with him, especially during battle. Most of them had no reservations, and would obey every order to the letter. Once, the 101st was called on to cross the Jordanian border to help the convoy of Israeli policemen on their way to Mount Scopus, which was held as an Israeli enclave in East Jerusalem under the terms of the cease-fire. The Jordanians were suspected of planning an attack. The 101st would enter East Jerusalem to attempt a rescue. They all understood that this would be tantamount to a suicide mission, with little chance of getting out alive. There was no hesitation on their part, because they accepted the critical nature of the assignment and because Arik would be with them.

The 101st was marked not only by comradeship and unfailing mutual support, but also by acts of mischief, and even serious insubordination and vandalism. Every weekend, Arik dismissed his men, organizing transportation home with a unit car. The last soldier took the car home. One weekend, the last soldier happened to live on a kibbutz in the Jordan Valley. Before he could make it home, however, he was stopped by the military police and informed that he was under arrest for driving the car after curfew. The kibbutznik responded with contempt, and was dragged from the car and beaten up by the military police. This could not be tolerated. Instead of enjoying his weekend leave, he collected his friends and returned to Camp Staph, where they planned their revenge. They drove to Tiberias and attacked the military police headquarters. They beat up the three policemen directly involved so severely that they required hospitalization.

Zvi Zur, Chief Manpower Officer of the IDF, contacted Shaham and asked what his boys were up to. Shaham, who had no idea about the incident, immediately called Arik. Although he censured Arik, making it clear that he should have filed a complaint against the military policemen, he refused to punish anyone. He informed Zur that he would take disciplinary action against the responsible men, provided that the military police did the same. The investigation ended there, with the military police threatening to sever all connections with the 101st. Arik gave his men a two week leave. Afterwards, he informed them that they had just completed two weeks of confinement in punishment for their deeds.

Arik formed and led this group, building its morale and fostering its sense of superiority. It was easy to sweep these men along because they were young, adventurous and generally naive. But above all, these men wanted to remain a part of what had become the IDF's most prestigious unit and believed that by so doing they would be serving the best interests of their country.

Arik continued to besiege the General Staff with pleas to use his unit and implement the many plans he had prepared. In truth, at general headquarters, there was a recognition that the IDF now had a crack special forces unit. Arik interpreted the paucity of assignments as an indication of the jealousy and envy of many of the senior officers on the General Staff, and suspected some of them of intentionally trying to trip him up.

Two men supported Arik: Moshe Dayan, soon to be appointed Chief of the General Staff, and David Ben Gurion, the Prime Minister. Dayan was happy that he finally had a real fighter as an officer. There were striking similarities between Arik and Dayan. Both were born in Israel and came from farming villages; both were audacious, imaginative and original. Ben Gurion, on the other hand, saw in Arik the realization of the new Israeli. The Prime Minister selected a Hebrew name for Ariel Scheinerman. He called him Ariel Sharon.

Chapter **4**

In January 1954, the Chief of the General Staff, Moshe Dayan, began to implement a plan he had devised many months earlier: the unification of the 101st into the paratroop battalion. While still Chief Operations Officer on the General Staff, Dayan secretly informed Arik of his plan to incorporate the 101st into the paratroop battalion and to appoint Arik as its commander. He devised this plan although he knew that Lieutenant-Colonel Yehuda Harari, the commander of the paratroop battalion, expected to receive the commission. Many of the officers of the General Staff believed Harari would be appointed. Meir Zorea, Chief of Training, even prepared a special program for the unification of the two units under Harari. But when he became Chief of the General Staff, Dayan formed this new unit and named Sharon head of the new 890th Battalion.

Sharon was faced with the problem of explaining this merger to his own men. He told them that he had been appointed head of the paratroop battalion. Only later did he reveal that the 101st was to be absorbed into this battalion. He invited Dayan to explain. The fact that the Chief of the General Staff was willing to come and talk to them was very flattering to the men and the meeting was successful. Dayan impressed upon them that they were indeed the elite fighting unit in the IDF, and it was now necessary to transfer some of their spirit and experience to the rest of the IDF.

Fearing that they would lose their independence and be forced to submit to the standard rules and regulations of the army, not all the men accepted this at first. Many had joined the unit to avoid military discipline. They were also aware of Arik's contempt for the paratroopers and for their commander, a contempt he, of course, had seen no reason to hide. A few weeks earlier, after returning from the paratrooper's base, Arik had commented that Harari could never be seen around the base because he was always in his office. Sharon, who was bursting with enthusiasm for the new position, explained that the 101st was never intended to be an army within an army, but rather to set an example of what a fighting unit should be. It was now necessary to demonstrate this to the rest of the army.

The situation in the old paratroop battalion was more complicated. It had been known as a top fighting unit in the army, and the more veteran commanders of the unit refused to accept the disgrace of their commander implied by the appointment of Sharon. In general, they did not look forward to the merger of their proud, highly skilled and professional unit with the wild and rowdy 101st. When Sharon arrived at battalion headquarters, he found letters of resignation from most of the officers of the unit. Arik reacted calmly, accepting the resignations and appointing his own men to all the newly opened positions. His only special effort was to convince the jump instructors to stay on. One of the few paratrooper officers to remain was Aharon Davidi, whom he appointed as his deputy commander.

The merger was complicated and potentially dangerous. Sharon was faced with the problem of absorbing the 101st into an existing battalion, of establishing a new command structure within the battalion, and of overcoming the internal opposition to the merger both by the paratroopers and by the men of the 101st. Sharon, himself, had to adjust to the new and larger role, while at the same time inculcating his basic ideas and means of training.

Sharon acted quickly and soon the 890th Battalion was unrecognizable. He followed a plan that he had prepared prior to assuming the position and implemented it with determination. He split the battalion up into companies and scattered these throughout the country for immediate, intensive training. The result was that the new battalion was never together during its first crucial days as a unit. He distributed the men of the 101st throughout, making certain that there would never be a sufficient concentration of them to allow for the unofficial establishment of a special unit within the battalion. The training program itself was carefully planned to improve the physical fitness and fighting ability of the soldiers. They had little time or energy for anything else.

Sharon personally supervised the training, and the unit quickly developed a reputation as being the toughest in the army – where only the best soldiers could survive. The training stretched their endurance and, as in the 101st, emphasized hand-to-hand combat and extensive field and night exercises. Sharon nurtured the special aura of the unit. He instituted evening social activities with huge banquets and singing around the fire; he recruited the most beautiful women from the neighboring collectives to serve in the unit, mainly as parachute folders; he scheduled the jumping exercises to take place near settlements where he wanted to recruit soldiers; and he held frequent discussions with the heads of the kibbutz movement to urge them to encourage their youth to volunteer for the paratroopers. In a remarkably short time these efforts succeeded. Top soldiers from other units began requesting transfers to the paratroopers, and members of the kibbutzim and moshavim, the cream of the Israeli youth, saw the paratroopers as a real challenge and a contribution to the country. The morale and fighting ability of the unit were the highest in the IDF.

Even while reorganizing and training the new paratroop battalion, Sharon spent countless hours preparing contingency plans for any type of raid imaginable. He continued to believe, just as he had with the 101st, that he must always be ready with a detailed plan of action for a reprisal raid or patrol. The difference was that he now had a large regular army unit at his disposal and was reporting directly to the General Staff. The unit soon showed signs of what was termed the "101st syndrome." Regardless of what assignment had been given to the paratroopers, it inevitably proved to be excessively extreme and of unexpected dimensions.

Most of the assignments given to the paratroopers during its first year were small raids and attacks in enemy territory. There was one larger scale•operation, however, against an Egyptian stronghold along the border opposite Kibbutz Kisufim, during which Sharon was wounded in the thigh. The attacking force, led by Sharon himself, entered the trenches surrounding the Egyptian post. Sharon had hesitated momentarily before jumping into the trench, and this provided an Egyptian soldier with just enough time to fire.

Besides these official activities, some of the paratroopers, in particular a handful of the officers, undertook a number of unofficial raids. A group of fighters led by Meir Har Zion set out on the night of March 5, 1955 to avenge the murder of his sister by Arab terrorists. They captured five Bedouins and slit their throats. Another group, disguised as UN observers, enticed a number of Jordanian soldiers to cross the border into Israel on the pretext of returning a Jordanian shepherd who had gotten lost. The raid was intended to capture the Jordanian soldiers and use them as hostages in an exchange for the paratrooper, Yitzhak Jibly, then held by the Jordanian army.

The General Staff began to suspect that these renegade raids were being conducted with Sharon's consent and assistance. They had to be stopped. The Chief Staff Officer, Meir Amit, demanded an explanation from Sharon, who insisted that he had nothing to do with the raids. Amit did not believe him, but there was little he could do against him. He did not drop the matter entirely, but decided to press for a court martial of Meir Har Zion for engaging in a personal vendetta. Sharon, in turn, secured the services of Shmuel Tamir, one of the top lawyers in the country, who raised the whole question of the IDF's reprisal policy at the trial.

Moshe Dayan was concerned and suspicious. He called Sharon to his office and recorded the conversation in his diary: "I called Arik on August 25, 1954, and told him that there is no authorization for any action across the border to take hostages to be used in an exchange for Jibly... we have to work together. If someone is dissatisfied with any action, let him step forward and propose an alternative. I will not be angry, nor will I be surprised, if a plan originally intended to accomplish one thing results in something altogether different as a result of unforeseen developments; however, under no circumstances will I condone the changing of a plan before it has been implemented, without prior approval. Arik said that he understood, agreed, and promised."

In 1955, Arik's second year as commander of the paratroopers, relations deteriorated between Israel and her Arab neighbors. Arab terrorist activity changed, and so did paratrooper reprisal. The fundamental antagonism of the Arab peoples to Israel and the formation of a new brand of Arab terrorist units, called fedayeen, resulted in a dramatic increase in the most vicious of attacks against Israeli civilians. The murders, the fear and the rage of the Israeli population, created public pressure for a more forceful response. With this as the background, Arik addressed his men:

"We have not succeeded in imposing any kind of peace on the Arab states; in fact, terrorist activities have increased to the point of being a daily phenomenon. Furthermore, these activities have also taken on a more organized structure, indicating the full support of the neighboring governments for them. We are faced with two choices: we can now show restraint, in the hope that the Arabs, too, will follow suit, or we can attack, and in so doing force them to reconcile themselves to the existence of the State of Israel. Until now Israel has not initiated any attack whatsoever, but has restricted itself to responding to terrorist activities. This has not prevented the Arabs from continuing their attacks against Israel. We can look forward to a new and larger wave of terrorist acts this year. In order to be able to fight back, Israel requires the paratroopers. You must be in peak condition to meet this obligation." Sharon was destined to provide the context for these comments.

Despite all his efforts, Sharon noted that there were still soldiers who did not meet the high standards that he had set. He therefore tightened the training program even further. At this point, however, soldiers protested the Spartan regimen and Sharon's unrealistic goal of getting an entire battalion to the same level as the small and highly specialized 101st.

Although Sharon was forced to dismiss those soldiers who could not keep up with the training, those who remained sincerely admired him. They loved his informality and engaging smile; they were captivated by his magnetic leadership and his military skills; they valued his willingness to support them; and they were swept up in the competitive atmosphere, where they all vied for the right to participate in the different missions. With his love for singing around the campfire and his participation in many of their social activities, Sharon symbolized a return to the romantic, adventure-filled days of the Palmah, the shock troops of the Haganah in pre-Independence Israel. The training itself, besides being intensive and exhausting, was somewhat out of the ordinary with its special emphases on night fighting, navigation and hand-to-hand combat. Sharon also continued to demand completely accurate and detailed reporting of all raids, with immediate dismissal from the unit for anyone who failed to comply. Together with the training, Sharon continued to indoctrinate: Israel was under constant threat from its Arab neighbors, whose only goal was the complete destruction of the country; the only way to combat this was by force; the paratroop battalion must play a central role in this defense.

While the soldiers were being drilled, very often outside the confines of the base, Sharon was busy in discussions and debates at the General Staff. Just as with the 101st, Sharon spent inordinate amounts of time trying to convince his superiors of the need to counterattack. However, unlike his days at the 101st, Sharon now enjoyed a much greater measure of influence. Moshe Dayan had great respect for his military skills and also identified with Sharon's basic approach to defense matters. Since their meeting following the raid on Kibya, Prime Minister David Ben Gurion was also charmed by the energetic young officer and what he viewed as the audacious virility of the young Israeli. Ben Gurion even visited Sharon in the hospital after he was wounded at Kisufim and told him that he could call on Ben Gurion for help. Sharon took advantage of this invitation and of

Ben Gurion's favors. When faced with opposition to his proposals at the General Staff, Sharon would circumvent the normal channels of command and go directly to the Prime Minister. Sharon often acted to nurture this image, parking his car near the Prime Minister's office even when he would not be meeting with him.

Circumstances at the time were ripe for Sharon's initiatives. On the one hand, Arab terrorism was increasing and becoming more virulent, resulting in increasing pressure on the political leadership to take concrete action to avenge, if not to prevent this; while, on the other hand, the leadership that had taken over the government and the army was much more receptive to the positions taken by Sharon. Sharon found understanding partners in Ben Gurion, serving as both Defense Minister and Prime Minister; Moshe Dayan, Chief of the General Staff; and Golda Meir, who had recently replaced Moshe Sharett in the Foreign Office. In the years 1955-56, the paratroopers, sometimes in combination with other IDF units, undertook a long list of missions beyond the borders, in Egypt, Syria and Jordan. As was the case at Kibya, many of these missions took on the most unexpected proportions, surprising both the government and the army, which had initially authorized them.

In February 1955, during a raid on an Egyptian army base in Gaza, 38 Egyptian soldiers were killed and 44 were wounded. Most of these were killed where Sharon had set up a blockade along a major route to the base, ambushing four trucks that were bringing replacements to the besieged soldiers. There were eight dead among the paratroopers. The Egyptian President, Gamal Abdul Nasser, stated that, as a result of this raid, he became convinced that peace between Israel and Egypt would be impossible, and he was, therefore, forced to turn to the Soviet Union for assistance and to sign an arms supply agreement with Czechoslovakia. Moshe Sharett, who was serving as Prime Minister at the time of the raid, recorded the following comments in his diary: "We have allowed the paratroop battalion to raise revenge to the level of principle...It has been formalized and even sanctified as a tool for collective revenge for the entire country. The spirit and training of this battalion have, in fact, become key factors in determining the policy of its use. Whenever a decision is made by the Prime Minister not to use this potent, uncontrollable force, the battalion is overcome by depression and rage to the point of threat to the rule of civilian government..."

In December 1955, Sharon was called on to plan a raid against five Syrian positions near the Sea of Galilee. Sharon's plan was very ambitious and called for the simultaneous attack on all five positions by combined infantry and paratrooper units, supported by the air force and the navy. The operation was a dramatic success because of Sharon's careful planning and the skill of the soldiers who took part in the action. Fifty-six Syrian soldiers were killed in the action and a further 32 were taken prisoner. The IDF lost six, with an additional 12 wounded. The overall dimensions of the action frightened Ben Gurion, who felt that it had gone too far. Moshe Dayan brought Sharon and Mordecai Gur, one of Sharon's officers in the action, to a meeting with Ben Gurion, to assuage his fears. But Ben Gurion remained unsettled and unconvinced by Sharon's explanations and commented after the meeting that the action was simply "too successful." Dayan explained to Ben Gurion that Sharon used a quota system in these types of raids, and that the quotas were always measured in dozens of enemy dead.

In another action, against the Egyptian army at Kuntila, 10 Egyptian soldiers were killed and another 29 were captured. Paratrooper losses were two dead and two wounded. This action prompted the Egyptians to move a reinforced battalion into the demilitarized zone near Nizana, in violation of the cease-fire accords. A meeting at general headquarters to review the Kuntila raid and subsequent developments, to which Sharon was also invited, commenced with criticism of the raid as grossly exaggerated: the army and the government were being dragged along by Sharon's initiatives. His defenders, however, retorted by reminding those present that in all cases the government and the General Staff had authorized these actions, and that Sharon had then gone out at the head of his force. Sharon expressed his consternation at the nervousness voiced by some of the participants at the meeting over the deployment of the Egyptian battalion, and proposed that they attack it and remove it forcibly from the demilitarized zone. Sharon's proposal was accepted.

Sharon created a polished instrument of war, an instrument which assured his success in implementing his original and often grandiose plans. It brought him the cudos of many people in the army, but none more so than those of his own soldiers and lower-level officers. He proved time and again that his plans were practical and successful. In one case they were called on to kidnap a Syrian to be held as hostage for the release of Uri Ilan, an Israeli who had fallen prisoner. Sharon's plan called for the capture of a Syrian army truck driver, by setting a fire in a barrel. As the truck approached, the paratroopers did as they were instructed, and the fire so confused the driver that he stopped the truck and they were able to capture him without firing a shot. In another case, to capture a hostage in the Gaza Strip, Sharon instructed them to place a new tire in an easily noticed spot on the road. He contended that no Arab would pass up the opportunity of stealing the tire. The plan worked just as he had predicted, and the Arab driver was captured easily. In one of the most famous cases, the paratroopers were called upon to remove an Egyptian army unit from a hill which Israel claimed to be in its territory. The plan called for a deep penetration into Egyptian territory in order to attack the encampment from the rear. A few minutes before the attack was to take place, Sharon had all his trucks turn on their lights and approach the hill from the front. Sharon assumed that the Egyptians would view this as a tank column. The plan worked beautifully, and, as the trucks drove around, the Egyptians began to flee, unable to provide any resistance to the real invading force.

Sharon constantly drew lessons from earlier missions. He instructed even his superior officers on the proper use of air and naval support, and he continued to hone the training of his own troops, working with them on improving trench warfare and the role of the foot soldier in combating tanks. Before any mission, Sharon would gather all the participating troops and brief them in great detail, seasoning his comments with explanations of the urgency and necessity of the mission. When they left on a mission, the soldiers of the 890th Battalion left confident that their commander had planned it carefully and that he would lead the force.

This period of raids and counterattacks enabled Sharon to exhibit his valuable military skills; it enabled him to vent his aggressions against a commonly recognized enemy; it kept him occupied day and night, saving him from the torments of boredom and idleness; and it placed him in the limelight, where he could relish the admiration and wonderment of his own soldiers as well as his enemies, both within and without. He loved to stand on the porch of his office, overlooking the center of the camp, as the companies bustled about assembling for battle: ammunition being loaded; jeeps cutting in and out, with officers and instructors shouting orders; water tanks and mobile kitchens being attached to the trucks; and guns and other arms being fired off in last minute tests. The soldiers themselves loved this frenzied preparation, for it marked the beginning of battle and the release of the insufferable tensions that built up in anticipation of the fight.

There was a small group of men in the paratroop battalion that saw Sharon in a different light. These men, mainly senior officers in the battalion who spent a great deal of time with Sharon, saw him as egotistical and overly ambitious, a man whose military initiatives were designed to meet his own personal needs, and who garnered all the prestige and praise, much of which rightly belonged to the soldiers and officers. These men noted his vulgarity and contempt for others, especially for superior officers who had deigned to disapprove of his plans or withhold their authorization. Yosef Geva, Commander of the Givati Brigade, and Meir Amit, Chief Staff Officer of the general headquarters, were the most frequent victims of these tirades. They recoiled at his irrational outbursts of temper or his repellent gluttony, and they despised his impetuosity in dismissing officers from the battalion for minor infractions, because they had temporarily fallen out of favor. They also observed his obvious pleasure at trying to trap one of his officers. In one case, the head of the command company of the battalion confessed to the battalion adjutant that he was going to take some food from the unit's kitchen for his wedding. The adjutant reported this to Sharon, who ordered him not to warn the company commander, but rather to let him carry out his plan and then to arrest him. Sharon's deputy commander, Yitzhak Hofi, argued this case unsuccessfully with Sharon, and finally appealed unsuccessfully to Zvi Zur, Commander of the Central Sector, to relieve him of his position. At another time, Hofi, in a conversation with Aharon Yariv, another commander, said Sharon was in need of psychiatric care, because he was clearly paranoid.

Those officers who were closest to him also attest to the fact that he often lied, that he was violent and would not hesitate to trample anyone in his way, that his relations with others were purely self-serving, and that he was ruled by his unbounded ambitions and his craving for adulation and prestige. His willingness to ignore orders was well-known. He would give orders to his officers to create provocations along the border in order to justify his reprisals. They report an incident on a mission in Jordan to attack a police station in Surif. The attacking force had already set out when a radio message was received from the General Staff, ordering Sharon to abort the mission. Sharon ignored the message, telling the other officers conspiratorially that he could not hear the order. Only when the central office repeated the message several times, did Sharon acknowledge the order. Less well-known is the fact that Haim Bar-Lev headed a military tribunal formed to investigate the numerous complaints of the soldiers of the 890th Battalion against Sharon, in which they alleged that they were subject to frequent humiliations at his hands. The prosecution began summoning witnesses, but the investigation dragged on and finally dissipated.

There were very few people around him when he responded obscenely to Shlomo Goren, the Chief Rabbi of the IDF, during the funeral of Yitzhak Ben Menahem, nicknamed 'Gulliver'. When his friend, Oded Zalmanson, rebuked him for this lack of respect, Sharon responded, "Who the hell do you think made Goren so famous? It was only after the paratroopers started operating and being killed that anyone ever heard of him!"

There were also few who stopped to understand Sharon's proposal to Uzi Eilam, a junior officer in the battalion and an accomplished violinist. While planning a raid on an Egyptian army camp in Gaza, Sharon asked him to position himself behind a hill near the fighting and play the violin. Although the proposal was made in jest, some of the officers pondered what it may have symbolized about Sharon's personality. Did it represent Sharon's conception of combat planning as a creative endeavor? Did it suggest Sharon's understanding of warfare as art, regardless of the number of dead?

It is true that few men at the time stopped to look at the dark side of Sharon's personality. In their service in the paratroopers they saw an opportunity of fighting the Arab enemy in the most effective way possible, as well as an opportunity for some adventure. They perceived themselves as partners in the secret effort to motivate the political leadership to take some concrete action. Sharon rarely faced open opposition within the unit, both because of their fear and respect for him, and because of their general agreement with his basic goals. Even the kibbutz members, who represented a large proportion of the battalion's men, voiced no opposition to Sharon's contempt for the political leadership or his planning attacks designed to kill as many people as possible. They saw the paratroopers as a framework for the realization of their ideals of self-defense and as an official arena for their adventurousness.

Although the battalion was beguiled by him, he had developed a number of enemies in the General Staff. Meir Amit, second in command, refused to accept the explanations of why every action conducted by Sharon somehow exceeded the proportions expected by the General Staff. There were frequent arguments as to whether Sharon willfully breached authority; this feeling pervaded the government as well. However, in no case were any of his opponents able to come up with proof. Sharon was invariably successful in providing a detailed explanation of how circumstances at the point of battle dictated expanding the scope of the original operation. In order to get approval for his plans, Sharon took advantage of the weaknesses of the cabinet members, capitalizing on their ignorance of the military and on the political dissension among the different parties. In particular, he made capital of the conflicts between Ben Gurion and Sharett, exaggerating the results of every Arab action against Israel by painting it in the most threatening way.

Sharon responded to the criticisms with a mixture of personal affront and transparent indifference, attributing the criticism to flagrant jealousy. He asked his supporters why he was being attacked, and why there was no recognition of the fact that everything he was doing was for the benefit of the country. He would declare that regardless of the criticism, nothing would change his mind or deter him from his goal.

The long list of Sharon's reprisals (supported by Ben Gurion and Dayan) had a fundamental impact on Arab-Israeli relations. Although they were unsuccessful in achieving their primary goal – to establish Israel as a fact to the Arabs, and to reduce Arab terrorism – they were popular with the people and with a number of key government members. These raids were, however, increasingly interpreted as proof of Israel's belligerence. Within Israel, people were gradually recognizing that strengthening the military in Sharon's way was leading to a dead end, and a very high price in human lives.

Two Jewish workers near Tel Mond had their ears cut off by terrorists who infiltrated from Jordan. The paratroopers, now raised to the level of a brigade, were given the reprisal assignment, and Sharon immediately planned an attack against a host of targets in the area. Moshe Dayan, however, ordered Sharon to limit the scope of the action to the destruction of the police station in Kalkilya, where the infiltrators came from.

Sharon called together the troops and briefed them on the mission. He explained that he had chosen the Kalkilya police station because, as a quasi-civilian target, it would show the residents of Kalkilya the dangers in providing refuge for terrorists. The plan called for a battalion under Mordecai Gur (who eventually became Chief of the General Staff and a leading figure in the Labor Party) to carry out the main action and blow up the police station. A second battalion, commanded by Raphael Eitan (who also became Chief of the General Staff, and who led the army during the Lebanon War) was held in reserve.

A company, commanded by Yehuda Reshef, was to set up a blockade deep in Jordanian territory, to prevent reinforcements from reaching the main scene of battle. Artillery batteries along the border were to provide support for Gur's force. Meir Amit, who was at the briefing, was put down by Sharon in front of the assembled troops, "Hey, you great military planner! Why don't you just shut up."

After an opening artillery barrage against the police station, Gur's battalion took control of the station and blew it up. As this was going on, Jordanian reinforcements along the Azun Road ran into the trap set by Reshef's unit. After surprising and delaying them, Reshef moved his men further down the road, once again setting a trap for the advancing Jordanian force. The third time, Reshef discovered that he himself was surrounded by Jordanian soldiers, unable to move.

At Israeli headquarters, Dayan worried about the safety of the soldiers in Reshef's company. The artillery support for Reshef was ineffective, and Dayan was about to make his way back to general headquarters to organize air support. Dayan was very upset about this, knowing that Prime Minister Ben Gurion did not want to risk a clash between the Israelis and the British. It was expected that the British would intervene on behalf of the Jordanians. Dayan accused Sharon of poor planning, and Sharon blamed Dayan for limiting the scope of the action. Sharon finally told Dayan that either Dayan should command the force himself, or he should leave Sharon alone. Dayan left Sharon in charge and returned to general headquarters.

Sharon organized a new force, made up of the men held in reserve, and sent them out to rescue Reshef, with Yitzhak Hofi in charge. After a tough battle, Hofi succeeded in freeing Reshef's company. On their way back to the border, they were ambushed, and bitter fighting continued until dawn when, finally, the Israeli force crossed back into Israel. Sufin, the scene of the ambush, had been one of the targets included in Sharon's original plan of attack, but Dayan had cancelled the plan. The losses on both sides were heavy: the paratroopers suffered 18 casualties and over 50 wounded, while the Jordanians lost 88 killed in action.

The magnitude of the losses and the scope of the fighting alarmed Ben Gurion and Dayan. Dayan was critical of Sharon's planning. He felt that Sharon had continued with his original plan, making no adjustments, even when ordered to limit his scope. This was especially clear in the mistaken order to send Reshef's company deep into Jordanian territory, without being able to cover its retreat through Sufin. In addition, Dayan felt that Sharon made inadequate use of artillery. Sharon countered that had the original plan been approved, the paratroopers would have taken control of all the key points around Kalkilya.

Dayan made no secret of his discontent, and at a general staff meeting he reported that what almost happened was far worse than what actually happened. Had the ammunition run out, there would have been no way of saving Reshef's force. Later, Dayan wrote about this incident: "The fighting ability of the paratroopers and their willingness to risk their lives do not relieve their commanders from the obligation to do everything to minimize the risks. In a discussion with the leading officers of the brigade, I said that the failure to make adequate use of the artillery was not only a tactical error, but worse than that, it was a failure to take advantage of the special conditions of the action."

Dayan's accusation was a severe one. Sharon had not shown sufficient concern for the lives of his own soldiers in planning and carrying out his mission. Until then, there had been no indication of anything but the greatest concern on the part of Sharon for the lives of his men. Sharon had never shown any concern for the lives of his enemies and, in fact, had little but contempt for any of his soldiers who did not shoot to kill. He censured a junior officer in the paratroopers, David Ben Uziel, for failure to kill two elderly Arabs he encountered during a raid. For Sharon, killing the enemy was a simple parameter in the equation of battle: killing the enemy reduces casualties; death is an aspect of war. Planning and commanding a battle was an intellectual exercise in which he tried to arrive at the best results possible – results were measured in numbers. As he watched the bodies of his dead soldiers being carried away after the battle at Kalkilya, he told the officers around him, "This is the other side of the coin."

Sharon claimed that the losses in the Kalkilya action were the direct result of Dayan's blunders. Sharon clearly implied that Dayan was merely trying to pass the blame. Sharon was invited to participate at a news conference to explain what happened at Kalkilya. To his friend, journalist Uri Dan, Sharon carped about the sudden interest the newspapers showed in him. Where had they been through all the successful raids and counterattacks: "They want me to explain the large number of losses. Well, they were unavoidable. I feel that we are seeing the end of the policy of reprisals and that I will have to defend myself against my would-be friends."

There would always be a gap between Sharon's actions and his willingness to bear responsibility for them. He viewed all criticism against him as the result of personal vendettas and totally irrelevant to the action in question.

Sharon's overall evaluation of the situation after the attack on Kalkilya was correct. It represented the end of the era of reprisal raids. The Arab armies had become adept at identifying Israeli targets and taking a high toll in casualties. Among the key decision-makers, the belief was that a war of much wider scope was inevitable if they were to put a stop to Arab terrorism.

CHAPTER 5

On October 26, 1956, in the middle of an official party given by the city of Ramat Gan honoring the paratroop brigade, Arik Sharon was alerted by the General Staff to be at the ready. Not one hour later he was called up by the Central Command, and before leaving the party he notified all battalion commanders to be ready. At central command headquarters, he was told about the assignment given to the paratroop brigade: one battalion was to parachute over the Mitla Pass in the Sinai Peninsula, while the rest of the brigade made its way by land toward the pass from the Egyptian-Israeli border via Kuntila and Temed.

Thirty-six hours later the 202nd Brigade was already making its way toward the demilitarized zone on the border. It was a strange-looking convoy composed of a motley assortment of civilian vehicles, some with signs still advertising their owners' wares, loaded with armaments and other military hardware. The severe shortage of military vehicles didn't stop Sharon from making his rendezvous on time. He enlisted civilian cars. The cars worked their way over the difficult terrain. Nothing slowed the progress of the troops.

The battalion commanded by Raphael Eitan stayed behind in preparation for the jump at the eastern end of the Mitla Pass, near the Parker Memorial. Although originally located at the western end of the pass, the jump site had been changed at the last minute to the east, when an Egyptian encampment was identified on the western side. Sixteen Dakota twin-engine planes took off at 3:30 p.m. on Monday, October 29, 1956 in the first combat jump in the short history of the Israeli army. Under escort of fighter aircraft, the 395 emotionally charged men of Eitan's battalion could make out their comrades on the ground assembling to cross the border. The shower of green and white mushrooms visible from a distance brought news of the jump over the Mitla Pass.

The chief press officer of the IDF was quick to publish the following communiqué: "The IDF has attacked fedayeen units at Ras el-Nakab and Kuntila and has captured key positions to the west of the Nahal intersection not far from the Suez Canal. These actions have been taken in response to Egyptian army attacks on Israeli land and sea transportation, attacks that were intended to sow destruction and deprive the citizens of Israel of their right to live in peace."

At about the same time, the paratrooper land force, led by Sharon, surprised the Egyptians at their base in Nahal with a frontal attack that lasted only twenty minutes. The brigade continued via Kuntila, Temed and Kilat Nahal without meeting any serious opposition as they drove to their tie-up with the parachute battalion. The entire brigade understood that this was not another limited raid into enemy territory, but all-out war. Under Sharon's guidance, the officers of the brigade explained the purpose of the war and its importance. Morale was very high and everyone was confident of the outcome. Eitan's battalion jumped, confident that they would be met within 24 hours, and the rest of the brigade set out confident that they would be able to meet this commitment. They all felt they were taking part in an important war that was, in many respects, the logical outcome of their own reprisal activities over the past few months.

Eitan's paratroopers spent the night of October 29 digging in. The following morning a battalion lookout patrol spied a column of Egyptian units approaching the Mitla Pass. Air assistance was called in, and the Egyptian column was destroyed. There was little other activity for the 30 hours that the battalion was separated from its home unit. As the rest of the 202nd Brigade reached the Parker Memorial, they noticed a sign that Eitan had put up: "Stop – Border Ahead! Please prepare your travel documents." The 202nd had been reunited and in so doing had completed its assigned task in the Sinai Campaign.

The General Staff intended the paratrooper maneuver to be a diversionary tactic. Their goal had been to have the Egyptians believe early on in the Sinai Campaign that, once again, Israelis were conducting a limited raid against isolated Egyptian targets. The jump over the Mitla Pass was also the prearranged signal to Britain and France to enter the foray in a combined campaign with Israel against Egypt. The 202nd Brigade was selected because stranding a battalion, cut off in the desert for over 24 hours, was deemed very dangerous, and only the paratroopers could be counted on to carry it off. Prime Minister Ben Gurion, who had fallen ill on the eve of the campaign, was particularly worried about the fate of these soldiers. When he was informed that the main force was slightly delayed in joining up with the isolated battalion, he even ordered Dayan to return the battalion to Israel immediately; but Dayan successfully mollified him. Aside from the danger to the battalion at the pass, the brigade was not expected to engage in any serious fighting. It had been presumed that the main force would not encounter any real opposition on its way to the Mitla.

Sharon was unaware of the underlying strategic and political considerations that had guided Ben Gurion and Dayan. He did not know of the secret treaty that had been signed with Britain and France, and therefore did not understand that the jump over the Mitla Pass had been intended to set the stage for the intervention of the two superpowers. In this respect he was no different from most of the members of the government, or of the army, all of whom had been kept in the dark during the long and difficult discussions with the governments in Paris and London. On the morning of October 31, Sharon began to understand that the paratroopers' role in the Sinai Campaign was over. It was a conclusion which he refused to accept. Sharon, together with his officers, yearned for battle, seduced even further by reports about the overall scope of the campaign and the actions of other brigades. He knew that in an earlier version of the battle plan the 202nd had been intended to attack the Egyptian army bases in the Gaza Strip, and that only recently had the plans been changed to the parachuting at the Parker Memorial. The paratroopers were capable of so much more, and Sharon refused to resign himself to such a secondary role in the war.

Sharon barraged the General Staff with pleas and requests for permission to engage the enemy from the moment he joined up with the battalion at the pass. His proposal was that his brigade attack the Egyptian forces across the Mitla and continue toward the Suez Canal. Dayan's refusal was peremptory. To assure that his orders were not only heard, but understood and obeyed, he sent the chief staff officer of the Central Command, Lt.-Colonel Rehavam Zeevi, on a special plane to the Mitla to meet with Sharon. Since the raid on Kalkilya, relations between Dayan and Sharon had been strained. Dayan was aware that missions given to Sharon often took on unpredictable and uncontrollable dimensions, and this was not the time for risk. Dayan also noted Sharon's tendency to transfer the blame for his own failures to others, and had even remarked on this problem at a meeting of the General Staff in the presence of Sharon, just prior to the war: "In the war, very difficult assignments will be given out, and there will undoubtedly be some failures. In these cases we may come across officers who shift the blame to what they see as the designated recipient: the Chief of the General Staff. This would be a serious mistake. Relegating blame to others is very easy, but every officer must be cognizant of the fact that in so doing he is sacrificing his own right to demand the supreme efforts required of his own soldiers."

When Zeevi landed, Sharon immediately started to bargain with him. After a long exchange between the two of them, Zeevi finally granted permission to send out a reconnaissance patrol, on condition that it not engage the enemy. The patrol that Sharon put together resembled a well-equipped fighting unit rather than a patrol and, in fact, was the same unit that Sharon had been preparing since the morning. The unit consisted of two motorized companies, a tank platoon, a brigade-level patrol unit on trucks and a mortar battery. The force was led by the commander of the 2nd Battalion, Mordecai Gur and Sharon's deputy commander, Yitzhak Hofi, joined as well.

Sharon's orders to the officers of this force also bore little resemblance to a patrol. They were instructed to advance to the western entrance of the pass and to capture and hold it. Should they face strong opposition to the advance, they were to stop their forward movement and try to break this opposition by using the mortars at their disposal. Sharon was convinced that there would not be very much resistance and that the capture of the western end of the pass would open the way for the brigade to the Suez Canal, where they would join the other brigades and share in the fame that would undoubtedly accrue to the victorious units in the Sinai war. The senior staff of the brigade was in complete accord with Sharon on this assessment.

Mordecai Gur gave the command to move out. The column was a strange sight, arrayed in a long line of halftracks interspersed with tanks, vans, trucks and jeeps; but the most striking feature was the relaxed atmosphere of the entire force. The side flaps on the halftracks were down, most soldiers wore work hats rather than helmets, and the soldiers of the brigade patrol were sunbathing in their trucks. It was as if they were doing nothing more than transferring the picnic from the eastern to the western end of the pass.

The 14 soldiers in the lead halftrack may have noticed the movements on the peaks overlooking the pass, but, if they did, the picnic atmosphere assured their complacency and the halftrack continued to lead the way deeper into the canyon of the pass. At 12:50 p.m., about 15 minutes after entering the pass, the three lead halftracks were hit by a lethal crossfire that seemed to come from all directions. The first vehicle was badly hit. The other two, including one driven by the force commander, Mordecai Gur, rushed to its assistance and soon found themselves trapped as well. There was little hope for the three halftracks as a hail of fire rained on them: bazookas, anti-tank cannons, machine guns, rifles and grenades had all taken aim on the helpless targets. The air filled with the sounds of the explosions and the screams of the wounded.

The trap that had been sprung on the hapless paratroopers

was set up by two battalions of the Egyptian 2nd Brigade. They were the same soldiers spotted a day earlier by Eitan. Eitan had called in the air force and it had successfully destroyed the advancing column, or so thought Sharon some 24 hours later. But Sharon had made a grave mistake. The air force had indeed destroyed the convoy of Egyptian vehicles as it made its way along the road above the pass, but the Egyptian soldiers abandoned their vehicles and spread out in the nooks and crannies overlooking the pass. They selected an ideal location for the ambush, a turn in the pass, not more than 60 feet wide, locked in by the high, sheer walls on the north and south of the pass, about two and a half miles from the eastern entrance.

The result of the ambush was tragic. The lead halftracks with about 40 men led by Mordecai Gur were trapped under intense fire. The second group led by Yitzhak Hofi successfully passed through the ambush and continued toward the western end of the pass, under the mistaken assumption that Gur was ahead of them. Aharon Davidi, commander of the 3rd Battalion, brought up the rear, with a force including the supply trucks and the brigade patrol, when he was attacked by the Egyptian air force. With little room for maneuver, it was as if the planes were using the ammunition and mortar trucks as practice targets. While this was going on, disruptions in the communications were preventing Gur from reporting on his position and clarifying the overall situation. The patrol instituted by Sharon was a serious and fatal blunder.

Using a radio from a tank, Gur succeeded in relaying his location and coordinating the counterattacks of Hofi, now to his west, and Davidi, to his east. He ordered mortar attacks against the precipices from which the Egyptians were firing and requested air support. Their effectiveness was limited by the nature of the terrain, and eventually Hofi and Davidi sent their men up the sides of the ravine to weed out snipers. For seven hours the fighting continued, hand-to-hand or at very short range, under the most difficult of conditions, with casualties mounting on both sides. The paratroopers lacked accurate intelligence about the exact whereabouts of the Egyptians and often found themselves fired upon from unexpected directions, and the Egyptian air force again attacked the supply trucks, totally defenseless on the floor of the pass. Gradually, as the day drew to a close, the paratroopers began to gain the upper hand.

By 8:00 p.m. the fighting completely died down. On the rocky ledges and peaks lay the bodies of over 200 Egyptian soldiers. The paratroopers managed to locate the bodies of 38 of their men and evacuated or treated a further 120 wounded. The rest of the wounded were left for the night, as the darkness made any further search impossible. Moans and screams continued all night, as the cold desert reaped its own victims. Two platoons were left to patrol the heights above the gorge over that long night. They were exhausted and numbed by the fighting, haunted by the sounds of their fallen friends. In the morning, the paratroopers set out to collect the last of the bodies. Attempts to contact the main force by radio were futile.

Sharon had spent the entire day in the rear, at the Parker Memorial. The bits and pieces of information that filtered in painted a complete picture of the catastrophe. He did everything he could to provide the assistance called for by his commanders in the pass, but he chose not to enter the pass and see for himself what was going on. He felt that he could better serve his trapped soldiers by organizing the activities in the rear. Under his command a makeshift air strip was prepared, and that same day planes were landing and taking off with scores of wounded.

Moshe Dayan was in a rage. Sharon's initiative in sending an attack force into the pass was further evidence of his insubordination and disobedience of orders. Dayan appointed Major-General Haim Laskov to investigate the events of the day. At the questioning, Sharon claimed that he was operating under the authority given him by Zeevi, who had been sent by Dayan, and who had not limited the size of the patrol to be sent out. He also noted that the location at the eastern end of the pass was a difficult one to defend and that he would, in any event, have had to move his forces to a more secure location. He mentioned that the original plan had called for dropping his force over the western end precisely because it was a more easily defensible position. The key claim of his defense was, however, that the force sent into the pass had not been sent to wage a battle. The fighting that took place was necessary to rescue the soldiers who had been trapped. He emphasized that he had instructed Gur, as commander of the force, not to engage the enemy and to continue to advance through the pass only if he met no opposition. Developments on the battlefield as a result of the ambush had dictated opening up the fighting in order to free the soldiers who had been trapped.

Dayan was not convinced and brought Sharon to a meeting with the Prime Minister. Ben Gurion asked Sharon if he did not think that the entire action was uncalled for. Sharon responded, "Now, as we sit here, it is possible to think that way, but under the circumstances there was no alternative."

Ben Gurion declined to arbitrate in what he saw as a professional disagreement between Dayan and Sharon. The tragic events were also balanced by what Ben Gurion viewed as the remarkable demonstration of military skill, dedication and loyalty by the paratroopers at the Mitla. Dayan was less enthusiastic. In his book, *The Sinai Diary,* Dayan gives his assessment of Sharon's responsibility: "There was no justification for the action because it was not the brigade's task to reach the Suez Canal... It was an unnecessary battle... The paratroopers attacked the Mitla Pass in violation of my orders and with fatal results. My major grievance is not the battle itself, but rather that they persist in referring to it as a patrol. I regret that I have not succeeded in developing a relationship of trust with the command of that brigade that would enable them to own up to the facts when they act in contradiction to my orders."

Shortly after the war, Sharon visited Mordecai Gur and Yehuda Reshef at the headquarters of the Nahal (a battalion that not only fought and underwent parachute training, but was also involved in establishing or maintaining new settlements in difficult border areas) which they now commanded. They could not control their criticism, attacking Sharon for his behavior at the Mitla Pass and for staying in the rear and not leading a rescue force himself. "You should hear what people are saying about you," Gur ended bitterly. Sharon turned to Reshef and asked him if he thought the same. Reshef responded by saying that he would be with Sharon in time of war, but he could not accept Sharon's norms of behavior.

Sharon summoned his officers to a meeting to air all their misgivings and criticisms. He invited past officers as well as the Commander of the Central Sector, Aharon Yariv, and the Chief Operations Officer of the sector, Avraham Tamir. Sharon convened them to sound off with complete frankness and, in so doing, put a stop to the murmur of grumbling discontent that had been going on behind his back. The senior paratrooper officers, Gur, Reshef, Davidi, Hofi and Eitan, picked up the gauntlet. Sharon's willingness to expose himself to their criticism, and this in front of a stranger, Aharon Yariv, surprised them but did not subdue the rebellion.

Sharon's approach certainly was evidence of his courage and his willingness to gamble. It was also a battle to preserve his leadership, for only by having a direct confrontation would he be able to remove their mistrust and recapture their loyalty. There was no real alternative but to let these men release their anger and bitterness, and, by doing so in public, it would be possible to end the discussion by reasserting his authority. But this unusual meeting may have been motivated by other factors. Did it not provide proof of his contention that he was constantly under attack? This very meeting was the clearest demonstration of a phenomenon which he had noted often: whenever a plan failed through no fault of his, those responsible for the blunder, or at least his partners in the failure, sought a scapegoat to relieve themselves of any responsibility. Dayan had behaved this way after the Kalkilya incident, and his own senior officers were behaving this way after the Mitla. But there may also have been a third explanation. Sharon was aware of the agitation going on among the brigade's senior officers, and he could assume that this had become known to the General Staff as well. He was attending to an illness within his command before it became debilitating, and he was doing so in the presence of a senior officer from outside the brigade. Word would certainly get back to the general headquarters that the problem had been solved.

The accusations made about him at that meeting were unpleasant:

You stayed in the rear at the Mitla Pass.

This was not the first time you remained in the safety of the rear. You failed to live up to the principle that a commander must lead his men into battle.

You relaxed at home even when the entire brigade was called to the base on an alert.

Your eating habits set a poor example for the soldiers.

Your reputation has been built up at the expense of the paratroopers, whom you refused to let share in the fame and limelight.

There is a wide gap between the courage and audacity of your plans and your own willingness to participate in them.

You are a coward.

Despite our disgust with your behavior, we will carry out your plans because you have been successful in getting the approval of the government and the General Staff.

Sharon listened to his officers berate him. In his rebuttal, he impugned their interpretations. He reminded them how he had repelled the assaults against him by officers of the General Staff and expressed his confidence that he would successfully overcome this crisis. He concluded his own comments by calling to account those of his officers who had been particularly hostile in their criticism of him.

These expressions of discontent with his behavior were the culmination of a process that had begun over two years before, and included almost all of the officers who were in close contact with Sharon during that time. The officers who discredited Sharon's leadership in the latter days of 1956 had by now become well-known fighters and commanders themselves. They did not hesitate to call his actions into question. The debacle at the Mitla Pass brought this to a climax. Sharon had not failed because he had sent the troops into the pass, for they themselves had encouraged him to do everything possible to get the approval of the General Staff for the action. Sharon failed because he had not taken the elementary precautions required for the safety of his men, and because he had not stood at the head of the force sent in to rescue the trapped units. They would not forgive him for sending troops into the pass without checking it first and without securing the heights above the narrow ravine. They acknowledged their own share in these mistakes, but the ultimate responsibility was that of the brigade commander – the same one who knew how to garner all the honors for himself in their successful campaigns. But more importantly, even when willing to acknowledge their own responsibility for the failure of the patrol through the Mitla, they still maintained a significant advantage over Sharon: they had rushed to the assistance of their comrades, while Sharon stayed in the rear and supervised the clearing of a field for a landing strip.

Agitation against Sharon among the officers of the brigade spread. They believed Sharon was tired and ready for another army position. They even approached Aharon Davidi with the plea that he try to convince Sharon that it would be in his best interest if he resigned, and ended his career with the paratroop brigade with a measure of respect, but Davidi refused. Yitzhak Hofi, deputy commander of the brigade, once again requested a transfer and once again was turned down. These grumblings of discontent among the senior staff of the brigade had come to the attention of many of the officers at the general headquarters. These officers had long been aware of how Sharon's tactical successes and audacious planning had dragged the country into a broad strategic posture – the policy of aggressive reprisal – which had proved of limited value. They wondered whether this activity had not dulled Sharon's ability to measure the cost in lives that his actions were taking. Even his most virulent critics recognized that he had raised the level of fighting among the paratroopers and, through them, throughout the IDF, but the continued embarrassments and surprises to the government and the army which had inevitably resulted from his actions were a high price to pay.

CHAPTER 6

Two months after the Sinai Campaign, Samuel Scheinerman died. To his dying day, he harbored a grudge against the people of Kfar Malal and even requested that his body be taken to the graveyard in the family van rather than in the wagon that served as the moshav's hearse. Arik and Margalit did, however, provide him with a grandson, Gur, who was born shortly before Samuel died. But the details of Sharon's personal life remain incidental to the life of the man, both because he lived a private, modest and undistinguished life, and because nothing ever really competed with the army in commanding his energy.

In the army, Sharon began to feel the effects of the ill will he generated. For the next seven years Sharon was relegated to secondary positions. Haim Laskov, who succeeded Dayan in 1958, refused to assign any important, responsible positions to Sharon, a decision based on his impressions after investigating the circumstances at the Mitla. Zvi Zur, who succeeded Laskov in 1961, behaved likewise. Sharon felt he could not continue as commander of the paratroopers, and in 1957 he resigned his commission and went to study at an officers' training school in Kimberley, England. This trip marked a turning point in his life: his rapid rise in the ranks of the army had ebbed.

Sharon's studies in Kimberley only reinforced his own sense of superiority. Most students would learn their lessons by rote. He proposed novel solutions to the military problems which they analyzed. His sense of frustration was only exasperated, when he returned to Israel and discovered that he was offered only second line-staff positions. The first such position was as commander of the infantry training section, a position which reported to Major General Yosef Geva, commander of the training branch of the General Staff.

Sharon had little opportunity to prove himself in his new job, for within a couple of months he was removed by Geva. The specific incident which triggered this dismissal was Sharon's failure to appear at a meeting called by Geva. When challenged by Geva to explain his absence, he related that prior commitments had made his presence impossible. Geva investigated this and came to the conclusion that Sharon was lying. His decision was to discharge Sharon. A number of factors combined together to influence Geva. He undoubtedly felt that he could not leave an officer unpunished for lying, especially a full colonel responsible for the training of hundreds of infantry officers. However, the severity of the punishment was almost certainly affected by the long-standing rivalry between them, dating back to the days when Sharon was commander of the 101st. At that time Geva had been commander of the Givati Brigade, and Sharon had never kept his low opinion of that brigade, or any of the other brigades, a secret.

News of the suspension reached Prime Minister Ben Gurion, who summoned Geva for an account of his decision. Ben Gurion defended Sharon, arguing that he was brave, original and a most imaginative military thinker. Geva responded by saying that that might be true, but that he was also undisciplined and a liar. They discussed the exact nature of the punishment, and Geva made it clear that he was removing Sharon from his current position, but not expelling him from the army. Ben Gurion requested that he find an alternative position for Sharon in the training branch and Geva acquiesced. Sharon became commander of the infantry school.

The new job was no better for his ego. Sharon could not reconcile himself to the fact that his fate was now in the hands of others, even if they were Chief of the General Staff and his commander of training. In the past he had always succeeded in maneuvering around or through those of his superiors who had stood in his way, but now he was facing a solid wall of opposition with no obvious cracks. He was convinced that they were giving vent to a personal grudge against him, motivated by their feelings of envy at his skills and successes in the past. Nevertheless, he decided to do his best in his new position and bide his time until circumstances changed.

At the infantry school he presented his now familiar ideas on training, with a special emphasis on the role of the infantry officer: the officer must always lead his men; he must be authoritative, in order to provide his men with confidence; he must know how to take advantage of his qualitative superiority in the face of an enemy that outnumbered him; and he must learn to respond quickly and intelligently to unforeseen circumstances. Sharon took advantage of much of the material prepared in the training branch designed to teach the officers how to contend with an enemy that had been trained by the Russians, as had now become the case with both the Egyptian and the Syrian armies. His students, junior infantry officers, admired Sharon as a military leader and authority; his fellow officers recognized him as an original thinker who made valuable contributions to discussions of military theory; but with his own officers at the infantry school, he quickly developed the reputation of being irritable, frustrated and fickle, given to rapidly changing, unpredictable moods.

Sharon led his staff by means of fear. Officers who reported to him did their best to keep their distance. He dismissed such large numbers of officers during his fits of temper, that a joke began to make the rounds that a General Staff vehicle was permanently on call to remove the disgraced officers. He was offensive and crotchety, and examples abounded to prove this. In one case, he summarily dismissed the commander of the school car pool for providing him with a jeep that was not in top condition when his own car had been taken in for repair. This officer was a civilian employed by the army and refused to accept this arbitrariness. He appealed to the National Labor Federation, and although Sharon tried to present his case as being a question of principle, he was nevertheless forced to accept the officer back. In another example, after changing the lunch time for the school to 12:30, Sharon himself would show up at noon. The first time this happened the master seargent responsible for the kitchen noted that in a question of life and death, all orders must be put aside. In another case, after forcing a change in one of the exercises, he proceeded to censure publicly those officers who had dared to make the change.

As his tenure at the infantry school increased, his dedication began to wane. He even began studying law at Tel Aviv University on a part–time basis. But this lassitude was compensated for by periodic bursts of frenzied activity and martial discipline. Sharon's malice was clearly evident at the staff meetings, where, although the victim changed, rancorous displays of personal insult and humiliation continued. In one instance he screamed at Zvi Zelner, an officer known for his slow speech and methodical thinking, "You're driving me crazy with your talking and your patience." His men took small consolation from the fact that his attacks on the senior officers of the General Staff were equally scathing.

Zvi Zur's appointment as Chief of the General Staff in January, 1961 did not alter Sharon's status. Zur, just as his predecessors, had great respect for Sharon's military skills, but he also shared their apprehensions regarding his all-too-obvious faults. On the basis of his performance with the 101st and the paratroopers, Zur concluded that Sharon lacked both a moral foundation and even a small measure of self-restraint. Zur viewed his approach to political and defense matters as simplistic to the point of calling into question whether Sharon would ever be ready to continue his advance in the ranks of the army to positions which would require decisions based on judgements of the overall defense situation of the country. This was particularly obvious in Sharon's need for immediate gratification and in his unwillingness to work toward longer-term goals and ideals. Sharon still had one mentor in the person of Ben Gurion, who continued to see in him a reincarnation of the Palmah generation; however, Zur refused to yield to the Prime Minister's requests that Sharon be given more responsible positions in the army.

After three years at the infantry school, Sharon entered a special training program in the armored corps. Once again, he distinguished himself with his uncommon thinking. His instructor, Yitzhak Ben Ari, attests to being continually surprised at Sharon's approach and at the solutions and tactics he proposed. The overall assessment of Sharon's ideas at this special course for senior officers was not uniform. Although his originality was granted by all, many of the officers saw unnecessary risks in the tactics he proposed. At the end of his requalification to the Armored Corps, Sharon was given the commission as commander of a reserve armored brigade.

Despite the new-found interest in the Armored Corps, the new position did not provide Sharon with sufficient occupation or dull his sense of frustration at his blocked military career. In one bitterly ironic incident, Sharon participated in a review of a reprisal raid conducted against a Syrian encampment in Nukyev by the Golani Brigade. He was very critical of Zvi Ofer, one of the commanders of the raid, for exceeding his orders. Others at the review contended, in Ofer's defense, that he had only responded to the unforeseen circumstances which had developed during the battle. As Major-General Meir Zorea, commander of the Northern Sector, started his summary of the discussion, he opened with a recital of the myth of Narcissus. The participants at this meeting, members of the senior staff of the IDF, were surprised and not a little confused by the detailed description of the beautiful youth of Greek mythology who pined away with love for himself and his own reflection. As he concluded, Zorea turned to Sharon and said trenchantly, "You are Narcissus. You are incapable of accepting the fact that someone else has successfully led a military action."

In preparation of a major review of the IDF's posture in the Sinai, Sharon requested of David Elazar, Commander of the Armored Corps (and Chief of the General Staff during the Yom Kippur War), that he be allowed to attend the meeting at the General Staff. Sharon argued that he was surprised at the failure to invite the senior field commanders, especially those with so much battle experience. Elazar hesitated and then agreed to let

Sharon raise the point with the Chief of the General Staff, who was expected at the Armored Corps headquarters the following day. At the meeting Sharon once again raised his consternation at not being invited to the meeting, but this time Elazar responded decisively, claiming that Sharon, as well as the other officers, had been given ample opportunity to voice an opinion. Under the circumstances, therefore, he felt that the decision of who should be present at the meeting to represent the armored corps must remain entirely in the hands of the corps commander. Sharon was to remain an outsider, excluded from all the important meetings held at the general headquarters.

A personal tragedy was added to Sharon's professional bitterness. On May 6, 1962, Margalit was driving in the small family car from Jerusalem to Tel Aviv when, near Abu Gosh, she suddenly veered out of her lane. A truck approaching from the opposite direction was unsuccessful in avoiding her. It was a head-on collision. She died in Shaarei Zedek Hospital in Jerusalem.

Sharon was overwhelmed by the news of her death; when he was told, he quietly walked away to a corner and cried. Yet mourners at the funeral recall that Sharon exhibited a totally unemotional facade. He approached the newly-excavated grave and removed a piece of paper from his pocket, tearing it into scraps – a note or a poem he had written for her.

The police investigation found Margalit responsible for reckless and negligent driving. The suit filed against the truck driver's insurance company was settled in a compromise out of court. Among their acquaintances, the accident was explained in different ways. Some felt that Margalit had simply been driving too fast, and as she pulled out to pass hadn't noticed the oncoming truck. Others explained it by emphasizing Margalit's preoccupation with the deteriorating nature of her relationship with Arik. Margalit's love for Arik was deep and powerful. She had an equally strong sense of jealousy. The focus of her jealousy was her own younger sister, Lilly. Lilly had immigrated to Israel as a youngster and spent her first few years at the Sharon home. When called up to the army, she served in the Paratroop Brigade, then under Arik's command. Tension grew in the Sharon home until eventually Lilly moved out. Margalit's acquaintances note that during the weeks just prior to the accident, Margalit was once again depressed and preoccupied, and had confided to a friend that her life had become miserable as a result of her all-consuming suspicion of a liaison between her sister and her husband.

One year after the accident, Arik married Lilly.

Unlike many of the senior officers of the IDF, Sharon was not a womanizer. This was particularly salient during his tenure with the paratroopers. These soldiers enjoyed an incomparable admiration and attracted many women, but their commander remained faithful to his wife. The sudden death of Margalit and Arik's precipitate marriage to her sister was the only event to cast aspersion on this reputation.

Lilly had grown up in the Sharon household. She had also developed an excellent rapport with Gur, the Sharons' son, and would often take care of the boy when Margalit was away from home on one of her trips around the country for her work. With the death of Margalit, Lilly easily assumed the job of Gur's stepmother.

CHAPTER 7

In 1964, following seven years of unmitigated frustration, Sharon was promoted and given a responsible commission. Yitzhak Rabin, who differed from his predecessors, as Chief of the General Staff, in his evaluation of Sharon and his ability to contribute to the IDF, appointed Sharon Chief of Staff of the Northern Sector. The appointment created a tremor of apprehension throughout the command, for Sharon's inability to get along with others had become legend. Avraham Yoffe, Commander of the Northern Sector, shared this nervousness, and in an attempt to assuage his officers, carefully delimited Sharon's authority before his arrival. In particular, he made it clear that Sharon would not have the right to dismiss an officer without his approval. In a short time, however, Yoffe's intentions proved insufficient in controlling Sharon.

Sharon quickly left his inimitable imprint on his surroundings, much as he had done in his previous positions. Sharon demanded total devotion and the strictest adherence to all his orders. He increased the work assigned to his officers and became impatiently irritable at any excuses given for failure to perform up to his demanding standards. Despite Yoffe's declared intention of controlling Sharon, Sharon did pretty much as he chose and suffered no interference. To the senior officers of the command it was clear that Sharon won this battle of wills.

He seemed to be everywhere at once, attending the meetings of the operations branch of the sector, participating in the frequent patrols along the Syrian border, and proposing new plans. It was as if the energy that had been throttled for seven years burst into a frenzy of activity.

Sharon began to focus on the deteriorating relations between Israel and Syria, in particular in view of Syria's attempts to divert the flow of water to the Sea of Galilee, Israel's major source of fresh water. He ordered the soldiers who patrolled the border to go up to the border and, by leaving footprints or some other sign, attest to Israel's sovereignty. For similar reasons he actively supported the farming of the land contiguous with the border, a policy which until then had been discouraged by the Northern Sector command, and which the government had refrained from adopting.

A road paved by Israel in the area of Derbashya, leading toward the Golan Heights, was a particular source of contention as the Syrians interpreted it as a violation of their territory. Whenever this road was used by a patrol, the Syrians fired. The northern command had already learned to prepare for these exchanges of fire, and the artillery batteries and the air force were placed on alert. Despite this tension, an attempt was made to contain these conflicts to the maximum extent possible, until Sharon arrived on the scene. Sharon responded to these attacks on the patrols with much greater firepower and would himself take part in the shooting. The General Staff was not appreciative of this escalation in warfare and sent orders via the operations branch of the Northern Sector to limit these engagements. When informed of the General Staff's decision by the Chief Operations Officer of the Northern Sector, Sharon challenged him, sarcastically demanding an explanation of what the exact difference was between a strong response and a limited one. Sharon finally interrupted the meeting in anger, telling the chief operations officer that he could now command the force himself. The next exchange with the Syrians was indeed restrained. The following day, the Chief of the General Staff, Rabin, visited the Northern Sector headquarters and summoned Sharon to a meeting. Sharon decried the policy of the General Staff and publicly announced his disappointment and resentment at the restraint imposed on him. To Rabin he also confessed that it was his goal to smash the Syrians.

The Syrians did not remain idle in this war of nerves and sent out men under the cover of darkness to farm in the no-man's-land along the cease-fire line. Israel responded by dispatching small raiding parties to uproot these crops and prevent the Syrians from establishing any measure of sovereignty on the land in question. These raids were extremely dangerous and difficult, often entailing the crossing of water ditches dug as obstacles by the Syrians and approaching precariously close to Syrian army positions. At general headquarters there were many officers who opposed this policy and its attendant risks of a major flare-up along the border. Sharon, however, actively supported this policy. In one instance, a paratrooper patrol returned from a mission to report that some equipment was left behind. Sharon ordered them to prepare for a return mission the following night to retrieve the lost equipment, lest it serve as proof in the hands of the Syrians of the policies being perpetrated by the IDF. Mordecai Gur informed Sharon of the General Staff's exception to Sharon's plans. Gur, a senior officer in the operations branch, told Sharon that the Syrians were likely to be ready for such a raid and would undoubtedly have set a trap for the returning soldiers. Under the circumstances, the danger to the soldiers, and of a major confrontation as a result, was too great. Sharon argued with him heatedly, but accepted the decision.

Towards the end of the summer, Israel used bulldozers to prepare drainage ditches for the winter flooding in the Tel Katzir region, a job which had to be performed under heavy cover by the soldiers of the northern sector. It was the general policy of the Northern Sector command to give the utmost consideration to the settlements in the area whenever planning actions with repercussions for them. In one case, when it had been decided to start work on the drainage at Tel Katzir, the Northern Sector staff received a request from a kibbutz near the Sea of Galilee asking that the work be delayed until the early afternoon. A large group of high-school children from Tel Aviv were visiting the kibbutz and would be in the fields picking grapes. The kibbutz was afraid that if any fighting ensued they would be unable to protect the children. The operations branch of the sector approved the delay. Sharon flew into a rage when informed of this decision, claiming that there was no danger of the Syrians intervening in any way. He gave the operations branch an order to send out the bulldozers at the originally appointed hour, but the order was not carried out: "We cannot afford the risk to the children from the possible Syrian shelling."

After ascertaining that the children had returned safely to the kibbutz, the bulldozers set out for Tel Katzir. When the Syrians failed to respond, Sharon could not help but gloat and called the chief operations officer to tell him that his worries were unfounded. Later that afternoon, however, with the digging still going on, the Syrians opened with one of their biggest barrages of artillery fire ever against the bulldozers, scattering the fire over a broad range of military and civilian targets. This time, Sharon recognized his mistake.

In preparation for an important trip by Prime Minister Levi Eshkol to a number of different countries, the Northern Sector command received orders to adopt a low profile for the duration of the diplomatic visits. During this time patrols were to avoid the routes along the border, deferring from any form of provocation. Responses to Syrian shooting were to be restrained. Sharon continued to demand the placement of heavy artillery and mortars along the border, and viewed such requests for restraint as key contributing factors to the defeatist attitude: "Only by pounding every Syrian who fires at Israel will there ever be quiet," he said.

Sharon's approach to the security problems in the north created a great deal of debate. Many of the senior staff felt that Sharon was escalating the conflict for no particular purpose. Many also disputed his determination of where the border between Israel and Syria actually was. Sharon countered with his grab bag of epithets: "defeatist" for the intelligence officer who would not support his definition of the border; "negligent" for a platoon commander who failed to engage the enemy on a patrol; "fool," "idiot" and "moron" were saved for the host of others who aroused his displeasure. Nor were his railings reserved for the officers of the northern sector. Sharon burst out laughing when he received plans devised at general headquarters, expostulating on how divorced those officers in Tel Aviv were from the realities of the situation, remonstrating against their unwanted and blundering interventions.

He shared these demeaning assessments with his own officers, but unlike his paratroop commanders, they were uneasy hearing this. Sharon had imposed a training and operations regimen that kept his officers busy seven days a week, day and night, yet he continued to lead by a reign of terror and fear. The sector was in constant turmoil, and many of the officers claimed that all the activity was serving no useful purpose other than to quiet Sharon's own sense of restlessness.

Among the officers of the northern command, Arik Sharon was known to be thoroughly unpredictable, given to sharply changing moods. One day he could be friendly and the next, for no apparent reason, he would turn hostile and malicious. When his superiors agreed with him he would be loyal; however, when differences of opinion arose, he would undermine their authority by demeaning them at every opportunity in front of his officers. The members of his staff came to learn that when his mood turned ugly, it was better to keep your distance. His audacity and perspicacity in planning missions against the enemy were recognized by everyone, but many also saw in these plans an undiscriminating and often impolitic courting of war with the Syrians. In only one instance did this opposition come to the surface, because, for the most part, Sharon's intimidation assured that this defiance would remain subdued.

At the end of a major exercise, Sharon asked his staff to gather data on the number of vehicles, buses and trucks that would be required to transport the entire Arab population of northern Israel (including members of mixed marriages) to the neighboring Arab countries. This was not simply a numerical exercise, but a request to prepare an operational plan for the relocation of these people. The request was justified as part of a contingency plan in the event that war should break out out between Israel and Syria. The agitation among the Arabs of northern Israel became a worrisome factor during the escalating tensions between Israel and Syria over the diversion of the rivers feeding the Sea of Galilee. The staff officers refused this request, claiming that it must be approved in advance both by the Commander of the Northern Sector as well as by the General Staff. They felt that the IDF would suffer acute embarrassment should the papers for such a plan be discovered among the sector's documents. One staff officer finally complied and provided Sharon with a straightforward numerical appraisal of the number of vehicles required for such a mission, but the rest of the staff made sure that all documentation relating to the subject would be destroyed.

Notwithstanding their opposition to many of Sharon's initiatives, as well as to his willful behavior, his staff officers were just as captivated by his charisma during battle as earlier officers had been. They noted that Sharon's plans were ultimately practical, that their fears of the enemy's response had been exaggerated, and that Sharon had an uncanny ability to predict the Syrians' reaction. The Northern Command also recognized the value of his untiring work and the increased self-confidence which he had instilled in the soldiers. Despite their skepticism regarding his loyalty and motivation, they also began to appreciate the efficacy of his policies. The lands being farmed had continued to expand, and their anxieties over the escalation of the conflict were proving unfounded.

The contradictions in Sharon's personality were conspicuous to anyone who spent more than a few days with him. When relaxed, Sharon could be warm-hearted, with an appealing smile. He still joined in on the occasional feasts, and eating huge platters of food, he seemed unaware of the rest of the world. They knew that he repeatedly visited the veterans of the 101st, often helping them out on their farms, and that he would be very considerate of personal requests referred to him by individual soldiers. They discovered that he took more than a passing interest in politics and that he maintained his contacts with former Prime Minister Ben Gurion. They were somewhat taken aback, however, by his opinion that the army should play a major, behind-the-scenes role in politics. One particular attribute never ceased to amaze these officers: Sharon's brazenness in contending with the opposition of his superiors in the command. He seemed both unconcerned with criticism and completely oblivious to facts and orders when this suited his purpose.

Clashes of the severity that had marred his command of the paratroopers following the debacle of the Mitla were infrequent. One incident does stand out. In a war-games exercise conducted in the north, Sharon commanded the force designated as the IDF and assigned to defend the northern border against attack by the Syrians. The enemy troops were represented by the armored corps under Major-General David Elazar. The judges, comprised of senior officers of the General Staff and led by Mordecai Gur, awarded the victory to Elazar's forces, claiming that they would have successfully threatened the national water carrier and conquered large portions of the north of the country. Sharon refused to accept this judgement, and in the presence of the Chief of the General Staff, Yitzhak Rabin, and most of the senior officers of the General Staff and the Northern Sector declared, "I cannot understand how the IDF allows a man, whose skills are at best appropriate for the commander of a company, to pass judgement on strategic maneuvers. Therefore, I refuse to accept the results of this exercise as determined by the commander of the games."

David Elazar replaced Avraham Yoffe as commander of the Northern Sector, but Brigadier-General Sharon did not have much of a chance to serve under him. He became commander of the training branch of the General Staff. He immediately set to revamping much of the training program then in use, adopting many of the features he had introduced in the paratrooper training. In particular, he reinstituted the commando training for all field officers, to improve their physical fitness and professional ability. Sharon felt that the current level among army officers was insufficient to combat the ever-growing might of the Arab armies. Once again, Sharon earned the respect of most officers for the work he was doing. But they also learned to beware of his violent temper and tendency to unbridled criticism.

In one of his first visits, in his new capacity, to the Officers Candidate School, the school commander, Colonel Meir Pail, told him he would not engage in any pretenses. Still, Pail invited the new commander of the training branch to assess conditions at the school the way they really were. Sharon readily accepted the invitation and arranged to examine one of the platoons. At the conclusion of the exercise Pail suggested that Sharon review the unit and make his comments. Sharon opened his remarks with a scathing critique of the school staff, its instructors and the cadets. The level of the cadets was pitifully low and their performance during the exercise unacceptable. A shocked silence overtook the participants at the meeting. Sharon completed his remarks and without waiting for any further comment got up to leave, when Pail spoke up, delaying his departure: "I am the school commander, and I would like you to hear my summary of the exercise."

Pail began by telling the cadets and the instructors to ignore what Sharon had said. Although he had touched upon some points of merit, Sharon's overall negative evaluation was grossly exaggerated and entirely unjust. Pail declared that the cadets were at a reasonable level and were steadily improving. To Sharon he added quietly that if he were determined to continue this way, he would be well-advised not to visit the OCS again as long as Pail was commander, for he would not let him poison the atmosphere there.

With his appointment as commander of the training branch, Sharon had become a full member of the General Staff, and one year following his commission he was promoted to the rank of Major-General, the highest rank in the IDF short of the Chief of the General Staff, bringing him on a par with his peers. Although this could have been perceived as a fulfillment of eveything Sharon had strived for, he remained impatient, irritable and moody. Sharon himself testifies that the source of this discomfort was his feeling that he was alone among the senior officers to have worked his way up the ranks.

The other generals had a simpler explanation: he was nasty, irritable and unlikable. They all recognized his considerable military skills, but were deterred by his oversensitivity to criticism. They all noted his inability to accept any criticism, however substantive and professional, as anything but a personal attack. This was so severe that the officers of the General Staff avoided discussions of any kind with him. His critics also saw him as egotistical and a chronic liar, whose relationships with others were invariably self-serving. His capacity for work was dismissed as the obsession of a compulsive workaholic.

Sharon did have a few supporters on the General Staff, who viewed him as the finest military thinker. In their estimation, it was his originality and courage that set him apart from the others: he was motivated by an almost fanatical patriotism and a sincere concern for the very existence of the State of Israel; this more than anything prompted his impatience, motivating him to do anything in his power to extirpate the incompetence and inadequacy which he saw around him.

CHAPTER 8

On May 20, 1967, Egyptian President Gamal Abdul Nasser shut the Straits of Tiran, closing the Red Sea to Israeli shipping. Two days later, Prime Minister Levi Eshkol conducted a tour of the three divisions deployed along the Egyptian border to prepare for the expected attack. Sharon was given an emergency commission as commander of one of these divisions.

Nasser closed the Straits in response to the serious deterioration of Israeli-Syrian relations, relations that had reached their low point about a week before, with Israel's downing of six planes over the Golan. Nasser's act of war inflamed sentiments throughout the Arab world, whipping the masses into a frenzy of activity in preparation for the final destruction of Israel and all its citizens. The Israelis saw this; fear and depression swept the country.

Eshkol's image of weakness and moderation, as well as his apparent indecisiveness, emboldened Nasser and encouraged the Arabs to believe in their dreams of a violent revenge. The mood in Israel reflected the confidence of the Arabs and the lack of determination on the part of Israel's political leadership. The IDF division commanders shared these sentiments as well, disconcerted by the fact that the government had no clear idea of how to respond to Egypt. Sharon did not accept this feeling of despondency, either on the part of the army or the government, and requested the permission of the Chief of the General Staff, Yitzhak Rabin, to speak to Eshkol.

The division commanders assembled at the staff headquarters of the Commander of the Southern Sector to meet with the Prime Minister. Rabin began with a proposed plan. The basic premise of the plan was that after capturing land in the northern Sinai, Israel would agree to withdraw on condition that Egypt reopen the Straits of Tiran. The plan did not reassure the division commanders. They saw it as weak-willed, showing a lack of confidence. Then Rabin allowed Sharon to address the Prime Minister.

Sharon explained that implementing this plan would be a grave mistake. Sharon admonished Eshkol to adopt a more ambitious plan – to destroy the Egyptian army in the Sinai and to free the Straits of Tiran by force.

A similar discussion took place at general headquarters a couple of days later. Rabin was on the verge of a nervous breakdown. Sharon, supported by Major-Generals Avraham Yoffe and Matityahu Peled, repeated his own conception of what Israel must do.

Moshe Dayan, who in early May was still only a member of the Knesset (parliament) and Eshkol's political rival, received permission to tour division headquarters along the Sinai border. When he reached Sharon's division, he noted the air of confidence which Sharon generated. Dayan asked if he could join Sharon in his command vehicle should war indeed break out. The division commander hesitated and then said, "Be my guest."

Dayan did not have the opportunity to join Sharon during the war. Under intense public pressure, Eshkol appointed Dayan as his Minister of Defense. This appointment tilted the balance in favor of those supporting the broader plan to capture all of the Sinai and free the Straits by force.

On Monday June 5, 1967, at 10:30 p.m., Sharon gave his artillery battery the order to open heavy fire on the center of the Abu Aguilah region. The target region was pummelled with over 6,000 shells in twenty minutes. Spotlights set up by Sharon improved the accuracy of the artillery. As the shelling ended, an infantry brigade began its clearing-up operation. So did the paratroopers and armored units.

The Egyptian command at Abu Aguilah dominated the central axis of the Sinai Peninsula as well as the roads leading north to El Arish and south to Kesayma. The Egyptians, in strict Russian military style, had deployed their forces in a fixed formation of heavily fortified bunkers covering an area of over 35 square miles. The southern perimeter was protected by a small chain of steep rocky mountains; in the north, there were impassible sand dunes. The units were arrayed in concentric circles of trenches, mine fields and bunkers – including one infantry brigade, six artillery brigades, over 90 tanks and a number of surface-to-air missile batteries.

Sharon's plan consisted of two stages. In the first, the Egyptian stronghold was to be weakened and the roads leading to it were to be blockaded, to prevent the arrival of reinforcements. In the second, the army was to be destroyed. The first stage would lead the Egyptians to ignore the preparations being made for the major penetration. The Egyptians would be convinced of the more limited nature of the strategy, especially since they undoubtedly perceived their position in an almost natural desert fortress as particularly strong.

The maneuvers were not uniformly successful: the paratroopers were discovered and left their mission partially unfulfilled, and the tank groups required three attacks before they succeeded in penetrating the Egyptian hold. But overall, Sharon's plan was executed well, and the entire Abu Aguilah command was captured, with over 1,000 Egyptians killed. Israeli losses were kept to a minimum. Forty died and about 120 were wounded.

Just before the outbreak of the fighting, Sharon rejected a proposal to delay his action until the following day to await air force support for his mission. One day after the fighting had begun, Sharon could look at his decision with pride.

Every senior field officer was given a mobile command shelter to serve as headquarters. These were modestly furnished with a couple of benches that also served as beds, a small filing cabinet, a large wooden table and a sink. The senior field commanders of the division visited Sharon's headquarters only for meetings and discussions; the division staff officers kept their distance too. The result was that the ambience surrounding Sharon's headquarters was set by his regular entourage of supporters, his personal cook and the journalists who accompanied him. (Among the journalists, one stood out: Yael Dayan, the Defense Minister's daughter.) Sharon's mobile shelter was akin to the setting of a royal court, with the leader surrounded by his faithful and admiring followers.

This aura of the successful general was somewhat sullied by the atmosphere of tension that surrounded the division's staff. Sharon worked his staff officers very hard. Three weeks before the war, Sharon managed to dismiss three chief operations officers. Sharon kept at his reserve a group of officers to cover the work he assigned and to fill the vacancies created by resignations or dismissals. The staff officers arrived at his headquarters afraid to incur his seemingly endless wrath; but one result was that they performed well, beyond what could have been expected. The staff officers were never really partners in the formulation of strategic plans. Sharon closed himself off in his command shelter, preparing plans and then calling staff meetings. The plans would be presented at these meetings for comment, but Sharon never set much store by these comments. The staff's function was to translate the plans he had devised into operational orders and then to exercise the units involved. Since he had prepared 16 different programs for the attack on Abu Aguilah, the staff knew little respite in the weeks before the war, often working days on end with no sleep. His demands seemed impossible, but somehow they had managed to meet them. One staff officer, Yosef Sokol, resigned after being censured by Sharon for missing a meeting, after having worked through a day and a night to prepare one of Sharon's plans. He withdrew his resignation after Sharon sent another officer to Sokol to apologize on his behalf.

The strain and fatigue, the mechanical nature of their work and the relentless fear set the tenor of the relationship between Sharon and his staff. In contrast, however, the field officers revered him, trusting his judgement and enjoying his company. Sharon reciprocated this feeling, as long as the officer was successful. For instance, Nathan Nir, a tank commander, had been assigned to outflank the Egyptians and set up a blockade. His first two attempts were unsuccessful. Sharon advised Nir's brigade commander, Mordecai Zipori, to replace Nir, but Zipori refused. The third attempt was successful. Later, Sharon praised Nir for a job well done, saying he knew all along that he was the best officer for that difficult mission.

The battle of Abu Aguilah provided Sharon with an ideal occasion to demonstrate his considerable military skills, his original strategic thinking, his courage and his ability for careful execution. It was his first commission as commander of a full division, the largest and most complex fighting unit in the IDF. His personal desire to flaunt his skills found support in the needs of the hour: Israel faced a real threat to its very existence. A weak-willed government, a diffident and confused military leadership, and his own contempt for the Arabs combined to underscore this unique opportunity.

The lessons to be learned from Dayan's rise to power in the weeks before the war were certainly not lost on Sharon. The broad public support that Dayan enjoyed as a result of his military successes forced his appointment as Minister of Defense. Sharon noted how public pressure and the personal prestige of a military hero transformed the government's policy and raised the morale of the country.

Many of Sharon's staff officers noted his concern for the way his role would be reported in histories of the war. His headquarters were constantly surrounded by reporters, and he also diligently documented his activities. He carefully collected all the plans he had prepared and paid particular attention to demonstrating his loyalty to his superiors and the spirit of their orders. Sharon had played an important role in the war and reported it accurately to the Military History Department of the IDF. One insignificant amendment was made to his report: Mordecai Zipori went through the considerable trouble of correcting a claim by Sharon that a blockade of a particular intersection had not been in place. Zipori noted that the blockade had never been ordered.

Before the Abu Aguilah operation had been completed, Sharon had already requested an additional mission for his division from the Southern Sector command. He was instructed to take the armored brigade commanded by Zipori southwest toward Hemed and Nahal. Sharon joined Zipori's forces, and they made their way slowly over the difficult terrain for two and a half days, stopping to receive supplies and fuel. Sharon managed to reach his goal a few hours before he was informed by Air Force Intelligence that an Egyptian brigade was moving in his direction and was being pursued by a much smaller Israeli force. He immediately improvised a plan to trap them.

Sharon ordered the pursuing Israeli unit to continue their approach and attack the Egyptians from their rear, driving them into the waiting tanks of Zipori's brigade. The armored infantry, with whom Sharon was riding, was behind the mountain ridges that would lock the Egyptians in. Sharon gave Zipori the order not to open fire until the major portion of the Egyptian force was trapped. The Israeli tanks opened fire from both directions and for eight hours demolished the Egyptian brigade, while the armored infantry pursued the Egyptian vehicles that tried to flee the trap. A few Egyptian tanks managed to break out of the trap, but then the air force came into the picture, knocking them out as well as participating in the main part of the fighting. By the early evening the fighting was over. The burned-out, twisted hulks of the Egyptian vehicles and tanks were strewn along a 20-mile stretch of road, punctuated by the bodies of hundreds of Egyptian soldiers, wounded or dead.

A few weeks following the Six Day War, a party was given for the senior commanders of the IDF to celebrate their victory. Sharon was visibly proud as most of the participants congratulated him.

CHAPTER 9

It was the eve of Rosh Hashanah (the Jewish New Year), in October 1967, when the sound of a gun roused Sharon from his seat; he dashed to the door to see what caused the noise. There on the threshold lay Gur, the son whom he loved more than anything else in the world, sprawled on the ground, unconscious and bleeding profusely from the head. Arik lifted him, screaming in agony for help, and rushed him to the hospital; but there was little the doctors could do to save the child.

Arik's emotional investment in his eldest son was enormous, and he wept uncontrollably at Gur's funeral. The boy was buried alongside his mother, Margalit. A broken man, Arik retreated to his home with his wife, Lilly, who was almost as grief-stricken as if she had been Gur's natural mother. There he mourned, with only his closest friends allowed to visit.

It was a pain which allowed him no respite. In the trunk of his car he carried a rake and a watering can, and whenever he passed the graveyard where Gur and Margalit were buried, he tended the graves. On the memorial days of their deaths, Arik, his family, and a small group of very close friends visit the gravesite for a modest ceremony conducted by Hasidim.

Gur was killed by a shot fired from Sharon's old hunting rifle. He had been playing with some friends when, according to the police investigation, the children had apparently put gun powder and scrap metal into the gun. One of them, Yaacov Keren, pulled the trigger while the gun was pointed at Gur. Sharon refused to be reconciled to the accidental nature of the tragedy and for years continued to blame the young Keren boy. Whenever he passed him, Sharon would call out "murderer" and threaten him with arrest. The boy's mother turned to friends and neighbors, requesting that they reason with Sharon and convince him to stop, but very few of these had the courage to confront him. Feeling there was no alternative, she turned to the Chief of the General Staff, Haim Bar Lev, and pleaded for his intervention. Bar Lev talked to Sharon, trying to explain the innocent nature of a child's game, trying to make him see that his anger was misdirected. But Sharon was unable to restrain himself. The intimidations continued, and finally the Keren family moved away.

The army was Sharon's refuge from pain, and he threw himself into his role as commander of the training section. Sharon prepared operational plans for the newly-occupied West Bank and Sinai peninsula, in the event that the fighting resumed. The key element was the crossing of the Suez Canal by mobile bridges which could be rapidly placed in position. A bridgehead would be established on the west bank of the canal, and armored forces would penetrate into the heartland of Egypt. These ideas were translated into detailed operational plans and then into training programs and war games involving the crossing of water barriers. Lessons were also drawn from the experiences of the Six Day War; adaptations were made to the new and larger quantities of arms the Arabs had acquired; and plans were prepared and exercised calling for the carefully coordinated use of combined forces from the different corps.

Sharon devoted a great deal of attention to the relocating of the training bases to the West Bank of the Jordan River, using Jordanian army camps. In many cases the barracks were in a shambles, but Sharon gave the order to make the best of what would be a temporary situation and began allocating training funds for the repair of these bases. Later, Sharon would comment that this policy had not been dictated by strictly **military** concerns, but rather by his attempt to meet a national obligation of settling throughout the West Bank. For the first few years following the war, the dominant expression of the Israeli presence on the West Bank was the soldier who lived on the training base.

Sharon's activities were not limited to the training section. His seemingly unlimited energy once again found an outlet in his contentiousness and belligerence. Many noted that, for the first time, the professional debates were accompanied by personal attacks and political maneuverings. The source of the disagreement was the way Israeli forces should be deployed along the Suez Canal.

Chief of the General Staff Haim Bar Lev contended that maintaining control of the east bank of the canal required that Israeli forces be present right up to the waterline. When the Egyptian war of attrition began to take the form of daily attacks on the Israeli forces there, he ordered the construction of a heavily fortified line of bunkers, which became known as "The Bar Lev Line." Sharon, in contrast, argued that it was critical to maintain flexibility and mobility. In Sharon's view, the canal defense should be based on highly mobile, armored forces in the general area of the canal, but not on the waterline itself.

This debate revolved around the key question of the room available for maneuver should the Egyptians attempt to cross the canal. Bar Lev's proposal was designed to discourage the Egyptians from making any move to disturb the status quo created by the war. However, it required relatively large forces along the canal and exposed them to daily attacks. Sharon's proposal, which called for nothing more than lookout posts along the waterline itself, was designed to trap and attack any invading Egyptian force on the eastern side of the canal, while its supply lines were extended. The perceived danger in this strategy was that superpower intervention might not allow sufficient time to destroy any invading Egyptian forces. A third alternative, a preemptive attack to destroy the Egyptian forces before they could even attempt to cross the canal, was dismissed on the assumption that diplomatic and public pressure would not be understanding of Israel's defense concerns when the battle front was so far from civilian population centers.

The debate intensified as Nasser's declared war of attrition began to take a larger toll of casualties. Sharon was part of a small group of senior officers (his main partner being Major General Yisrael Tal) who opposed the dominant military conception as voiced by Bar Lev. Sharon claimed that the increase in casualties was further proof that the current position along the canal was untenable. Sharon argued that the conflict was between the old-fashioned "Maginot Line" mentality of the Chief of the General Staff and the newer and original strategy that he embodied. The disagreements at times also took the form of a clash between the "armor" men, with their heavy-handed, complicated way of thinking, and the lean and flexible "infantry" men, typified by the paratroopers and led by Sharon.

These debates were not contained within the General Staff. Sharon made it a point to inform the press in detail of his criticism of the direction of the IDF and what the alternative, preferred strategy would be. The unprecedented leaks to the press from General Staff meetings were clearly attributed to Sharon, who could be seen at these meetings recording various comments in his small, orange notebook. This unprecedented breach of confidence, and the overall degeneration of the General Staff debates to personal attacks, set the stage for a very unusual meeting.

Bar Lev convened a meeting to discuss the security situation along the canal, a meeting chaired by Defense Minister Dayan. Not long after the meeting began, Major-General David Elazar, Commander of the Northern Sector, took the floor and announced that he was disgusted with Sharon's continued deprecation and smearing of the Chief of the General Staff and a number of other officers. Elazar reminded those present that he, too, had been the recipient of these personal affronts (evidently referring to Sharon's criticism of him for not having captured more Syrian territory in the Golan Heights during the war and for not driving out more of the Arab residents of the Heights). Taking their cue from Elazar, the other generals at the meeting were quick to join the fray. They denounced Sharon for his lack of loyalty and comradeship, for his use of the press to force changes in military policy, for his habit of making offensive personal accusations, and for the ugly atmosphere he created at the meetings. In the heat of these accusations, Sharon was even charged with dereliction in the performance of his duties as head of the training branch because he devoted all his time to personal intrigues.

For a while Sharon listened impassively, but as the line of accusers stretched on, he abruptly stood up and asked bitterly whether the General Staff meetings had now become the stage for "This Is Your Life – Arik Sharon." Throughout this lynching, Chief of Staff Haim Bar Lev remained silent, giving a clear impression that he was a partner to the sentiments expressed. Only the commander of the Air Force demurred, and after Sharon left, announced emotionally that he would not be part to the wholesale denunciation of one of the staff members. Dayan called the meeting back to order and announced that the deliberations would continue without Sharon, and the discussions returned to the original agenda of improving Israel's response in the war of attrition. A week later there was a follow-up meeting, but all attempts to ignore the hard feelings of the previous meeting proved impossible. Bar Lev refused to overlook Sharon's angry departure and summarily cancelled his commission as head of the training branch, appointing Yitzhak Hofi in his place. Sharon responded by taking a leave of absence.

It was not Bar Lev's only attempt to rid himself of Sharon's presence on the General Staff. When he was first appointed Chief of the General Staff in January, 1968, he was surprised by Sharon's overtures of friendship, but during their joint tenure at general headquarters, relations between them soured. Despite Sharon's unconcealed ambition to be commissioned as the head of one of the key commands in the IDF, Bar Lev continued to pass him over, keeping him as head of the training division. As Sharon's belligerence became particularly pronounced, Bar Lev even tried to force him out by exploiting a bureaucratic loophole. Sharon had failed to fill out a standard army form requesting an extension of his service, and Bar Lev was only too happy to force his retirement. Sharon appealed to Dayan, but his intervention failed to help. Bar Lev was intent on ridding himself of Sharon. Sharon then spoke to Prime Minister Golda Meir, but she refused to intervene in the affair and left it to the discretion of her Defense Minister.

Sharon decided to fight back. He signaled to Menahem Begin and Yosef Sapir, the heads of the right-wing bloc of parties known as Gahal (made up of the Herut and the Liberal parties), that he was about to retire from the army and would be interested in joining their parliamentary list with an eye to the forthcoming elections. Pinhas Sapir, the kingmaker of the Labor Party, feared just such a move on Sharon's part and persuaded Bar Lev to relent and keep Sharon out of the way in the army. Sharon was summoned to a meeting. He apologized for his behavior at the General Staff meeting and promised to improve his relations with his colleagues. Soon thereafter, Bar Lev appointed Sharon head of the Southern Command.

This was not Sharon's first contact with Pinhas Sapir. A number of years earlier Sharon had made a special point of making Sapir's acquaintance. These connections could also be very valuable in promoting his own career, within the army as well as in politics. In a country as small as Israel, the ruling elite in the army and in the government knew each other well, and senior officers in the army frequently met with members of parliament or the government.

Sapir finally agreed to join Sharon on a tour of the West Bank. Sharon had been trying to convince Sapir, then Minister of the Treasury, to join him and see for himself the importance of this territory in terms of the development of the country and its defense. Sapir had been known for his reluctance to take any step that would perpetuate and finalize Israel's hold on these lands. They left in the morning in a military vehicle, accompanied by Sharon's driver and Yossi Sarid, Sapir's assistant (later one of Sharon's bitterest opponents). Sharon gave Sapir the grand tour throughout the West Bank. On the way, they stopped outside Ramallah and lunched on army rations that Sharon had prepared in advance. The entire day was a unique experience for Sapir. Making their way back toward Israel, Sharon suddenly turned to Sapir, saying he was convinced that Foreign Minister Abba Eban was an American spy. Sapir kicked Sarid in the leg and indicated to him by touching his temple with his finger that Sharon must be insane.

Sharon was certain that his new appointment would be an ideal jumping-off point in his pursuit of his real ambition, Chief of the General Staff. He threw himself into the job with energy and devotion, making sure that he kept on the best of terms with Bar Lev. As the war of attrition escalated, Bar Lev gave him an order to fortify the positions on the canal bank, and Sharon amply demonstrated his own industriousness and perseverance in carrying out these orders. Within days, Sharon had organized the enormous resources required for this considerable and often dangerous task: hundreds of workers with their heavy machinery worked on the infrastructure, the water lines, the communications network, the fortifications and the trenches. Sharon did not hesitate to phone the commander of the construction department of the IDF in the middle of the night, to demand an explanation of why a truck had been late in delivering the necessary building materials.

While overseeing the construction of the Bar Lev Line, he formulated fresh mobile defense tactics based on the newly-designed tank shelters and the artillery. He initiated paving a number of key roads to assure mobility from one section of the canal line to another, as well as to the waterline itself. The forces felt his presence. He visited the front lines often, supervising, giving advice and encouragement, and often probing into the smallest of details. Visits to the canal line became a popular pastime for the members of the Security and Foreign Affairs Committee of the Parliament. At such times the old Sharon was clearly recognizable, mocking and ridiculing the wisdom and understanding of these so-called leaders.

Sharon was completely loyal to Bar Lev's policies. He maintained that if the Egyptians chose to impose a war of attrition, it was incumbent upon the IDF to extort the highest price possible until Egypt was convinced that it could not accomplish anything with this policy of aggression. The latter stages of this war of attrition did, in fact, include the destruction of almost all the Egyptian canal-zone cities, invasions and raids deep into the Egyptian heartland, and numerous air battles, including direct confrontation with Russian pilots, who were piloting Egyptian aircraft.

In August 1970, Israel and Egypt agreed on a cease-fire. Sharon turned his attention to terrorism originating in the Gaza Strip. One terrorist attack, on a family driving innocently through the city of Gaza, resulted in the murder of the two children and the wounding of their mother. It was this attack that prompted Dayan and Bar Lev to direct Sharon to "establish order" in Gaza. Sharon planned this program systematically, assigning it to an elite commando unit. The Gaza Strip was divided into squares which were given code names. The unit was to comb the area, square by square, until it was certified that no terrorists were left. Sharon ordered that the lower branches of the trees in all the orchards were to be cut off, improving the soldiers' field of vision and eliminating potential hiding places. He ordered that the caves and bunkers that had served as havens for fleeing terrorists be sealed off. He also resorted to such stratagems as having soldiers, dressed as local Arabs, call on suspected families and engage them in conversation to find out how deeply they were involved with the terrorist organizations.

Sharon achieved his goals by working systematically and relentlessly. For months he remained at his post at night, sleeping at his headquarters, to supervise search and destroy operations. On his orders, every adult male in Gaza was stopped and subjected to a thorough search. Periodically, curfews were imposed on the refugee camps, and all residents were assembled for hours on end for purposes of identification. Paths through the refugee camps were widened and the population thinned out, to make it harder for the terrorists to find refuge. He personally briefed the commando squads before they left on their patrols and would often participate himself. He seemed always to be there when problems arose, providing solutions, encouraging soldiers, and demanding results.

Sharon was accused by Palestinian organizations of secretly killing fedayeen who had been captured alive. He adamantly denied this, although he admitted that his soldiers had orders to shoot to kill all terrorists and not to make an effort to capture them alive. A quote attributed to Sharon began to make the rounds, "The only good terrorist is a dead terrorist." A rumor could also be heard, some say instigated by Sharon, that he would roam the Gaza Strip with a list of wanted terrorists in hand, crossing off the names as they were eliminated. Within seven months Sharon and his men ended terrorism in the Gaza Strip.

The commando units had scoured every home, every cave, bunker and orchard. They discovered huge caches of guns and ammunition as well as detailed plans for attacking civilian targets within Israel. The fierceness of these patrols had terrified the residents of Gaza to the point where they became reluctant to either participate in further terrorist activity or provide active support for those who did. The results spoke for themselves. Seven hundred and forty-two terrorists were killed or captured between July and December, 1971. In June, 1971, 34 terrorist incidents were recorded: in December of that year, only one. Between June, 1967, following the Six Day War and Israel's taking control of the Gaza Strip, and June, 1971, when Sharon took direct control of these actions, Israeli security forces put 179 terrorists out of action. In six months Sharon had more than quadrupled this number, silencing key regional and local terrorist commanders. Moshe Dayan praised Sharon and attributed the success in smashing the terrorist organizational structure in the Gaza Strip to him.

The secret of Sharon's success in these operations was his willingness to confront the terrorists directly. Unlike his predecessor, he placed little importance on pressuring the political leadership of the Gaza Strip, or on armored patrols through the cities and camps as a show of force. He ordered foot patrols and thorough searches, which inevitably exposed both sides to hand-to-hand combat. In order to save the lives of his commandos, he ordered them to minimize their risks: before investigating a suspicious bunker, a hand grenade was thrown in first; one group covered for another, using more rather than less fire power. Suspects who did not respond to an order to stop were fired on with intent to kill. These policies created a certain discomfiture, and the Chief of the General Staff sent observers to review these actions, but nothing untoward was found.

Sharon's actions in wiping out the terrorist activity were performed in direct opposition to the policies of Lt.-General Yitzhak Pundak, the commander of the Gaza region, who argued for the limitation of all police and military involvement in the Gaza Strip. Pundak called for a program of improving the living conditions and material welfare of the residents of the region and normalizing relations between Israel and the local population, thereby reducing the attractiveness of joining in the terrorist and other underground operations. His program strove to rebuild the local economy, to introduce social welfare services and youth programs, and to modernize the key agricultural sector of the economy. Sharon's approach was the antithesis of Pundak's and was based on the premise that the only way to combat terrorism was to deter the local population from cooperating with the terrorists with force and fear. Sharon did not hesitate to uproot an orchard or other crop in his pursuit of the terrorists. The senior officers on assignment in the Gaza region were trapped between implacable foes and conflicting orders. Ultimately, a tacit coalition was created between Sharon and Pundak's men, who cooperated fully with Sharon in designing and implementing his strategy.

The local population was trapped between the terror of the IDF and that of the PLO. Local PLO leaders used flagrant torture and the most horrifying forms of murder to intimidate the locals from any show of cooperation with the conquering forces of their enemy. Bodies were found impaled on stakes, torn to pieces or bloated to the point of rupture. Sharon's tactics were less crude, but no less effective. Thorough searches were conducted by stripping suspects in public; weapons caches were sought around houses by excavating trenches around them, even when this would irreparably weaken the foundations of the houses; and curfews would be imposed for days, while crops began to rot for lack of attention. Sharon supervised personally throughout.

There was no doubt as to the efficacy of Sharon's program; however, it was beginning to generate opposition within the ranks of the army. This was not limited to Pundak. Yitzhak

Abadi, the senior field commander charged with implementing Sharon's programs, became disillusioned with the extremity of the actions and the hostility it was engendering among the Arabs of the Gaza Strip. In particular, he maintained that the worsening economic situation was driving the people to engage in terror for pay. He proposed that the tough policies of Sharon be supplemented by some form of economic support and compensation for the innocent majority of the population. Abadi, who had served under Sharon in the paratroopers, held Sharon in the highest personal regard for his leadership and military and organizational ability. Still, his cruelty to the local population reached a point Abadi could no longer accept. Abadi, who had personally been assigned to the Gaza Strip by Defense Minister Dayan, now requested that he be relieved of his commission.

Dayan summoned Abadi to an interview to explain his resignation. Abadi explained that he could no longer be a partner to Sharon's reign of terror. Dayan did not respond directly, but a few days later Sharon called Abadi to a meeting and asked him to repeat his conversation with Dayan. The two of them reviewed the situation in Gaza and the right to speak one's conscience in the army. The meeting was an emotional one, and both were often on the verge of tears. Less than a week later, Sharon notified his senior staff that the Minister of Defense had decided to transfer responsibility for the Gaza Strip from the Southern Command to the Central Command.

Sharon was also responsible for a number of raids conducted beyond Israel's borders during this time. In March, 1970, rockets were fired from Jordan at the potash plant near Sodom, and Sharon obtained approval to respond forcefully to this attack on one of the country's most sensitive factories. Sharon personally led the reconnaissance patrol, and the subsequent raid captured the Jordanian village of Safi, opposite the potash plant on the Jordanian side of the Dead Sea. The IDF held this land for over one month and did not withdraw until Jordan guaranteed to prevent all further terrorist activity in that area, an agreement negotiated under the auspices of the U.S. In another case, Sharon in effect established Israel's sovereignty over an area whose ownership was in dispute. In the Arava, the long desert border between Jordan and Israel, Sharon claimed the land by moving his forces there and patrolling the disputed area on a regular basis. Later Sharon noted that he had never received authorization for this minor conquest, but that Dayan had been fully aware of what was going on.

Based on just such a tacit understanding with Dayan, Sharon also undertook a program to evict the Bedouins who had settled in northern Sinai, southwest of the Gaza Strip. As the two men flew over the area one day, Dayan casually remarked that it would hardly be a tragedy if there were no Arabs living there. It would then be possible to fence off the area, creating a security belt around the heavily populated Gaza Strip. Sharon did not ask the Defense Minister if his musings were in fact an order. He assumed that if he asked for an explicit sanction to act, Dayan would refuse. Sharon understood that Dayan preferred to be circumspect, to avoid being put on the spot should his ideas lead to political difficulties.

Sharon proceeded to implement what he envisioned as a long-term strategy for the mitigation of the Palestinian threat to Israel via the Gaza Strip. Sharon's plan called for isolating the Gaza Strip from the Sinai peninsula, severing the continuity of the Palestinian population within Gaza by introducing Jewish settlements in its midst, and thinning out the population of the refugee camps. Sharon began by forcibly evacuating thousands of Bedouins from northern Sinai and encouraging the establishment of new settlements in their place. He justified this action on the basis of national security: the imperative to isolate the Gaza Palestinians from their sources of arms in the Sinai. He also vigorously supported plans for Jewish settlements in the Gaza Strip, to blur the unequivocally Palestinian character of the area. Years later, Sharon boasted that under the cloak of the war against terrorism he had effectively extended the Israeli border into northern Sinai, and that as a soldier he had dictated a national policy which the government had no choice but to approve.

The Bedouins were evicted from the northern Sinai with a vigorousness and violence that stirred many Israelis to protest.

These protests began among the Israeli kibbutzim in the Negev and spread throughout the country. Newspapers were filled with touching accounts of the helpless Bedouins as they faced the might of the IDF. The public shouted for answers to the very embarrassing questions raised about Israeli policy toward the residents of the occupied territories, as well as to army brutality.

Sharon went on the offensive against his detractors, visiting a number of kibbutzim in the Negev to explain and to argue for his policies in the region. He pointed out that the Bedouins had moved to the area only a few years before, after the Six Day War. He reminded the kibbutzim that they themselves were occupying land that had been abandoned by Arabs who fled during the War of Independence. He pointedly asked why they had never protested Palestinian attacks against Jews or against Arabs who chose to live peacefully alongside their Israeli neighbors. Sharon marshaled wealth of facts and figures.

David Elazar, wno replaced Bar Lev as Chief of the General Staff in January, 1972, was unconvinced by Sharon's able defense and decided to investigate the many charges raised against the IDF's conduct in Gaza and the northern Sinai. He was particulary concerned about the eviction of the Bedouins. He appointed Major General Aharon Yariv to investigate Sharon's deeds. Sharon told Yariv sarcastically that he could conclude his report immediately: "I gave the order and I won't deny it." Aside from a relatively mild verbal censure, Elazar took no action. Dayan was somewhat surprised by Elazar's mild and tolerant handling of Sharon and asked Yariv on one occasion how he would explain this, but Yariv declared that as Defense Minister, Dayan certainly did not require his assistance in communicating with his Chief of the General Staff.

Although she was very critical of Sharon at government meetings, even referring to him as a threat to democracy, Prime Minister Golda Meir supported Sharon's actions in evicting the Bedouins and setting up a security zone between Gaza and the Sinai. In one protest demonstration held at a kibbutz in the Negev, Meir addressed the assembled people: "After it became clear that the evacuation of the Arab residents had been undertaken without authorization, without a decision by the competent authorities, and in a manner inconsistent with our beliefs, the Chief of the General Staff appointed a committee of inquiry well before these protests and demonstrations. The program approved for the relocation of these people was a very expensive one. My conscience is clear regarding the fact that the minings and murders were worse than the eviction of innocent people."

Sharon saw this public uproar as evidence of sheer hypocrisy – to make him the scapegoat for implementing national policy. He was certain that the eviction of the Bedouins was perfectly in accord with the government's program to settle the northern Sinai. The posturing of the politicians and senior officers of the IDF was typical of their attempts to shirk off all responsibility for anything remotely unpleasant. From Sharon's perspective, his willingness to bear complete responsibility for the actions taken was also necessary in order to defend his own men, who were forbidden by law from responding. The attacks were another link in a long chain of attempts to cast aspersion on his own character, and fit perfectly with his conception of the injustices done him in the past.

The Bedouins appealed to the Israeli Supreme Court to stop this eviction and allow them to return to their land. Sharon prepared the key portion of the government's case, basing his defense on grounds of security. He presented a profusion of data that purported to show that Rafiah, where they were, was a key center of terrorist activities conducted both against Israel and against the peaceful majority of the Arab population of Gaza. The Rafiah salient was described as the main avenue for the introduction of arms from Egypt into Israel and the occupied territories. The Supreme Court, basing its decision on the arguments for the security of the nation, rejected the Bedouins' appeal.

This trial did not represent the end of the affair. Many opponents of the government's policy were severely critical of the biased picture and gross exaggerations of the government's brief. Their claim was that most of the attacks alleged to have originated in the Rafiah salient had come from the city of Rafiah in the Gaza Strip and not from the Bedouin encampment to the south; that the IDF had, in fact, hired hundreds of these Bedouins for various jobs, including guard duty; that the mines uncovered were left over by the Egyptians after their withdrawal in the Six Day War; that it was highly unlikely that the IDF would have allowed the Bedouins to accumulate such large quantities of arms; and finally, that the IDF had demonstrated in the Gaza Strip that it was capable of wiping out terrorist activity without evicting whole populations. The inevitable conclusion drawn by these opponents was that the evacuation had not taken place because of national security reasons, but in support of the government's intention of transferring control of the northern Sinai to the Jewish settlers.

After Nasser died and was succeeded by Sadat, the Chief of the General Staff appointed a high-level team to review policy alternatives for peace with the new Egyptian leader. The team included Aharon Yariv, Herzl Shafir and Ariel Sharon. Sharon presented a detailed proposal under which Egypt would have complete civilian control over the entire Sinai peninsula, while the Israeli army would continue to maintain military control for a period of 15 years. During this time, each side would have the opportunity of examining the other, with the goal of shortening this period of military occupation as some measure of mutual trust was developed. Egypt would commit itself to reopening the Suez Canal and reconstructing the canal-zone cities, and Israel would withdraw its forces from the canal waterline. Sharon's proposal startled everyone on the General Staff: how could this moderation be reconciled with his belligerence toward Egypt since the Six Day War? Did this provide a view of a new and hitherto unknown diplomatic skill, or was it rather a cynical adaptation to the changing mood of the country? Was it an expression of fatigue at the continuing war of attrition, or was it a devious way of making Israel's control of the Sinai permanent? Sharon's real motives were never discovered. The proposal formed the basis of the General Staff's recommendation to the government, but it was rejected by Prime Minister Meir. With the cease-fire that ended the war of attrition, Sharon adopted a position completely opposite to the one he had proposed to the General Staff. He now called for the rapid settlement of the eastern Sinai and for the effective annexation of this area and the Gaza Strip.

In May 1973, a red alert was declared in the army in the face of what seemed to be Egyptian preparations to attack Israel across the canal. This state of emergency enabled the Southern Command to test its readiness and examine its battle plans in case of war. These plans were based on the premise that the IDF would attempt to transfer the fighting to the Egyptian side of the canal as soon as would be possible. Sharon made plans to cross the canal and had even marked off a number of locations that had appeared to him to be the best crossing points. The alert was gradually reduced, and a few days later was removed, as it became evident that the Egyptians had only been involved in a major training exercise.

The state of alert had renewed Sharon's contacts with Defense Minister Dayan, and he took the opportunity of sounding him out about his future prospects within the IDF. Sharon very much wanted to stay in the army and eventually to serve as Chief of the General Staff, either in the next term or the one following. Dayan made it clear that the government did not see him as a candidate for the position. Sharon then asked that he be granted permission to continue as commander of the Southern Sector for an additional year, but Dayan once again disappointed him, telling him that he would be relieved of the commission when the normal three-year term had ended, toward the end of 1973.

Sharon acted with dispatch and sent off his letter of resignation shortly after this meeting. His resignation was accompanied by a well-organized public relations campaign in which he claimed that he was being driven out of the army and had been prevented from competing on a fair basis for the position of Chief of the General Staff. In a very long newspaper interview at the time, Sharon claimed that the IDF had become a powerful army, but that the government continued to function from a position of weakness. He contended that the government should adopt a much more forceful foreign policy, and, had it more self-confidence, it would have succeeded in preventing the terrorist activities directed against Jews and Israelis outside of Israel. He stated his personal wish to serve the country as the

Minister for Jewish Affairs, a new cabinet position which he favored; however, he denied any immediate plans to enter politics.

These declarations, as well as his precipitate resignation from the army, were the result of his plans for entering the political arena. The Labor Party government apparently had little respect for his skills as a military leader and, therefore, were easily willing to see him leave the army. His political goal was to remove this government. Although he undoubtedly must have understood that the opposition of Meir, Elazar and Dayan to his appointment was based largely on his personality and lack of diplomatic skills, he continued to attribute his rejection to their differences in defense policy.

Sharon hastened his departure from the army because parliamentary elections were approaching. Although publicly denying any such intentions, he maintained close contact with the leaders of the liberal wing of the Likud, in the hope of getting a top position in that party. Israeli law forbids a government employee, including members of the armed forces, from seeking election unless they resign their positions at least one hundred days prior to election day. At his carefully-staged farewell party, Sharon declared:

"...New circumstances have arisen which have forced me to leave the army. I would like to emphasize that this was done completely against my will. I emphasize this because I owe an explanation to the many people who encouraged me to continue my military service...There has been no war in which I have not served. I have been privileged to serve the State of Israel for over 25 years at all the critical points in its development. It has been a great period of time...I have felt the elation of victory. I have felt the terrors of overwhelming fear and the pain at the loss of close friends. On a personal level this period of time has also contained everything – wonderful happiness and deep sorrow. We have enjoyed the happiness of victory and the feelings of love and debt which follow great victories, but we have also felt the terrible pain of the personal tragedies that have befallen us. I have probably experienced these shifts from happiness to pain more than anyone.

"If there is one thing I am proud of, more than anything else that has taken place during the past three years, it is that I have avoided joining any particular group (within the IDF) and have worked alone instead. I always maintained that the only group I belong to consists of my family: my wife Lilly, my mother, my sons, Omri and Gilad.

"I have always maintained that a man must voice his opinions and then be willing to fight for them. Our military men are not just soldiers. In fact, I have been engaged in matters of state for almost 30 years. These matters have always been settlements, borders, water, etcetera...It would be only natural for me to continue to fight for these goals in the future...My father would have been very proud of my service in the paratroopers. My home and the settling of the land have influenced me more than anything else. My service in the elite units of the army has never ceased to be a challenge, to which I devoted myself heart and soul..."

Sharon's speech was carefully worded, but its main point was to focus on the injustice done to him. Whereas his approach to the army had always been professional and practical, a coalition of generals and politicians had formed to oppose him on purely personal grounds. Sharon's successor at the southern command, Shmuel Gonen, was nonplussed by these comments, and when Sharon asked him to come up to the stage to say a few words in honor of the occasion, he explained to the gathered crowd that he was a bit surprised by Sharon's comments and didn't know how to respond. He confined himself to wishing Sharon good luck.

On the morning of July 15, 1973, Sharon drove to the headquarters of the Chief of the General Staff in Tel Aviv to receive the official notification of the cancellation of his commission. He then drove to the Southern Sector headquarters in Beersheba, where the command was officially transferred to Gonen in a modest ceremony before an honor guard; the requisite pleasantries and good wishes were exchanged. Later, a soldier drove to Sharon's home to deliver his new papers as a reserve officer, an official letter of departure from the Chief of the General Staff, and a standard oath of secrecy to be signed upon discharge from the army. It was to have been Sharon's last day in the army, a farewell to 25 years of military service in the IDF.

When he arrived home he changed his clothing and went out to meet the host of journalists waiting for his return: "Well that's it. Now I have to tend to the lambs, the sheep and the horses on my ranch. For 28 years I have been a soldier, but in the final analysis I am a farmer."

Two weeks later he received his official membership in the Liberal Party. He had no intention of spending the second half of his life on his giant farm – over 1,000 acres, it is probably the largest privately owned farm in the country. He was confident that he would be able to create the greatest revolution in Israeli politics since the founding of the state: the creation of a right-wing bloc that would finally throw the Labor Party out of power.

CHAPTER 10

Sharon's plunge into the world of professional politics was preceded by an important consultation with two close friends and advisors in the United States, Meshulam Ricklis and Sam Saks. When the city of Ramat Gan had adopted the Paratroop Brigade a number of years earlier, Mayor Krinitzi had turned to Ricklis and Saks for financial assistance, and it was then that they met Sharon. Ricklis and Saks were typical of a number of wealthy American Jews who diligently nurtured their special relationships with key Israeli public figures. As a former Israeli citizen who had emigrated to the U.S., Ricklis had a further reason for maintaining a connection with his homeland. The two had helped Sharon financially on a number of occasions, including the mortgage on his ranch. They believed that outstanding public figures such as Sharon should be freed of their financial dependence on the Israeli political system. Sharon told them about his fate and the fact that his career in the army had effectively been blocked, and they both encouraged him to pursue a new career in politics, to assure his involvement in the shaping of Israel's future.

As Sharon made his decision to enter politics, he was convinced of his ability to create a better future for the country. His primary concern was for the defense of the country, but he was convinced that Israel had developed into a major military power and that this strength should be used as the basis for its policies.

The Israeli political scene was dominated by the Labor Alignment, which united the different labor parties. The Labor Alignment had ruled the country since its founding. The major opposition party was Gahal, formed in 1965 by the union of Herut and the Liberal Party. Aside from the religious parties, there were also varying numbers of much smaller splinter parties formed by maverick politicians who could not find their way in the mainline political groupings or, more often, had become disaffected and broken away from them. Two such groups were the National List headed by Yigal Horowitz, which had broken away from the Labor Party and had undergone a number of reincarnations, and the Free Center Party, headed by Shmuel Tamir, who had broken away from Herut.

Sharon contacted these two leaders before he left the army to sound them out about his idea for the formation of a major right-of-center political bloc to include their parties as well as Gahal. He believed that only such a union of forces would have a reasonable chance of defeating Labor's hold on the government. The major stumbling block to the creation of this kind of coalition seemed to be the ill will that existed between Herut, led by Menahem Begin, and Shmuel Tamir. Any proposal for cooperation between the two was dismissed.

Begin was no stranger to Sharon. Sharon had often worked behind the scenes in the government to influence political decisions that would have an impact on the army. Their relationship became much closer when a national unity government was formed just prior to the Six Day War and Begin joined the cabinet. Begin had been one of the leaders to apply pressure on Bar Lev to promote Sharon and was a very attentive follower of Sharon.

Beyond these formal associations, there was an interesting personal connection between their families. In 1904, when Theodor Herzl, the father of Zionism, died, the rabbi of the Lithuanian community of Brest locked the doors to the synagogue to prevent a memorial service. Like many of the Orthodox leaders of the time, he disliked Zionism, feeling it was a denial of everything he believed in. But three young Zionists broke into the synagogue and conducted the memorial service for Herzl despite the rabbi's protestations: Dov Begin (Menahem Begin's father), Mordecai Scheinerman (Sharon's grandfather), and Zion Neumark. Nine years later, Mordecai Scheinerman's wife Bluma, a midwife, delivered Dov Begin's son Menahem. Menahem Begin, born in the Diaspora, was educated in eastern Europe in the traditions and culture of Polish Jewry and had been a member of the Revisionist camp in Zionism from childhood. Sharon, fifteen years his junior, was born in Israel on an agricultural settlement and had been an army man all his life. It is true that Sharon received a Revisionist education at home, but he was a full member of the labor movement as a youth.

Begin, just as Ben Gurion, was charmed by the unrefined and gruff Sharon, the tough officer who was a symbol of courage and energy. He was native-born, raised on a farm to manual labor and had learned to live by his sword, capable of fighting the young country's enemies and willing to risk his life on behalf of the Zionist dream. For many of the politicians of Begin's generation, Sharon and other soldiers like him were the realization of their vision of what the emancipated Jew would be like. These army officers were the "resolution" of the Diaspora complex of these veteran politicians, who still carried with them the nightmares of persecution, pogroms and the Holocaust. Beyond these considerations, there was of course the political one. Begin recognized the electoral potential of Sharon, so he welcomed him into Herut and the Gahal right-wing bloc.

Sharon was determined to bring about an alliance among the right-wing parties. He read the political map of the country well and understood that the people were looking for a serious alternative to Labor. From the creation of the State of Israel until mid-1973 the Labor parties in their various organizational configurations had held control of the government. The creation of Gahal from Herut and the Liberal Party was just such an attempt to present a political party of sufficient critical mass to attract the voters. Although it enjoyed a moderate success, it still had only 26 mandates in the current parliament, versus 58

for the Labor parties (out of a total of 120). Sharon's task, as he
now saw it, was to force the three right-wing parties to unite in
one bloc and put aside the personal animosities which so plagued
them. This pressure would have to be focused on Begin, the
leader of the largest of the groups, and by far the dominant
figure among them, to accept the rejoining of Shmuel Tamir.
Sharon went to the public, calling a press conference, to
announce his plan to create this bloc and to express his own
views on the current issues of concern.

The press conference became a major media event, attended
by scores of reporters. After presenting his proposal for the
creation of a new political grouping, he proceeded to outline a
detailed platform for this party. The platform was a potpourri of
ideas, a mixture of serious political thought with platitudes and
campaign fabrications. He called for "toughness in security and
foreign affairs, but liberality, tolerance and democracy in
internal questions"; he criticized the "backward quality of life in
Israel," and as proof cited "the lack of night life, the dirty
streets and the primitive education system"; he spoke of the
widening "social gap," and as proof claimed that over 200,000
children suffered from malnutrition; he talked of the need to
preserve Jewish values without imposing religious laws
governing the observance of the Sabbath; he supported granting
equal rights to the Arab minority; he called for a changing of the
guard in the political parties, with the elder statesmen making
way for the younger generation; and he spoke of his concept of
the government of Israel as the ruling authority for Jews
throughout the world, with a clear responsibility to take action
to prevent such incidents as the public hanging of Jews in Iraq.
On the question of the territories occupied during the Six Day
War, he made a clear distinction between Judea and Samaria
(the West Bank), and the Gaza Strip, which he declared must be
made an integral part of the country and held indefinitely, and
the Sinai peninsula, which should be held only so long as was
necessary for security reasons. In this context Sharon spoke of
the need for massive Jewish settlement of the West Bank,
including the areas immediately adjacent to the main cities, in
order to prevent the creation of a geographical belt of Arab

communities. He cautioned against ignoring the Palestinian problem, but said such a solution must be sought without compromising Israel's security or territorial integrity. His presentation of this problem was not without hope. He spoke in vague terms of granting the Arabs of the West Bank the option of becoming Israeli citizens or of remaining Jordanian nationals, and he mentioned other possibilities requiring Jordanian cooperation, such as the establishment of a Palestinian canton on the West Bank.

Two weeks after the press conference, Sharon registered as a member of the Liberal Party. He was presented with his membership card by Elimelech Rimalt, an elder statesman, at a ceremony held in Sharon's honor. Rimalt emphasized that the membership card was not simply a piece of paper, but a symbol of one's loyalty to a particular political philosophy. Sharon delivered a brief speech of gratitude and acceptance and stressed that he would continue to work toward the creation of a major political party that would "transform the country."

When Sharon had previously met with Begin and his close associates to present his plan for the creation of a "Likud" (consolidation) of the right-of-center parties, Begin answered as expected: although the proposal had its merits it would not be reviewed formally as long as it was presented by someone outside of Gahal. He suggested that Sharon join the Liberal Party and then make his proposal. Sharon responded that he had no interest in joining the party in order to be a part of a permanent parliamentary opposition. He must be convinced of the possibility of consolidation first. The meeting was a tense one, and Begin was particularly irritated at the ultimatum in everything that Sharon was saying. He added that Gahal would not give an unequivocal answer to Sharon's demand, because even if Begin was convinced of its worth, it was by no means clear that it would be supported by the hundreds of thousands who voted for Gahal in the last election. The meeting ended as a stand-off. Begin and Sharon held a second, private, meeting, in which Sharon successfully regaind Begin's trust. The Gahal leadership began to discuss the formation of the Likud, and Sharon joined the Liberal Party.

The times were propitious for Sharon's initiative. The leaders of Gahal were tiring of their role as a permanent opposition party, while Sharon, a popular general with a broad base of support, was holding out what seemed the only hope to alter this situation. This feeling was even more acute among the leaders of the Liberal Party, who were disappointed in the results of their participation in Gahal. Sharon very ably took advantage of this situation to pressure leaders of both groups. Throughout the weeks of political maneuvering he alternated between appeasement and intimidation, between flattery and admonition. Sharon's skill and agility at this form of combat were preeminent, and he successfully evaded the pitfalls of this duplicity.

Sharon successfully manipulated the press throughout this period. He assiduously briefed the journalists about the progress of the negotiations and courted them by providing details of the intricate maneuverings of the different combatants. The fact that the press committed itself to a clear stance on the issues involved by supporting the move to a political consolidation of the right-wing parties assured Sharon's position as the spokesman for the movement as a whole and as the authority on the role and responsibility of each of the participants. Sharon certainly exploited the press to apply pressure on Begin and make his threats real, but, just as important, the journalists provided him with a platoon of intelligence officers, affording him daily, up-to-the-minute reports on what was going on in each of the contending camps.

On September 5, 1973, Herut followed the lead of the Liberal Party and announced its support for the formation of the Likud. The decision was based on the principle, supported by Sharon, that Tamir's Free Center Party would receive the same consideration as the National List in placing its members on the electoral list for the upcoming parliamentary elections. The following day Sharon was appointed national campaign manager for the Likud.

Sharon himself testifies that the source of his success was his willingness to gamble all his political assets, a position which he states was possible because he was ready to foresake politics altogether and retire to his ranch. Under these circumstances, Begin had no alternative but to accept Sharon's threats as real. In fact, Sharon could no sooner have foresaken politics than Begin himself could have.

Sharon, dressed in an open shirt and wearing sandals among the tie-and-jacketed Gahal leadership, sowed dissension among his negotiating partners. He managed politics much as he had commanded in the army, with courage and audacity, and did not hesitate to viciously attack the Gahal leadership.

This ridicule of the Gahal leadership was not all histrionics, for Sharon apparently held most of these men in contempt. He could be heard criticizing party functionaries who had reached positions of national influence by intrigue and special interests. He was particularly critical of the servility and sycophancy of these leaders, who hopped with alacrity at Begin's slightest whim. Begin was described by Sharon as a man completely divorced from reality, whose main strength was in his florid rhetoric. This did not stop Sharon, however, from engaging in fulsome flattery of the Gahal leadership as he reported to the press on the successful establishment of the Likud. Even as the years passed and his ties to these men became permanent, Sharon's disdain did not wane.

On September 14, 1973, after some last-minute dealing to avoid a new crisis, the following communiqué was issued: "We the representatives of Gahal, the National List, the Free Center, and the Labor Group for Greater Israel have decided to form a common political body – 'Likud' – within Parliament, the municipalities and the National Federation of Labor. We will work together for our common goals of the preservation of the wholeness of the Land of Israel, security and peace, the elimination of poverty, the development of the economy and the attainment of a reasonable standard of living for all, the improvement of the quality of life and the environment, the reformation of the structure of municipal government, and the guarantee of democracy by the creation of an alternative to the ruling Labor Alignment…"

As the campaign was about to begin, Sharon was excited about the opportunity of fulfilling his ambition of revolutionizing the political history of the country and ending Labor's hold on the government. He was certain that should the Likud be successful he would receive a key seat in the cabinet. On September 19, Sharon declared, "Israel now awaits a period of unparalleled quiet in terms of national security. This time must be used to handle other pressing problems. In terms of our country's defense, we are now in the most advantageous position Israel has ever seen and, in fact, given the nature of our current borders, we face no security problems whatsoever..."

CHAPTER 11

On Friday, October 5, 1973, a general alert was called throughout the IDF. The General Staff decided on this precautionary measure in the face of the unusual activities of the Egyptian and Syrian armies. As a matter of routine, the southern command notified all reserve division officers of the alert. Sharon received his notification while in his office at Likud party headquarters in Tel Aviv, and he immediately made his way to the southern command to review the air photographs of the western side of the Suez Canal. In retrospect, Sharon claims that as soon as he saw the photographs he understood that war was inevitable.

Until the state of alert was declared, the General Staff had been convinced that the activities and preparations observed in Egypt and Syria were all part of a major exercise on the part of these armies. Junior intelligence officers who pointed to the offensive nature of these preparations were overruled by their superiors. The state of alert was considered as merely a precaution, for, even on October 5, the commander of the Intelligence Branch of the army considered the possiblity of war remote.

After reviewing the aerial photographs, Sharon ordered his staff to go into a state of preparedness for a general call-up of the thousands of soldiers in his division. He himself left for his

home in Beer Sheba to spend the quiet Yom Kippur weekend
with his family. That afternoon he received further reports
which, once again, he claims in retrospect convinced him that
war was imminent. The following morning Arik and Lilly went
for a drive to their ranch and spent the early hours of the
morning touring the grounds. At 9:30 a.m., the division
command received the order for a general call-up; the General
Staff was finally convinced that Egypt and Syria would attack
within the next few hours. Sharon toured the emergency depots
with Lilly and his two sons. At 1:55 on the afternoon of Saturday
October 6, the Egyptian army opened the war with a heavy
barrage of fire and began its crossing of the canal. Sharon knew
that it would take at least two full days for his division to be
mobilized, but the fighting had begun less than five hours after
the call-up had started. Sharon spent the early hours of the
evening over a dinner at home prepared by Lilly for himself and
a number of his staff officers. At midnight he left for the Sinai.

Small, secondary units began moving south and west along the
desert roads. Sharon ordered his men not to wait until the
mobilization was complete, but to move out as soon as a
company was ready. The tanks and other armored vehicles made
the long and abrasive trips on their own tracks, for there were
not enough tank carriers to transport the units to their
destinations.

Immediately upon his arrival in Sinai, Sharon began to quarrel
with Shmuel Gonen, Commander of the Southern Sector.
Sharon was aghast at the failure to deploy the regular troops
stationed in the Sinai in accordance with the emergency plans,
and he quickly began to realize that the southern command had
no control over the troops stationed along the canal and very
little concrete information about the positions and strength of
the attacking Egyptian armies. Sharon admonished Gonen to
deploy his division in preparation for a crossing of the canal,
arguing against Gonen's plan to split these limited forces and use
them as reinforcements for the units that had been under such
heavy fire since the start of the fighting. Sharon strongly
disputed Gonen's plan, arguing for the concentrated use of his
force to undermine the Egyptian bridgehead. Sharon sensed that

the southern command had been overwhelmed by the panic and confusion of the surprise attack. Beyond the professional disagreement between Sharon and Gonen, the tension between them was the result of the very recent reversal of roles. Just three months before, Sharon had still been commander of the Southern Sector and Gonen had been one of his officers, but now Sharon reported to Gonen. Sharon was convinced that he still understood the situation in the southern sector better than anyone else and certainly better than Gonen had been demonstrating until then.

Sharon's division was located in the center of the Sinai peninsula, while to its north was a division commanded by Major-General Avraham Adan and to its south the remnants of the division commanded by Major-General Avraham Mendler. As soon as he arrived in Sinai, Sharon began to pressure Gonen and David Elazar, Chief of the General Staff, to allow him to break through to the canal to free the soldiers trapped in the bunkers along the waterline. In Sharon's plan, after freeing these soldiers he would cross the canal and establish a bridgehead on the western side of the canal, thereby throwing the Egyptians off balance. Later, Sharon would recount that he saw this action as particularly important because he had personally promised the trapped soldiers that he would free them. He would further support this claim by stating that the principle of never abandoning soldiers in the field, a principle to which he had steadfastly adhered since the battle of Latroun, was at stake here. Sharon had been the only senior commander to succeed in calming the terrified soldiers in the bunkers. One reservist trapped in a bunker under heavy Egyptian fire, Max Maman, could be overheard on the radio, his panicked cries reflecting the feelings of all the soldiers trapped along the canal; but no one was able to calm him until Sharon spoke to him. Sharon's personal assurances not only pacified Maman, but also stopped the incessant calls from the other units along the canal. Sharon pleaded and beseeched Gonen and Elazar to allow him to keep his promise to Maman, and, after once again being turned down, he even appealed to Dayan and Begin, though this time to no effect. Sharon could be heard mumbling "Damn the person who ever made Gonen a general!" Within the first twelve hours, Sharon had submitted three different plans for his division, all including the liberation of the trapped soldiers, but all were rejected.

The army faced a cruel dilemma: whether to approve the initiatives of Sharon or wait for the mobilization of two additional divisions to be sent to Sinai. In the early evening of the second day of the war, Sharon received a message notifying him that a helicopter had been sent to bring him to a meeting in Beer Sheba. But the helicopter was delayed, and while Sharon and his staff sought an alternative aircraft, the crucial meeting convened.

Sharon missed the discussion. The helicopter that had been sent to collect him ran into mechanical difficulties and arrived two hours late. As Sharon rushed to headquarters, meeting Elazar and Rabin on their way out, Elazar stopped to brief him on the results of the meeting and to report on the very difficult situation in the north, where depleted Israeli forces were holding off a major Syrian assault. Sharon asked Elazar if he would go back into the room with him so that he could present his plan for attack. Elazar responded curtly that he did not have the time because he was in a rush to get to a cabinet meeting. Further, if Sharon were to undertake such an attack, his forces would be out of position for the operations assigned to his division the following morning.

Sharon presented his ideas once again to Gonen. In a marathon meeting that lasted past midnight, Sharon finally convinced Gonen to let him send a force to free the soldiers along the canal, provided that this force return by the next morning and be available to participate in the planned operations for the following day. In so doing, Gonen was deviating from the original orders he had received from Elazar not to approach the waterline. At 5:45 a.m., these orders were countermanded. New intelligence indicated that the Egyptian forces had been reinforced, and the program to free the soldiers was postponed indefinitely. Sharon was shocked and frustrated.

Sharon saw Elazar as one of his key rivals and as a prime mover behind his inability to reach the position of Chief of Staff.

At their inauspicious meeting, Sharon noted Elazar's antagonism, his formality and his refusal to hear him out. The personal insult, the anger at what he considered the blunders of the government and the General Staff, and the awareness that these elements would eventually serve him well in an election campaign combined to formulate Sharon's attitude to the war. He set out to the battlefield motivated by these emotions and considerations.

As in the past, Sharon's staff provided him with an audience of admirers that listened attentively to his every word. From the moment that his staff began to organize, they heard his contemptuous insults of Gonen and Elazar as well as his promise that at the end of the war he would bring those responsible to account. Sharon's headquarters were marked by a calm assurance, especially notable in contrast to the general atmosphere of panic that had engulfed the other command centers. Sharon radiated a sense of confidence that seemed to calm everyone around him. When he noticed any sign of impatience and desperation among his men he would call a meeting to encourage them, recounting stories from the long, but ultimately successful, War of Independence. Sharon's staff, consisting of many officers who were not officially associated with his division but who had joined him for the duration of the war, provided him with an enthusiatic and supportive audience. Their response reinforced Sharon's conviction that he had been called upon to save his country from the catastrophe brought on by the incompetence of the political and military leadership that had blocked his advance to the rank of Chief of Staff and had forced him to resign from the army. The events of October 8 only further confirmed this impression.

On Monday, October 8, at 10:45 a.m., Sharon received orders from Gonen to begin to move south toward the Giddi Pass and then to break through and cross the canal at the city of Suez. This order had been approved by Elazar, who had insisted the previous evening that Sharon not move his division until it was clear whether Adan's division in the north would require his assistance. The order to move south was in accordance with the Chief of Staff's general strategy: Adan had been fighting the

Egyptians for over an hour and a half, and by his estimate would not require assistance from Sharon's division, thereby freeing Sharon to begin to move south. Before pulling out, Sharon reminded Gonen about the soldiers still trapped in the central sector of the canal.

About an hour after Sharon began his march south, Adan reported that he was facing strong opposition, his losses were mounting and he needed air assistance. Adan did not request ground support from Sharon's division, so Gonen didn't alter Sharon's orders. Adan's forces once again attacked the Egyptian forces but failed. That afternoon, Adan engaged in some of the bitterest fighting of the war, as Sharon's division continued its progress south, pursued by confused orders from the southern command: Sharon first received orders to attack the Egyptian forces opposite him, the Egyptian Third Army; then he was instructed to capture an Egyptian bridge and cross the canal into the city of Suez; later that afternoon he received orders to reverse direction and attack the Egyptian forces in the north of Sinai. Finally, he was instructed to halt his division altogether. Given this, Sharon refused to obey any orders unless he received them in writing. At 5:00 p.m., the Chief of Staff of the Southern Sector arrived at Sharon's headquarters by helicopter with new orders. Sharon responded in anger, decrying Gonen's abilities as a commander and asking that these comments be brought to Gonen's attention. Gonen's orders were to reverse direction and move the division back to where it had been the previous day. Sharon's request to free the trapped soldiers along the canal was also rejected.

These maneuverings imposed on Sharon's division generated ill will between Sharon and Adan, the division commander responsible for the northern sector of the Sinai. As Sharon's division prepared to pull out on its march southward, a request for assistance was received by Ami, a company commander in Sharon's division, from Gabi, a brigade commander in Adan's division. Ami, whose company was stationed alongside Adan's division, wanted to assist but had to receive formal approval from his superior officers. Sharon personally gave the order not to stop to provide assistance as the orders from the southern command were clear about the need for the entire division to march southward. Gabi, the brigade commander, was in serious trouble and appealed to Adan and the brigade commanders in Sharon's division to give him help, but his requests went unanswered. Gabi shouted, "My men are being slaughtered and you're all arguing!" Ami ordered his company, as he later testified "with a bloody conscience," not to provide assistance, but to join the rest of his division in the move south. His junior officers questioned why they did not assist the beleaguered brigade. Ami asked Sharon why they were ordered not to help Gabi's brigade. Sharon responded that he should leave matters of conscience to the division commander. They had been called upon to rush to the Mitla and Giddi Passes to ward off a major attack and prevent an Egyptian breakthrough. Sharon's division reached the passes and discovered them empty.

This was not the only conflict between Adan and Sharon. As Sharon brought his division back to the central sector of the Sinai from where he had started in the morning, he saw that the Egyptians had captured strategic points originally held by Sharon. After the war, a bitter debate resulted between the two division commanders as to who was responsible for this. Sharon claimed that he had been given clear orders to move his entire division south and that it was therefore Adan's responsibility to cover the abandoned positions he left. Adan countered by claiming that the positions should never have been abandoned by Sharon's forces until Adan had sent new forces to replace them. Adan even testified that Sharon's junior officers were surprised by the order to abandon their positions before Adan's men could assume responsibility, but that Sharon had personally ordered them to do so.

As Sharon's division finally arrived at its starting point once again, Adan requested Sharon's assistance in fighting the Egyptians in Adan's sector. Sharon conducted a long telephone conversation with Gonen about Adan's request and concluded that he would not go to Adan's assistance. Gonen supported Sharon's analysis and conclusions.

That night around midnight, the division commanders met with Gonen at headquarters. Exhausted, with bloodshot eyes and hoarse voices, they were angry and frustrated with the events of the war until then: Sharon, because his force had not been used at all; Adan, because he had not been entirely successful in meeting his strategic objectives. Although Adan presented the situation of his division as a partial success, he understood that in comparison with the optimistic designs the plan had not been realized. The losses inflicted on the Egyptians by his division were considerable; his own losses, however, were far more than expected. And he came nowhere close to crossing the canal. Elazar and his adviser, Aharon Yariv, arrived at the meeting a little later. Elazar was very critical of reports he had received during the day, none of which indicated the true picture of the fate of Adan's division. On the basis of this misinformation, he had approved the movement of Sharon's division southward. Elazar could still feel the bitter taste of disappointment as he reported to the government that his reports of the progress of the fighting in the morning had in fact been unfounded. After the war, Adan testified that he had reported the situation accurately and that the responsibility for the misinterpretation was entirely Gonen's. Gonen contended that he had based his assessments on Adan's reports and that the misunderstanding was a result of Adan's failure to read the battle accurately. Sharon would lay the blame on the mismanagement of the campaign from the very beginning. He had insisted from the very beginning that the two divisions should be used in a concentrated manner, bringing to bear the full might of their forces against the Egyptian alignment in the north of the Sinai. He saw the primary strategic goal as the crossing of the canal, both to undermine the Egyptian forces and to quickly destroy anti-aircraft missile sites west of the canal. At the conclusion of the meeting it was decided to await the reinforcement of the two divisions by the continued mobilization of the reserves. The order was given to the men in the bunkers along the canal to abandon them and retreat if possible. Only the men of one bunker were successful. A small force from Sharon's division met the soldiers after they had made their way through the Egyptian forces surrounding them and brought them back to safety. Sharon and his staff monitored the fighting at

Max Maman's bunker as it presaged the demise of that bunker; all the division officers shared in the horrible feeling of impotence and paralysis.

To Adan and Gonen, Sharon appeared to be a self-serving general who was not enthusiastic about assisting a colleague; a reckless general intent on crossing the canal without properly assessing the strength of the enemy forces; and an officer who followed orders selectively, obeying only those that he approved. To Sharon, on the other hand, the events of that day only proved his contention that Adan, Gonen and a host of other officers were simply incompetent and certainly incapable of commanding a war. He was in a rage over the everchanging and conflicting orders he had received and was more than ever convinced that, just as he had claimed, the IDF should have opened with a counterattack immediately at the onset of the war, before the Egyptians had the opportunity of establishing themselves on the east side of the canal. In his evaluation, Adan had failed because he had attacked in the wrong direction and not read the alignment of the Egyptian forces correctly. He was certain that Adan had more than ample forces, had they been used properly, and that there had been no point in dismembering his own division to support Adan's. Finally, he felt that had the Chief of the General Staff and the Commander of the Southern Sector come to the front to see what was actually going on, instead of remaining behind in their headquarters, they would never have made the decisions they had made.

Sharon's criticism was not a secret. His entire staff could overhear his ridicule and contempt for the Commander of the Southern Sector and the Chief of the General Staff, who that very day had announced that the IDF was about to "break the bones of the Egyptian army." They fully agreed with Sharon's evaluations and smirked as they heard the reports of the IDF Spokesman about fighting in the Sinai. Sharon had his own cadre of reporters following him, waiting attentively for his every comment, and he promised to reveal everything to them as soon as the war was over.

Meanwhile, on October 9, Gonen became convinced that

Sharon had overstepped all reasonable bounds of behavior and should be discharged. To rescue the trapped soldiers from the bunkers along the canal, Sharon had ordered one brigade to return to the site of the fighting to recover the tanks that had been hit. Two other brigades were ordered to attack the Egyptian forces simultaneously, resulting in a major operation over a very broad front and using the bulk of his division. This was in direct contravention of orders received from Elazar, who had called on Sharon not to engage the enemy actively, but to dig in where he was. Sharon claimed that his attack came after he had broken an Egyptian assault on his position. Gonen ordered Sharon to halt his progress toward the canal in pursuit of the Egyptians, and to disengage. Sharon implored Gonen to allow him to capitalize on his advantage and continue his pursuit of the fleeing Egyptians. In a later investigation of the events of that day, Sharon claimed that he had been granted permission by Gonen to tail the fleeing Egyptian forces and snipe at them. In any event, he insisted that his actions were designed to protect his division from the Egyptian infantry, which was armed with anti-tank missiles. Gonen argued in contrast that Sharon had been given clear orders to take static defensive actions only. This "tailing" operation had continued for over four hours over a wide area of the desert. When it became apparent to Gonen that Sharon was continuing to attack, he unsuccessfully tried to contact him by radio and was forced to board a helicopter to deliver the order personally to Sharon. Sharon responded bitterly that he would obey the order; but Gonen remained convinced that Sharon continued the attack anyhow.

Under cover of his alleged "tailing" operations, a patrol from Sharon's division reached the canal. The patrol had progressed cautiously, not meeting any opposition, and apparently had come upon the breach between the Egyptian Second Army in the north and the Third Army in the south. Sharon understood that he had found a way for the IDF to reach the canal and cross it with relatively little opposition. He immediately called Gonen and proposed that the patrol be left in its position and further reinforced in preparation for the transfer of much larger forces through this strip the following morning. Gonen passed on

Sharon's request to Elazar, who unequivocally ordered Sharon to retreat. Sharon made one more effort to convince Gonen that he would be able to hit the Egyptian rear by surprise and upset all their plans. He argued with Gonen that he was convinced that such an operation could topple the Egyptian forces entirely. He beseeched Gonen to let him attack, assuring him that his concerns were strictly practical, that he had no political motives and no expectation of returning to the army – only to win the war as quickly as possible. Gonen passed this request on a second time to the Chief of Staff, who once again rejected it and ordered Sharon to retreat and prepare for a major defensive battle. Sharon obeyed.

Among Sharon's staff, the feeling of frustration and anger was increasing. They were convinced that their commander understood the battle better than any other general involved and that his superior officers were intentionally halting his initiatives for totally extraneous reasons. They were certain that it was within the power of their division to reverse the trend of the war and to save the country from dire circumstances. The blame for the failure to capitalize on this advantage, in their eyes, lay clearly with the senior command of the IDF.

After the war, Elazar explained the rationale behind his thinking: he was convinced that the Egyptians were planning a major armor attack to the east, and he had therefore decided to establish a defensive wall consisting of the two divisions of Sharon and Adan. Although he too had planned on a counterattack intended to take the IDF across the canal, this had been scheduled to take place after breaking the anticipated Egyptian assault. Elazar feared that crossing the canal at the time suggested by Sharon would have left the entire country exposed to an Egyptian thrust to the east. Sharon, on the other hand, argued that the failure to allow him to maintain control of the strip along the canal and the order given him to stop tailing the Egyptian forces indicated the lack of imagination shown by the Chief of Staff and the Commander of the Southern Sector, and their failure to free themselves of preconceptions. Sharon also contended that the very fact that he was in the field facing the Egyptians enabled him to see the real picture of the fighting.

Beyond the professional dispute, Sharon suspected that the reason he was not granted permission to carry out his plan for the crossing of the canal was the wish to deny him the laurels of the victorious general. Sharon's premise was that both Elazar and Gonen had been influenced by political considerations, based on their personal antagonism to him and the election campaign that immediately preceded the war. The result was that a strategy had been devised to grant Adan the opportunity of crossing the canal first, thereby tying Adan's name with the IDF's victory over the Egyptians.

Gonen, fed up with Sharon's insubordination, phoned Elazar and asked that Sharon be removed. Elazar discussed this with Minister of Defense Dayan, quoting Gonen's complaint in detail. Elazar supported Gonen's military analysis. Dayan, however, interpreted events differently. He confessed that in his opinion Sharon's initiatives were far better than the hesitations of the other division commanders. According to Elazar, Dayan still agreed, notwithstanding, that Sharon was motivated primarily by how history would record his actions. Both Dayan and Elazar rejected Gonen's request. Dayan went further and proposed to Elazar that Sharon replace Gonen as commander of the southern command, but in the face of Elazar's opposition they agreed that, instead, Bar Lev would be sent to the southern command to provide Gonen with support.

Haim Bar Lev had ostensibly been sent to the southern command as the Chief of Staff's representative. It was hoped that he would improve the management of the war and assure some measure of control over Sharon. The General Staff was angry with Sharon's actions on the 9th of October because of what they viewed as the excessive casualties and the losses in tanks. They envisioned a solution with Bar Lev replacing Gonen, and Gonen replacing Sharon. The lone dissenter against this anti-Sharon coalition was Major-General Yisrael Tal. Tal argued that Sharon's actions on the 9th were entirely successful, that his losses were far less than those reported by the General Staff, and that his attack had proven that it was possible to penetrate the breach between the two Egyptian armies and destroy the Egyptian bridgeheads on the western side.

When Bar Lev arrived at headquarters he found that neither Gonen nor his chief aide, Brigadier-General Uri Ben Arie, were on speaking terms with Sharon. Orders were being passed on to Sharon through other staff officers. He noted that Gonen and Ben Arie were carefully monitoring Sharon's division's radio communications because they would not rely on Sharon's reporting of his activities and because they were afraid that Sharon would take actions in contradiction to his orders. Bar Lev also saw that Sharon was continually being forced to take military action which ran counter to his understanding of the situation. Bar Lev interviewed each of the division commanders in order to get an unbiased picture of the developments in Sinai. Sharon poured out his criticism in the severest terms against the General Staff and the Southern Command. He condemned the static posture adopted by the IDF and its failure to attack, and suggested instead that his division, in combination with Mendler's, attack the Egyptian Third Army. Gonen rejected this plan and Bar Lev supported him. In the face of the strained and often ugly relations that existed between Gonen and Sharon, Bar Lev thereafter made it a point to provide Sharon with clear and detailed orders at every stage.

On October 10, Bar Lev held a major meeting of his division commanders and staff members to review the situation in the Sinai. Once again, Sharon was completely open in his criticism, underscoring the fact that since the war had broken out, the IDF had not once taken the initiative. He proposed that his division penetrate the breach between the two Egyptian armies and establish a bridgehead on the western side of the canal, which could then be expanded and reinforced for a major invasion of Egypt. Adan disagreed with Sharon, claiming that there had been two initiatives and that both had failed: his own on the 8th and Sharon's on the 9th. Adan opposed Sharon's proposal on the grounds that the losses would be too high. Mendler, on the other hand, was even more adamant than Sharon in calling for a counterattack. He proposed that the three divisions engage in a concentrated assault on the Egyptian Third Army, intended to drive them out of Sinai, and then continue westward across the canal. Bar Lev listened quietly and then declared unequivocally that the three divisions would continue digging in and refrain from any offensive activities. He ordered Sharon's intelligence units, in consort with those of the southern sector, to continue collecting information on the alignment and movements of the Egyptian forces.

The following day Sharon and two of his brigade commanders met with Bar Lev in order to outline the details of his proposal to attack in the region of the Bitter Lake. Bar Lev asked many questions, making no secret of his reservations. When he finally asked the two brigade commanders directly what their opinion of the plan was, he noted that neither was particularly confident or enthusiastic about Sharon's plan. In retrospect, Sharon claimed that their hesitancy was solely the result of Bar Lev's negative attitude toward the plan and that they were only adapting their opinions for him. After the war, many of Sharon's officers attested to their opposition to Sharon's plans and to his assignments. According to their testimony, especially in the first days of the war, many of the officers in Sharon's division felt that his plans went against their own better judgement. This was the clearest indication of the change in relationship between Sharon and his officers in comparison to the Six Day War. In 1967, although there had been a great deal of tension between Sharon and his staff, the field commanders all willingly accepted his authority. In 1973, in contrast, the field commanders felt that Sharon was seriously underestimating the strength and ability of the enemy and seemed to be oblivious to the casualties that his initiatives would cost. They were acutely aware of the overtones of personal rivalry that existed between Sharon and Adan and between Sharon and the staff of the southern sector, and felt at times that Sharon's initiatives were dictated by these considerations, regardless of the cost to his own soldiers.

Among the division's staff, however, Sharon enjoyed the support of most of the officers, who openly identified with his evaluation of Gonen's incompetence and Elazar's failure as a military leader. Sharon's feeling of persecution intensified during this period. He read newspaper accounts that were critical of him or of his wife and interpreted this as proof of the political battle being waged against him. He was convinced that the IDF

Press Officer was intentionally preventing the journalists from visiting his division by referring them to Adan's division instead. On October 10, Sharon sent a journalist attached to his staff, Micah Shagrir, to Tel Aviv to make certain that his division's exploits would be accorded their due in the reporting on the fighting in Sinai. Shagrir prepared a report that quoted an Israeli soldier as saying, "the Israelis have learned to broadcast like the Arabs, and the Arabs have learned to fight like the Israelis." Although Shagrir's report was cut off in the middle, it did provide a more honest hint of what was actually going on in the Sinai. Sharon was also aware of the fact that his relationship with Gonen had become the topic of rumors circulating in the army and in key political circles, and he was irate at the interpretations given them. He learned that he was being slandered because of his alleged insubordination and that the IDF was even considering discharging him from his current position. This merged with the professional disagreements he had with Elazar, Bar Lev and Gonen. In contrast to them, he contended that the IDF had sufficient forces in Sinai to mount a major assault across the canal without in any way jeopardizing Tel Aviv. He contested the decision of the General Staff to wait for the anticipated Egyptian offensive before commencing their counterattack. He was particularly suspicious of the imposition of a cease-fire that would make the Egyptian early gains a permanent fact of life. In his mind, the strategy of the General Staff indicated that it was floundering. As was his wont, he made no effort to keep this criticism to himself, but shared it in all its detail with his staff. After the visits of senior officers from the southern command, he'd comment that they were more like squad leaders than like generals, frightened of the possibility of armored battle. Sharon promised to take care of things after the war, giving a clear signal that he saw these conflicts as political in nature.

On October 11 Gonen called a meeting of all the senior officers in the southern command, including the division commanders, to present the IDF's plan for the crossing of the canal, Operation Stoutheart. The idea of crossing the canal and **penetrating** deep into the heartland of Egypt, in the event that the Egyptians were to open a war along that front, had been a major element in the strategy of the IDF since the Six Day War. To the General Staff it had been clear that in any major conflagration, it would be necessary to carry the war over to the west side of the canal and that the fighting could not be limited to containing the Egyptian offensive. On the basis of this assumption the IDF had prepared itself, purchasing the appropriate equipment for such a crossing, paving roads that led up to the canal and building mobile bridges that were to be used to transfer the armored units across. Gonen had ordered that the mobile bridges be assembled on the 9th of October, and now on the 11th he was presenting his plan for the crossing to his senior officers.

Sharon and Adan had reservations about the site of the crossing selected by Gonen, but in the face of Bar Lev's support for Gonen's plan they withdrew them. In Gonen's plan Sharon's division would establish bridgeheads on both sides of the canal, initially using the temporary bridging equipment and then the two major mobile bridges. With the bridges in place, the two divisions, Sharon's and Adan's, would cross and gather for a major thrust into Egypt.

With the plan accepted in all its essentials, Bar Lev presented it in detail before Moshe Dayan. Bar Lev emphasized that although he firmly believed that it would be better for the IDF to await the expected Egyptian offensive before attempting to cross the canal, he felt that the uncertainty regarding the Egyptian intentions made it impossible to wait for them to make the first move. Dayan, depressed and unsure because of the surprise of the war and its inauspicious first few days, initially vetoed this plan. He wasn't convinced. Even if the canal crossing were successful, the Egyptians might not plead for a cease-fire. Dayan was not, however, decisive in his arguments and ultimately stated that the decision belonged to the Chief of the General Staff. Dayan opposed the crossing, but did not do so forcefully. Elazar refused to accept this equivocating as policy and demanded an answer. Dayan agreed to bring the question before the Prime Minister, Golda Meir.

On October 12, the Cabinet and a number of senior officers

from the General Staff gathered in Golda Meir's office to decide the question of the southern command's plan. Should Sharon's division be given the go-ahead to establish a bridgehead on the canal and then cross over with Adan's division? Would this enable them to knock out the anti-aircraft missile batteries on the western side of the canal? Would this bring about the turning point? Bar Lev argued that this was the only alternative open to the IDF. Some disagreed, because of their lack of confidence in the ability of the IDF to establish and hold the two bridges needed to make the crossing. As the meeting continued without a decision, reports came in about Egyptian preparations for their long-awaited thrust to the east. It was decided to postpone a decision on the canal crossing until after the Egyptian situation was clarified.

Sharon did not accept this. He said to Bar Lev and Elazar, who came down to his command post, that the decision was wrong and that the IDF should not allow itself to be maneuvered into a defensive posture, but should take the initiative and attack the Egyptian lines east of the canal, with the intention of crossing it. Elazar disagreed. So did Bar Lev. Dayan, on the other hand, met with Sharon on October 13th and returned to Tel Aviv conviced that the crossing was a good idea. After the war, Sharon claimed that his conversations with Dayan had reconstituted some of Dayan's self-confidence, lost in the first days of the war.

Despite Sharon's complaint that the southern command prevented journalists from visiting his command post, he was surrounded by many reporters, most of whom were avid supporters. Sharon treated them politely, devoted time to them, and openly discussed battle plans and his reservations about his superiors. The reporters were allowed to stay in the command post and monitor the reports from the front via the division's communication system. Sharon conducted both the war and his relationships with commanders and colleagues openly. Sharon would say later that he had treated the reporters patiently since he maintained that information should not be withheld and that the people should be told the truth about matters of life and death. On Saturday night, October 13th, the reporters were briefed by Sharon. The division commander wished to convince his listeners that he was justified in his demand to open an immediate attack against the Egyptian troops east of the canal and pave the way for the crossing. Everything indicated that the Egyptian armor attack would be initiated the next day, but Sharon still refused to wait for it. To the reporters he explained that the most important mission facing the IDF was to reestablish its deterrent power and to destroy the Egyptian army. These targets could be obtained only by the reoccupation of the eastern bank of the canal and by seizing areas west of the canal.

On Sunday, October 14th, the ninth day of the war, soldiers in Sharon's division noticed four Egyptian helicopters landing commando troops southeast of the front line. This was a clear sign of the Egyptian intention to break out to the east. One of Sharon's units attacked the Egyptians and killed them. At 6:00 a.m., Egyptian artillery started shelling the Israeli division and half an hour later over 100 tanks of the Egyptian 21st Division started towards Sharon's forces. Sharon's troops were well-deployed and conducted a careful and well-planned battle against the Egyptian armor. At the end of nine hours of intense combat, 120 Egyptian tanks were destroyed or captured in Sharon's sector. A similar fate awaited the Egyptian units in the areas commanded by Adan and Kalman Magen (who had taken Mendler's place after Mendler had been killed). The Egyptians abandoned 264 tanks. Only 6 tanks were damaged on the Israeli side. That evening Bar Lev called Golda Meir and announced that it had been a good day for the IDF: "Our forces have returned to themselves and so have the Egyptians." The armor-to-armor battle proved Bar Lev's and Elazar's assumptions correct. It was worth waiting for the Egyptian attempt to break east, to wear down their units and improve the chances of Israel's counterattack. Sharon, on the other hand, continued to maintain, even after the war, that the waiting period was unnecessary and that if the IDF had initiated a counterattack immediately, it would have prevented the Egyptians from strengthening their hold on the east bank of the canal. He found it difficult to reconcile a policy of caution with reality. At the end of the day of combat he mocked Bar Lev's and Elazar's premature fear of the Egyptian armor and their warning about the Egyptian ability of reaching Tel Aviv. Sharon did not refrain from reminding his audience that during his tenure as head of the southern command, he had to work hard to persuade the General HQ to pave many of the roads in Sinai, whose importance to the movement of the Israeli troops was clearly proven on October 14th. Sharon's scorn towards the supreme command at the end of the battle of October 14th was unfair. He ignored the fact that Bar Lev and Elazar saw a potential danger of penetration only if his own suggestions had been accepted and the canal were crossed before the armor-to-armor battle and the concentration of sufficient IDF forces east of the canal. Elazar and Bar Lev wanted to cross when it would be possible to allocate enough forces to curb any Egyptian attempt to penetrate towards the center of the country.

Faithful to his method, Sharon demanded, even in the midst of the battles of October 14th, to be allowed to develop the war he was waging against the Egyptians into a wide and deep counterattack towards the other side of the canal. He screamed over the radio at the southern command, "The Egyptians are coming back to themselves and we must take advantage of it. They are fleeing their tanks." Bar Lev called on him to act cautiously and Sharon responded with rage: "You warm your butts in the command shelters. You don't go out to the field to see the situation. I saw them run. They're crumbling!" At one point Sharon said to Bar Lev, "Today I saw the 21st Division and, if I may be allowed to use a rude expression in front of a minister of this government, they are the same assholes they used to be. They came, we screwed them and they ran away." Bar Lev was more cautious and emphasized that the Egyptian fighting ability must not be belittled, mentioning the heavy losses which the Egyptian infantry had inflicted on the IDF during the first days of the war. Sharon did not limit himself to pleading. He instructed his brigades to take advantage of the armor battles to advance toward targets which were occupied by the Egyptians on the east bank of the canal. The southern command objected to these maneuvers, among other reasons, so as not to expose the breach that had been discovered between the two armies. They tried to reach Sharon for a long time, but failed. In retrospect, the southern command declared that they could not contact Sharon because he deliberately ignored their calls, assuming that they would instruct him explicitly to withdraw his forces.

At about 11:00 p.m. the southern command completed an updated edition of Operation Stoutheart to cross the Suez Canal. According to the new plan, Sharon's role was further increased. In addition to penetrating towards the canal, occupying bridgeheads on both sides, installing bridges and crossing, his mission now included the widening of the breach between the two Egyptian armies. In other words, Sharon was instructed not to be satisfied with the momentum of penetration towards the canal, but to open a safe corridor between the two armies, through which the IDF troops could reach the canal and cross it without fear of the Egyptians closing ranks and cutting off the Israeli units west of the canal. According to this updated mission, Sharon's division was to seize two fortified Egyptian strongholds: "the Chinese Farm" and "Missouri," which commanded the two main roads leading to the waterfront on the west side of the canal. The occupation of these positions was aimed at assuring the free transportation of the bridging equipment to the canal. Orders stated that should Sharon's division encounter difficulties in enlarging the wedge between the two armies, Adan's division would become the first to cross the canal, while Sharon's division would continue covering the bridgehead east of the canal, guaranteeing access.

"Operation Stoutheart" was mainly Sharon's idea. During his years as head of the southern command, Sharon had authorized a crossing site called "the Court," in the area of Dver-Swar, north of the Bitter Lake. Sharon selected this site since it provided a convenient approach for the crossing equipment to the edge of the canal. Sharon had prepared "the Court" in anticipation of the crossing, and one of its embankments was constructed so that it would be easy to break through. Two years later, on October 14, 1973, his plan was finally to be tested by reality. Sharon based his crossing plan on a two-division effort, which aimed at several objectives: first, penetration to the canal at the rear of the Egyptian forces arrayed along its east bank, in order to form the bridgehead; second, the opening of two axes for the transportation of the bridging equipment to the waterfront; next, the dispatch of the paratroopers through the open roads to the other side of the canal; and finally, the construction of two bridges. All this was to happen while a special force engaged the Egyptians in battle, to alleviate the anticipated pressure on the engineering units constructing the bridges. This basic strategy was supported by detailed operational plans for Sharon's forces, including an effort to deceive the Egyptians about the real objectives of the Israeli attack.

The crossing plan which Gonen prepared was based in principle on Sharon's concepts as found in the files of the southern command, but it was anchored in the IDF military concept of the late 1960's, according to which an attempt would be made to cross the canal in the event of an Egyptian attack.

With his nose red from a cold and his eyes half-shut in concentration, Sharon briefed his units in detail on the crossing of the canal and provided them with a carefully worked-out timetable. One brigade, commanded by Tuvya Raviv, would serve as a decoy by attacking at 5:00 p.m. on the west, while at nightfall, under cover of the decoy, a second brigade, commanded by Amnon Reshef, would move along the breach between the two Egyptian armies and attack from their rear, heading north to stop the Egyptian Second Army from moving south. At 8:30 p.m. Danny Matt's paratrooper brigade was scheduled to start crossing the canal on rubber dinghies. On reaching the western bank, the brigade was to deploy as a cover for the bridgehead, and an hour later the first tanks were to start crossing the canal on special rafts. While the bridgehead was being established on the west side of the canal, the other units in the division were to clear out and widen the breach between the two armies and secure the continued access to the bridgehead on the canal. These activities were to be concluded by about 11:00 p.m., in time for the placement of the two main bridges which were to be transported to the canal. One bridge was to be formed by rafts, and the other was to be constructed from the heavyweight rollers which the IDF had designed and conducted exercises with during the two years preceding the war. The transfer of the bridging equipment to the canal was to be carried out by Haim Erez's brigade in coordination with the engineering units, whose task it would be to construct the bridges. According to this plan, the entire operation would last 12 hours. On October 16th, at 5:00 p.m., the two divisions commanded by Sharon and Adan were to be established on the other side of the canal, striking at the Egyptian anti-aircraft missile batteries.

On Monday, October 15th, at 5:00 p.m., Arik Sharon realized that he would not be able to meet his planned schedule. The delivery of the bridging equipment was delayed on the roads leading toward the canal, blocked by the thousands of vehicles moving slowly along these roads. The convoy which carried the crossing equipment was stuck among them. Sharon and his chief staff officer, Avraham Tamir, considered three alternatives: either delay the start of the operation by 24 hours; start the operation as planned, but only carry out the penetration to the waterfront and the enlargement of the breach between the two Egyptian armies, postponing the crossing to the next day; or carry out the original plan even if the bridging unit arrived late. Sharon consulted Bar Lev and received his approval to delay the crossing until midnight, although in the original plan the paratroopers were to cross the canal by 8:30 p.m.

Sharon took a great risk in this new plan. He started the operation designed to place the paratrooper brigade on the west side of the canal, knowing in advance that he would not be able to reinforce or support it. In the absence of bridges, the paratroopers were to fight alone deep behind the enemy lines. Later, Sharon would explain that he took this gamble because he wanted to capitalize on the success of the battles on October 14th, and because he feared that any delay might bring the cancellation of the entire operation. Sharon was also guided by his conviction that the very breakthrough to the west would have a decisive effect on the battle and that, in any event, a sufficient number of tanks could be transported by rafts.

At 5:00 p.m., Sharon's and Adan's divisions opened a heavy

artillery barrage, under cover of which the crossing operation started. As planned, one brigade averted the Egyptians' attention from the movements of the other brigade, which started its penetration towards the canal and the rear lines of the Egyptian forces. During the first four hours, the operation proceeded as planned, and the division's patrol unit reached the canal. But then problems started to arise: the paratrooper brigade did not reach the crossing point on schedule; the Egyptians began to react and disrupt the activities of Reshef's brigade; and the road which was cleared for the transportation of the bridging equipment was blocked again by the Egyptians. Despite these disruptions, Sharon ordered Danny Matt, the paratroop brigade commander, to load his men on the dinghies and cross to the western bank of the canal. A few minutes after 1:30 a.m., October 16th, Matt transmitted the code word "Acapulco," meaning: we have reached the western bank of the Suez Canal. Within the following hours, Matt transferred his entire brigade to the west side and strengthened his hold of an area of about two and a half square miles. By dawn, the IDF had a bridgehead west of the Suez Canal. At 3:00 a.m. Sharon arrived with 10 tanks, and an hour later 10 more tanks had reached the site along with rafts and two bulldozers. Sharon instructed the bulldozer operators to break through the embankment at its thinnest part, marked by red bricks. He himself mounted the bulldozer for a few minutes and began breaking through the embankment. At about 7:00 a.m. the first tank arrived on the west bank, quickly followed by the nine others, all transported on the rafts. At Sharon's request the southern command allowed him to transfer Haim Erez's armor brigade to the western bank as well, including 21 tanks and seven APC's. They all crossed on the rafts and immediately reinforced the stronghold established by Danny Matt, enabling them to deepen their penetration and begin their attacks on the Egyptian anti-aircraft batteries.

Even in the midst of the clamor of battle, Sharon found the time to call Lilly and tell her what was going on. During the entire war, Sharon called his wife three or four times a day. Those who followed him during the war realized, as did other soldiers who had fought by his side in previous wars, that his roughness and bad temper would disappear the moment he talked to his wife. On the morning of the crossing, Sharon asked his communications officer to call his home so that he could talk to his wife. The officer handed the receiver to him, and Sharon hurried to announce: "Lilly, listen to this. We did it! Danny has already crossed and Haim is on the other side with the tanks. Can you hear me, Lilly? Is this Lilly?" As it turned out, the officer had reached a wrong number, and this startled, unknown woman learned of the crossing before most of the senior officers of the IDF.

With the initial crossing complete, a huge feast was set up and a crate of beefsteaks was brought into Sharon's command post. As he ate the meat, a soldier brought in coffee and Sharon smiled and said, "I'm on a diet, so please serve the coffee without sugar."

On the morning of October 16th, it became apparent that Sharon's plan had not been fully implemented. His forces had not succeeded in breaking through to the canal and establishing a bridgehead and a secure corridor of approach. Although he was successful in moving along the breach between the two armies and crossing the canal, this maneuver now seemed extremely dangerous to the command. Moshe Dayan even suggested that Matt's brigade return to the east. Gonen declared that had he known that this would be the outcome of the crossing plan, he would not have suggested it in the first place, but nevertheless, the paratroopers should not retreat. Bar Lev agreed. He maintained that even if the construction of bridges on the canal was delayed, the momentum of the crossing should not be slowed. The southern command, nevertheless, decided to change the missions assigned to the two divisions and to order Adan's division to carry out the task which Sharon's forces had failed to accomplish: to shatter the Egyptian lines east of the canal and to widen the breach sufficiently to allow the bridging equipment to pass without being exposed to Egyptian fire.

The transfer of the missions from Sharon to Adan reflected the southern command's disappointment with Sharon. Bar Lev and Gonen were forced to work with the knowledge that

Sharon's combat reports did not always match reality. Sharon's report that one of the main roads to the canal was open proved to be a hasty evaluation, as the Egyptians quickly seized it again. Sharon estimated that the occupation of the road would take his units an hour and a half, but he could not come close to meeting this estimate. While Sharon maintained at an early stage that the Egyptians were collapsing, they actually soon recovered and fought back. Sharon declared that his forces could handle the penetration to the west as well as the crossing, but his superiors soon realized that he needed support from Adan's division and that he had failed to report the delays in the transportation of the bridging equipment. The command attempted to change roles, to charge Adan with the crossing and leave to Sharon the responsibility of creating a corridor and covering the east bridgehead, but Sharon insisted that he was capable of performing both missions. The vague annoyance of the southern command about Sharon's insistence began to turn into open discord by the late morning.

Sharon estimated that his forces had created the necessary conditions for the transfer of both divisions – his and Adan's – to the other side of the canal. Elazar, Bar Lev and Gonen maintained that he had failed to do so. The command had hoped that on the 16th the IDF would have at its disposal two bridges across the canal as well as two well-established bridgeheads on both banks. Instead, Sharon accomplished only the penetration into the rear lines of the Egyptians east of the canal and the preliminary crossing. He maintained that the rest of his division, as well as Adan's division, could be transported to the other side of the canal on rafts, but the southern command objected. Bar Lev contested bitterly that this was a war and not a raid. Gonen no longer placed any credence in Sharon's reporting, ventured into the field and, bypassing Sharon, began giving orders directly to Sharon's brigade commanders. The opinion of the command was that Sharon was driven by one goal only: to be the first to cross the canal and to be remembered by the public as the general responsible for the turning point in the war. Bar Lev, Elazar and Gonen thought that Sharon's position was precarious and irresponsible. Gonen said that unless at least one bridge were constructed within 24 hours, there would be no alternative but to return the units to the east side of the canal. Sharon interpreted this attitude as another indication of limited military thinking and lack of decisiveness. He proclaimed that as long as the enemy was unaware of the extent of Israeli penetration, as many units as possible should be transferred to encircle both Egyptian armies.

By 11:00 a.m., the casualties had reached 200, and the number of damaged tanks had mounted to 50. This information was not relayed to the command, but Elazar and Bar Lev realized that Sharon's plan had been disrupted. Bar Lev forbade Sharon to float more tanks to the west bank. Sharon flew into a rage. Within a few hours, even the junior officers of his division were aware of Sharon's opinion of his commanders. The news of his vindictive and bitter criticism travelled so fast that it would even reach the General Staff on the same day. Sharon claimed that the command was wrong in stating that his units were encircled, claiming that it was just as correct to say that his forces were encircling the Egyptians.

Elazar, Bar Lev and Gonen were so aggravated by Sharon's behavior that Elazar felt compelled to protest to the Minister of Defense. Elazar emphasized to Dayan that, as a result of Sharon's stubbornness, Bar Lev was constrained to make compromising decisions which contributed little to solving the many problems faced in the war. As an example, he mentioned Bar Lev's decision to let Sharon transfer some of his unit to the west, while leaving his main forces on the east side of the canal, whereas the correct solution would have been to concentrate Sharon's entire division on the eastern bank and to transfer Adan's division to the west. Elazar also complained about the humiliations and insults that emanated from Sharon's division, which invariably blamed the General Staff for the conduct of the battle and for not profiting from Sharon's successes at the start of the penetration. Dayan did not respond directly, but told Elazar that he had a great respect for Sharon's military ability and for his special talents in clearly assessing the situation in a battle. Dayan further added that, in his mind, Bar Lev's thinking was unnecessarily rigid. They both agreed, however, that this was not the time for an internal war among generals.

Meanwhile, Adan's forces did not succeed in opening the roads to the canal. Units from Sharon's division, including his own forward command post, fought hard to ward off Egyptian attempts to hit the Israeli stronghold east of the canal. On the night of October 16th, a paratrooper brigade commanded by Uzi Yairi waged a heavy battle on "the Chinese Farm" to enable a raft convoy to reach "the Court." The raft bridge was not completed until more than 24 hours later because of the heavy Egyptian bombardments, while the roller bridge was not erected until 48 hours later because of a mechanical failure and the difficulty in the towing itself. After the war, Colonel Joseph Geva was asked to check the reasons for the delay in the construction of the bridges over the canal, and his unequivocal conclusion was that one of the main causes of this failure was the mutual distrust which had developed between Sharon and the General Staff. Sharon suspected them of scheming against him, while they distrusted his reports. The bridging equipment reached its location thanks to officers in the field who acted independently of the southern command's instructions.

This mutual distrust took on many forms during the war. In one instance, Gonen ordered Sharon to continue towing the roller bridge westward. Sharon responded that the breakdown would take at least a few hours to repair. Gonen retorted promptly that he personally had just come from the area where the equipment had broken down, and that it would not take more than a half hour to repair it. When Adan and Sharon were called upon to make coordinated attacks, Adan complained that he got no cooperation from Sharon. On October 16th in the afternoon, Gonen ordered Sharon to attack "the Chinese Farm" and part of "Missouri." Sharon responded that his tanks lacked sufficient fuel and ammunition, but Gonen suspected that Sharon was merely trying to avoid the mission. After the war, a bitter debate broke out about the cause of the delay in crossing the canal. Sharon blamed Elazar, Bar Lev and Gonen for their general management of the war; they blamed him.

On the morning of the 17th, the first barges reached the canal and it was finally possible to erect a bridge. Sharon took advantage of this and began transferring tanks to reinforce and strengthen his forces on the west side. Gonen ordered him to stop and to first complete his basic assignment of expanding the bridgehead on the east side and securing it from further attacks by the Egyptians. Sharon was irate but obeyed. He could not understand why the southern command refused to allow him to support the troops who had crossed the canal and had faced constant heavy fire from the beginning.

While Sharon was still at "the Court," the Egyptians opened up with a heavy barrage, first with Katyusha rockets and then with mortars. Panic began to set in and cries of "take cover" could be heard from all sides. Those who found themselves together with Sharon were very impressed with his coolness and composure under fire. Apparently in complete control of the situation, he gave orders to the driver of his half-track to back the vehicle up, but the tires were stuck in a crater from the recent bombardment. With Sharon shouting orders and the driver maneuvering the vehicle, another shell landed near them, upsetting the half-track. Sharon received a vicious head blow from the machine gun attached to the half-track and was knocked unconscious. When Brig.-Gen. Tamir saw Sharon bleeding profusely from the head, he called out in confusion, "It's a head wound! The division commander is dead!" A few moments later, Sharon recovered consciousness and asked for a medic to bandage his wound, and then immediately began giving orders to get them out of the fire. The driver, who by then had managed to get the half-track moving, found a position with a reasonable amount of cover and there Sharon stopped to listen in on the radio communications and find out how badly the bridgehead had been hit. The damage seemed severe. The roller bridge was hit, and the southern command ordered the division to slow its progress. In addition there was a sad personal note: his close friend, Zeev Slotzky, was critically wounded and dying. Sharon was visibly overcome by the news about Slotzky, and many contended that it was the only time he showed any emotion about a war-related death or injury. With a growing blood stain on his head bandage, Sharon began his quarrel with the southern command about their orders to slow their movement in crossing the canal. He screamed over the radio, "Get your fucking asses out of the bunker and take a look at what's going on here!" Impressed with the vehemence of Sharon's rage, a meeting was hastily arranged for that afternoon including Elazar, Bar Lev, Gonen and the commanders of the divisions in the Sinai.

Riding in his half-track with a fresh bandage around his head and his silver white hair blowing in the wind, Sharon presented an inspiring picture as he made his way to the meeting of the senior commanders. As he passed among the soldiers of his division they all waved and cheered, wishing him good health. They were happy to be a part of the division commanded by Sharon. Sharon continued to nurture this atmosphere throughout the war, frequently using open radio communications for his discussions and debates with the southern command so that as many soldiers as possible could overhear him. Sharon was clearly campaigning. When asked why he had not been wearing a helmet, he responded testily, saying that helmets were for those sitting in the rear in their bunkers.

The meeting was held at Adan's headquarters, a site in the middle of the desert surrounded by helicopters, half-tracks with antennas reaching up to the sky, and a variety of other vehicles. All the senior officers in the IDF who had anything to do with the war in the Sinai were present. Bar Lev attacked Sharon early in the meeting saying, "Let's talk straight and to the point. There's no connection between the plan you proposed and what you carried out."

Sharon was clearly hurt by this allegation. Much later he would recount that he was on the verge of slapping Bar Lev across the face. He firmly believed that his success in crossing the canal was vital and that the tremendous strain and constant work of the past three days merited at least a "thank you," or some measure of recognition on the part of his colleagues. "Pretty soon you'll be claiming that I wasn't even involved in the battle," Sharon responded sarcastically.

The discussion that took place focused on the future strategy of the IDF for the war in Sinai and on the crossing of the canal. Sharon and Adan initially agreed that one division should cross

the canal while the other widened the access to it and secured
the bridgehead on the eastern side. It was only a question of
who would do what. To Sharon it was clear that he should cross
the canal while Adan fought the Egyptians on the east; to Adan
it was equally clear that the plan that he cross, while Sharon
widened and established the bridgehead, should be maintained.
Bar Lev even proposed a compromise - splitting the divisions,
with brigades from each taking part in both missions. The Chief
of the General Staff objected to the compromise and
admonished Sharon to complete the mission of establishing the
approach corridor and the bridgehead on the eastern side before
making any move to cross the canal. Sharon argued that no time
should be lost in crossing and attacking the Egyptians from the
rear. Rather than wait for the completion of the roller bridge,
more tanks should be transferred across the canal by raft.
Sharon went even further: it was not necessary to dedicate a
whole division to securing their hold on the eastern bank. The
bulk of the two divisions should cross the canal and attack the
Egyptians from their rear, for by doing so, the entire Egyptian
alignment would be undermined and the fighting on the east
would prove unnecessary. By his calculation it would be
sufficient to leave two brigades to hold the bridgehead: one from
his division and one from Adan's. Adan disagreed and contested
that the eastern bridgehead was a critical stage in the war and
more than merited the allocation of a full division to assure its
proper completion. In his opinion, Sharon's division should hold
the east bank while his division crossed the canal. Bar Lev
recalled Sharon's report following his initial crossing of the
canal. Sharon had informed the senior command that the
Egyptian forces were collapsing all around him. The blatant
inaccuracy of Sharon's analysis convinced Bar Lev that he could
not rely on Sharon's optimistic prognosis. The march westward,
however effective, would not cause the collapse of the Egyptian
army unless accompanied by the smashing of the Egyptian forces
on the eastern side as well. Bar Lev, therefore, also supported
Adan's analysis and called for securing the access and the
bridgehead by capturing "Missouri." In Elazar's summary, he
called on Sharon to secure the eastern side and on Adan to cross

the canal.

That afternoon Dayan undertook a review of the situation by touring Sharon's forces on the western side of the canal. When he returned to headquarters, he was irate: the roller bridge had been in place for over an hour, and Adan had made no attempt to send troops across. After the war, Adan would explain that the delay was the result of organizational difficulties created by the failure of Sharon's units to replace those of Adan's who held key positions on the eastern side. Adan's units were engaged in constant battle and could not simply disengage for the attack to the west without endangering their entire position in the east. Adan was so irate that he turned to Gonen and formally complained about Sharon's actions. Gonen tried to reach Sharon by radio but was unsuccessful and, once again, bypassed Sharon's authority and gave orders directly to Sharon's brigade commanders. He reported to Elazar that, in his estimation, it would be impossible to continue to exercise control over Sharon's division in this manner and suggested the posting of southern command observers on Sharon's staff, in order to report on Sharon's activities and assure that Sharon fought in the same war they were fighting. Bar Lev was just as exasperated as Gonen, and he too told Elazar that in his opinion Sharon should be dismissed from his command. As Elazar was about to make his way to the northern front, Bar Lev added that unless some solution was found to the "Sharon problem," he would also make his way to the north. After the war, it became clear that Elazar failed to take any concrete steps against Sharon because he was afraid of the very strong public support that Sharon enjoyed, and because he understood that Dayan would oppose any such action.

At 10:00 p.m. Adan's forces finally began to cross the canal, and joined the brigade from Sharon's division that had been fighting on the western side of the canal for three days. Adan's bitterness toward Sharon would last for a long time. Whereas he had been more than generous toward Sharon, showing him full cooperation at all stages, Sharon had intentionally impeded him and had prevented him from fulfilling his missions properly. Adan referred, in particular, to Sharon's failure to replace his units in the east in a timely fashion, and to his failure to release units originally from Adan's division, that were temporarily attached to Sharon and which now were to be returned to Adan's command, as he prepared to cross the canal. Sharon would counter that Adan was part of the clique of "old-fashioned Palmah leaders" headed by Elazar and Bar Lev. Sharon continued to believe that this clique had intrigued against him personally, restricting his every move, and was in general motivated by their desire to prevent him from enjoying any of the laurels of the war.

On Thursday, October 18, "the Chinese Farm" finally fell to one of Sharon's brigades, which then continued its movement north to expand the corridor even further. At the same time a second force, commanded by Sharon's second-in-command, Jack Eban, began opening another corridor, enabling the placement of a second roller bridge on the canal. The balance of Sharon's forces on the western side of the canal were to move south in parallel with Adan's division, but Sharon proposed a change that was accepted by Bar Lev. Instead of reinforcing Adan's forces, his men would strengthen the bridgehead on the west and start to push the Egyptians slowly northward to Ismailiya. That night the command gave Sharon authority to transfer more troops to the west, despite the fact that the key Egyptian stronghold in the east, "Missouri," was still in enemy hands.

The following day, October 19, international political pressure began to be felt, and the senior military command became anxious. It was critical that the political stage be delayed until the key military objectives could be achieved: removing all Egyptian forces from the eastern side of the canal and establishing a firm hold on the newly captured territory to the west of the Suez. At first Sharon proposed that his division move out of their bridgehead, in a fan, in the general direction of Cairo, but Dayan recommended that they be content with the narrower objective of moving to the north and surrounding the Egyptian Second Army. Bar Lev and Gonen both felt that the key mission was the removal of the Egyptian stronghold at "Missouri," both because it continued to threaten the Israeli bridgehead and because it represented a holdout in the face of the Israeli pressure to force the Egyptians to retreat. Sharon was, therefore, instructed to move northward in a narrow strip along the canal and capture the high points opposite "Missouri." The assumption was that this would facilitate the removal of this very stubborn Egyptian stronghold.

Elazar visited the southern command headquarters and once again heard Gonen request that Sharon be dismissed. Gonen claimed that Sharon had failed to obey orders to move northward on both sides of the canal in order to apply the maximum pressure possible on "Missouri." Gonen protested that Sharon was moving northward on the western side only. The Chief of the General Staff responded that he had no intention of creating a turmoil among his own officers in the middle of a war and made his way to Sharon's headquarters to see for himself what Sharon was doing. In Elazar's testimony after the war, he stated that he was very impressed by what he saw. Sharon gave him a very graphic depiction of the battles his division had fought since the first day of the war and described in detail the difficulties it currently faced in its march northward on the western bank. The terrain was at points nearly impassable and slowed his troops down considerably, while the Egyptians facing them continued to fight tenaciously. Sharon's description impressed Elazar, even though it stood in direct contradiction to Sharon's earlier prognosis, passed on through Yisrael Tal to the General Staff, that the Egyptian forces opposite him would soon collapse. Upon his return to the southern command, Elazar informed Gonen that he could not blame Sharon for the slow pace of his advance because he was facing intense opposition all along the way. In light of these developments and the unexpected tenacity of the Egyptians, the southern command began to reformulate its strategic goals. There were now two major objectives: the first and key one was to conquer "Missouri" and widen the eastern bridgehead; the second was to continue the march south on the western side of the canal and surround the Egyptian Third Army.

On Saturday, Dayan once again visited Sharon's headquarters on the western side of the canal. Dayan enjoyed the time he spent at Sharon's division. Sharon immediately bombarded him with a host of different plans for the continuation of the war. The key element of these proposals was his call to surround Ismailiya and cut off the Second Army from Cairo. One day earlier, Elazar had estimated that such a mission would take ten days at most. In the midst of this discussion, they were suddenly attacked by two Egyptian helicopters that dropped napalm on the paratrooper brigade within which Sharon kept his headquarters. It served to demonstrate, if such a concrete demonstration were actually necessary, that the war was far from over; however, it had no impact on the confidence that radiated from Sharon and which had such an ameliorating effect on Dayan.

Sharon's proposal to attack Ismailiya and cut off the Second Army from Cairo was rejected by both Dayan and Elazar. A number of Dayan's aides who accompanied him on this visit felt that Sharon had not made this proposal seriously. It was their impression that this grandiose plan had been suggested for the very reason that Sharon was certain it would be rejected. According to this version, Sharon had a clear understanding of how difficult such a task would be, but had refused to acknowledge this in public. By making such a proposal he would appear to be confident and to be thinking in the daring and courageous mode he so diligently nurtured. Regardless of whether this supposition is correct, a number of officers on Sharon's staff cornered Dayan's aides to entreat them not to approve their commander's plan. Whatever the posturing that may have been going on, Dayan was visibly impressed with the energy and vitality that Sharon showed, and even remarked that Sharon's spirit and optimism were certainly contagious. In actual fact, there was no real opportunity to test the plan, because time was running out both politically and militarily and the pressure for a negotiated cease-fire was increasing daily. Although Sharon's division had already moved northward by a few miles, he was ordered to shift the battle back to the east and attack "Missouri." Sharon argued against this decision and, just as he had done throughout the war, he sought to enlist the assistance of Menahem Begin, notifying him of what was going on and requesting that he intervene with Dayan on behalf of Sharon's position.

The following day Dayan visited Sharon's headquarters again, but this time he found Sharon in a "furious rage," as he later said. Sharon had been ordered to stop his advance to the north and bring his soldiers back so they could attack the Egyptian stronghold at "Missouri" on the eastern side of the canal. Sharon argued that this was a crucial mistake, for it was far more important to encircle Ismailiya and reach Qantara, thereby cutting off the Second Army from the main roads connecting it to Cairo and its supply bases. The attack on "Missouri," on the other hand, would entail heavy casualties and result in questionable military and political gains. Israel would have a much better chance of forcing the Egyptians to retreat if it were successful in isolating the Second Army than if it captured "Missouri." Elazar, Bar Lev and Gonen all saw the picture differently, as they argued against Sharon's suggestion. They interpreted Sharon's opposition to the attack on "Missouri" as a reflection of his vainglorious desire for an ostentatious mission and the personal adulation that would be his reward. They also added that the vehemence of his argument was attributable to his anxiousness over the successes of Adan and Kalman Magen, his fellow division commanders in the south of the Sinai. They completely disagreed with Sharon's evaluation of the military situation and of the importance of "Missouri." It was their opinion that the capture of this key position on the canal would undermine the Egyptian posture along the entire canal.

With Gonen carefully monitoring Sharon's plans and movements to ascertain whether he was indeed obeying orders, at 3:15 p.m. one of Sharon's brigades, commanded by Tuvya Raviv, began its attack on the Egyptian position at "Missouri." The attack failed and Raviv's forces retreated. At southern command headquarters a hurried analysis was performed of the reasons for the failure. Although Sharon had given clear assurances that he would be reinforcing Raviv's brigade, he had sent only five tanks to its support. Despite Raviv's entreaties to provide him with further assistance, his division commander refused to comply. The southern command contended that had Sharon attacked with a larger force, the attack **would have been** successful. Gonen therefore tried to reach Sharon on October 21 to order him to prepare for a renewed attack the following morning, but this time with much larger forces, drawn from the brigades on the western side of the canal. Gonen was informed that Sharon was asleep and that they were unable to wake him. Gonen went to seek out Sharon and finally delivered the order personally. Sharon immediately began to argue with him, but Gonen retorted that it was a direct order and Sharon stopped arguing. Bar Lev tried to assuage Sharon and described the action as part of a larger plan. He told Sharon that there was no reason to do anything that night, but rather to be ready by dawn of the following morning. Sharon relented and agreed to transfer his tanks back to the eastern bank of the canal.

An hour later, Sharon contacted Dayan and poured out his anger and frustration with the southern command and the orders he had been given to attack "Missouri" the following morning. Dayan asked Major General Tal to investigate the problem and try to settle the dispute. Tal contacted Elazar and advised him not to ignore Sharon's sense of foreboding regarding the next day's attack. The Chief of Staff accepted this advice and postponed the attack, informing the southern command that the plans for the attack on "Missouri" should be held in abeyance and would be subject to Sharon's approval.

Early in the morning of October 22, the United Nations Security Council called for a complete cease-fire along the Suez Canal to go into effect that evening. The government of Israel, in turn, accepted this decision and ordered the IDF to stop all fighting at 6:52 p.m., on condition that the Egyptians did so as well. The General Staff became a beehive of activity as it became apparent that with the institution of the cease-fire the IDF would find itself in a position in which its key military goal had not been met. The Egyptians still held key positions on the eastern bank of the canal. The southern command was therefore ordered to do everything possible to complete the encirclement of the Egyptian Third Army in the southern region of the canal and to attack and remove the Egyptian forces from their stronghold at "Missouri." This was to be accomplished with as few casualties to the IDF as possible. Sharon conducted his own private war against the government's acquiescence to the U.N. decision. He criticized the government for cooperating with the U.N. in salvaging the Egyptian army and withholding a major victory from the IDF. Sharon beseeched Begin to fight the government's decision and expressed his feeling that the IDF would have won a complete and total victory had it not been deterred by its goal of undermining Sharon. Shortly after receiving notification about the cease-fire, Sharon's division set out toward Ismailiya. Sharon was determined to capture this key city before the cease-fire came into effect.

Despite all the efforts of Sharon and his division, he failed to capture Ismailiya. The division had encountered problems throughout its march. They were under constant artillery attack, while the difficult terrain slowed their movement significantly. The division was formed into a long train as they negotiated the water ditches, railroad tracks, orchards and fields that forced it into a narrow avenue of advance. As they reached the outskirts of Ismailiya, Sharon gave Amnon Reshef the order to enter the city with his brigade. The men were exhausted. Casualties would almost certainly be very high, and there was little chance of successfully completing the mission. At 7:50 p.m., an hour following the appointed start of the cease-fire, all units received the order to stop firing. It was apparently also Sharon's personal signal to start his own battle against the government and the senior command of the IDF in earnest. To the reporters who accompanied his division he declared that Ismailiya could have been captured three days before, had the time available to them been utilized properly. Instead, a cease-fire was imposed, without the IDF having attained any of its key goals in removing the Egyptians from the eastern side of the canal. Had he been allowed to attack the city earlier, it would have been possible to surround the Egyptian Second Army completely and cut it off from all sources of supply. To the officers of his own staff he was even more outspoken. He accused the senior commanders of the army of incompetence. They were slow in making decisions and failed to read the developing battles accurately. The war was about to end with Israel, as a whole, paying the penalty of their blunders.

Sharon, supported by a number of faithful journalists, would continue to argue that he had been given permission to attack Ismailiya only three hours before the expected end of the war. In such a short period of time, it was, of course, impossible to complete this key mission, despite the near-Herculean efforts of his men. Sharon's followers would also contend that he had been given government assurances, in particular by Yigal Allon, that the IDF would not be bound by any timetables established by the U.N. The General Staff and the southern command would counter that Sharon had been given five full days to implement his plans in the region. By Sharon's own request, his division's battle plans had been altered after the crossing of the canal, and he had been authorized to march northward toward Ismailiya instead of supporting Adan's division in the fighting to the south. No one in the southern command did anything to prevent Sharon from succeeding in meeting the very goals he had set for himself, except for the one short-lived attempt to capture "Missouri," which had diverted only a small portion of his division. Sharon's division fought a very difficult battle in its approach to Ismailiya, but had failed. No one argued with the bravery of the division's soldiers or the difficulty of their mission; no one stood in their way, however, except for the enemy. There were also those who would argue that the reason for Sharon's failure went beyond the objective circumstances of the attack. Whether because of his personal wars, or because of some other reason, according to this argument, Sharon had failed because of mismanagement of the attack.

More than 36 hours would pass before the cease-fire actually became effective, and during this interim the fighting was fierce throughout the region. Sharon's division was particularly prominent, both in the intensity of its action and in the extent of its movement. Israel contended that the fighting during this period was a direct result of Egyptian provocations. Regardless of the cause, the IDF significantly improved its position during this time. In the south, the siege of the Egyptian Third Army was completed, while in the north, Sharon's division continued its advance northward, although he failed to complete the encirclement of the Second Army. Sharon did not take advantage of the following days to rest, but rather continued to badger the senior command of the IDF to take concrete steps to remove the Egyptians from the eastern side of the canal. By his argument, the Egyptians would not agree to any real cease-fire, let alone some form of peace, as long as their success in capturing parts of the eastern bank was preserved. He proposed to Dayan that his forces be allowed to move west and capture large tracts of land in the heart of Egypt. His responses to what the IDF termed "Egyptian cease-fire violations" were especially aggressive, despite the explicit instructions he had received from the new commander of the Southern Sector, Yisrael Tal, to avoid any further outbreaks of fighting with the Egyptians.

As the fighting subsided, signs began to appear on the division's vehicles: "Arik King of Israel." A wave of support and admiration swept over most of the soldiers in Sharon's division as they gave expression to their feeling that their commander had changed the face of the war. Many were grateful for having been in his division, believing that in some respect they owed their lives to the military skills of Sharon. A handful of officers who had spent the war in close contact with Sharon looked upon things differently, however. They felt that there were times when Sharon's personal ambition completely subdued his logic. Overall, Sharon was impressed and flattered by the adulation of his men and saw it as further evidence of his leadership ability.

In the days following the war, Sharon's attacks on the government and the senior command of the IDF became virulent. His verbal assaults knew no restraint. Whether to his own subordinates in the army, to visiting journalists from "The New York Times," or to visiting education teams from the IDF, he blasted the senior command of the IDF and the government for the horrendous blunders of the war. As he puffed on his cigar and sipped his cognac, he expostulated on the need to replace the entire General Staff and the Defense Minister, Moshe Dayan. In his interview with visiting American reporters he explained how his superior officers were responsible for the failure to complete the siege of the Second Army because of the delay in transferring his forces across the canal. He emphasized that not a single senior officer had visited the front lines to see for himself what was going on. He blamed the senior command for the failure of the march northward to Ismailiya because of the unwarranted delays and indecisiveness. He disagreed with the conception that the crossing must take place on stationary bridges rather than by making use of the rafts on which he had sent his first tanks across. Finally, he disputed the need to acquiesce to the cease-fire, as well as the government's unduly serious interpretation of the Russian threats aired during the latter part of the war.

Granting interviews to American journalists was an unprecedented act on the part of an officer still in uniform. Until Sharon's outburst of October, 1973, no officer had ever taken essentially internal quarrels to the press. Elazar was irate and immediately started proceedings to cancel Sharon's reserve commission. Sharon interpreted this as another stage in the establishment's personal vendetta against him.

Sharon continued to serve as division commander for another three months, until January 20, 1974, during which time the two armies reached a tense but stable relationship. As he prepared to leave his position, he published his final orders of the day without prior approval from the Chief of Staff:

"...It was our division that initiated and assumed responsibility for the most difficult, complex and cruel mission of the war: the crossing of the canal. The crossing of the canal brought about the change and was the turning point in the war. The crossing of the canal brought us the victory in the war. We must remember that our victory in the Yom Kippur War was the greatest of all our victories. If, despite the blunders and the mistakes, despite the failures and obstructions, despite the loss of control and authority, we nevertheless achieved our victory, we must therefore recognize that this was the greatest victory the IDF has ever known. We fought, and hundreds of our best fighters died in battle, and even more were wounded, but we were victorious...At the conclusion of the fighting I informed you that I would stay with you as long as it was necessary to remain in the reserves. I promised to stay with you, but today I am forced to leave. To you soldiers, the real heroes of this war, I owe an explanation. The war has ended, the preliminary discussions about an arrangement with the Egyptians have ended as well, and now I feel it is essential to fight on another front. It is essential to fight, with all due strength, to prevent further wars in the future. Therefore I am leaving. I would like you to know that I have never served with fighters like you; you have been the greatest of them all...I leave you in sadness. I wish you all a speedy return to your homes, but if it should prove necessary to fight again, I promise to return to fight together with you."

For the first time in the history of the IDF, Lt.-General Ariel Sharon had drawn a direct connection between his military service and his political aspirations. His last communication to his soldiers was a clear call for their support in the political career he had chosen.

CHAPTER 12

A few hours after the publication of Sharon's last orders of the day, he participated in a major political demonstration organized by the Likud in Tel Aviv to protest the recently-signed agreement for the separation of forces along the Suez Canal between Egypt and Israel. This rally represented Sharon's return to open political activity, which had been cut off by the outbreak of the Yom Kippur War. Sharon made ample use of the information and impressions he had acquired during the war. He attacked the government for its manifest weakness in agreeing to the terms of the separation of forces which left the Egyptian army in possession of the eastern bank of the Suez Canal and accused the government of the blunders responsible for the very outbreak of the war. The crowd cheered Sharon's speech wildly, interrupting him frequently with chants of "Arik, Arik." At the end of the rally, he was surrounded by hundreds of ardent supporters singing "Arik King of Israel." Sharon made his way through the throngs in his now familiar strut, visibly proud but also a little nonplussed by the degree of the response he had elicited.

Sharon's order of the day, his speech at the political demonstration and an interview he gave to *Harper's Magazine*, all reiterated that the senior command had been prompted by purely political motives in its misguided policy concerning the crossing of the canal in the war. In response, the Chief of Staff cancelled Sharon's commission as a division commander and the General Staff even began a review of the possiblity of prosecuting Sharon formally. The Advocate-General of the army, Colonel Zvi Inbar, and the legal advisor of the Ministry of Defense, Yosef Chahanover, reviewed the case in light of the written opinion presented by the Attorney General, Meir Shamgar. In their opinion it was impossible to prosecute Sharon formally, despite his violation of army laws and regulations, because since his election to the Knesset on December 31, 1973, Sharon was protected by parliamentary immunity to prosecution. It was therefore decided to publish a formal response by the spokesman of the IDF in which the cancellation of Sharon's commission would be announced.

As Sharon sat patiently through the application of the make-up in preparation for a television appearance, the Chief of Staff's adjutant phoned him and informed him of the decision of the General Staff and the upcoming announcement. One hour later, the spokesman of the IDF made the following announcement: "The orders of the day published by Major-General Sharon as well as the comments attributed to him by *Harper's Magazine* are an affront to the other commanders and units and are a direct attack on his commrades-in-arms and to the fraternal spirit among soldiers. Despite this violation of good order and of military discipline, the Chief of Staff has decided not to institute disciplinary proceedings against Major-General Sharon following his release from active reserve duty and the cancellation of his commission as a division commander." Sharon responded by denying all the charges raised against him and adding, "the announcement of the Chief of Staff is merely a continuation of the campaign against me. Its motivations are essentially political, although there are also elements of jealousy and hatred among officers which have become, to my regret, among the clearest characteristics of the term in office of the last Chief of Staff... As regards the cancellation of my commission, it seems that those responsible for security have learned nothing from this last war. The level of the soldiers and the officers is not determined by their political affiliation, yet I cannot see the cancellation of my commission as anything but a purely political act." In the forthcoming days, Sharon would become even more explicit in his evaluation of his own contribution and skills, and added in a newspaper interview, "it is foolish and irresponsible not to allow someone like me to reach the highest levels of command in the army. How many other officers of my caliber are there in the IDF?" The government and the General Staff, however, remained consistently opposed to Sharon's return to the army and he continued his active career in politics.

Sharon was elected to the Knesset along with 38 other candidates on the Likud list. The election results were, however, a bitter disappointment for Sharon, as his dream of converting the Likud into a potent political force capable of removing the Labor Alignment from power remained unfulfilled. The public was not as quick to punish the Labor bloc for the blunders of the Yom Kippur War as he had expected and, instead, had provided the Labor Party with a broad base of support. Sharon was, therefore, forced to spend the next few years as a legislator, involved in routine, endless debates in parliament and in the boring process of legislation, being thrown into daily contact with the political hacks and party operatives. It was a difficult period for Sharon, as his whole personality rebelled against this inactivity. Unable to be content with taking part in the quiet, slow processes of democracy in the Israeli Knesset, he yearned for action, for responsibility for something concrete. Sharon was soon discovered to be an impatient politician who held his colleagues in the parliament and in his party in complete contempt.

Not long after the election in December, 1973, Sharon renewed his efforts to convert the conglomeration of parties that made up the Likud into a unified political party. In March, 1974, he resigned as head of the policy committee of the Likud, whose task it had been to formulate the framework for the unification of the party, in protest against the pace of work and the lack of progress. He accused his own party, the Liberals, of being consumed by marginal issues and ignoring the key questions facing the country. He completely stopped attending meetings of the Liberal Party and agreed to participate only in meetings of the entire leadership of the Likud. He declared that unless the Likud was reconstituted as a single political party, he would not agree to run in the next elections as part of its list.

As a member of the Foreign Affairs and Defense Committee of the Knesset, Sharon participated in the discussions on the interim peace arrangements between Israel and Egypt. At one of these meetings, in which Foreign Minister Abba Eban was called upon to testify before the committee, Sharon demanded churlishly of Eban to present the full "map of retreat" agreed upon by the government. Eban refused to answer, protesting Sharon's ill-mannered insolence. In response, Sharon rose and left the meeting. In retrospect, Sharon recalled that he often left these meetings just prior to their conclusion in order to avoid having to give any of the members a lift in his car and possibly exposing his utter contempt for his fellow members of the Knesset.

When Golda Meir resigned as Prime Minister in response to the criticism of the previous government within the Labor Party, and Yitzhak Rabin was elected to replace her, Sharon called on Rabin to include the Likud in the latter's government and thereby institute the sorely needed changes in the army and the leadership of the country. When he became convinced that his courting of the new Labor leadership was not achieving the hoped-for inclusion of the Likud in the government, Sharon went on the offensive and termed Labor's attacks on the Likud as a throwback to the pre-Independence period when the Haganah pursued and hunted the underground fighters of Etzel.

Following two particularly vicious terrorist attacks in Kiryat Shmoneh and Maalot in which dozens of children were killed, Sharon called for the establishment of a modern 101st Unit to fight the terrorists wherever they may be. "I know how to do just that and I have experience," Sharon declared. In June, 1974 Sharon led a group of Jewish settlers in their attempts to establish an unauthorized settlement near Nablus. As the soldiers on duty in the area tried to prevent these illegal settlers, Sharon advised them to disobey their orders. When members of his own Liberal Party protested his involvement in the illegal settlement and his incitement of the soldiers to disobey direct orders, he responded acidly: "There is a lot of self-righteousness among different elements of the Likud... there are those who have hypocritically joined the campaign against the settlements near Nablus. They have disseminated a host of lies and half-truths regarding this issue." In general, he succeeded in alienating the entire leadership of his own party, Simha Erlich, Elimelech Rimalt and Arieh Dulzin, until finally Rimalt responded by declaring the "we will not be able to sit at the same table if Sharon continues to use this style of expression."

To the button-downed members of the Likud, Sharon was a raging bull. He refused to accept the rules of the game calling for quiet discussions, addressing one's opponents politely, mutual respect among political adversaries and subtle parliamentary maneuvers. Sharon burst in with a new and brutish style that offended his partners. Sharon threatened, warned, swore and protested, mocked and insulted. He disagreed openly with the platform of the Likud leaders and aired his criticism publically through the media. The reason for his dissatisfaction was their refusal to respond to his demand to disband the four parties which together formed the Likud and to reunite them as one party. His activity was also a result of the boredom which he felt while in the Knesset. Since the election, he realized that the Likud had been condemned to the opposition while he continued to seek a more active occupation. This activity he now sought within the army.

Although expelled from the army, Sharon persisted in seeking an avenue of return. The defense situation seemed to be auspicious. The Agranat Commission had found both David Elazar and the Chief Intelligence Officer guilty of serious misjudgements leading to the outbreak of the war and the poor state of preparedness of the army; ruthless terrorist attacks were taking place against the population in northern Israeli settlements; and the preconditions for a separation of forces between Israel, Egypt and Syria were far from satisfactory. During Elazar's tenure, Sharon's initiative had little chance for success because of the bitter relations that existed between the two of them and because of a series of formal complaints that

Gonen had filed against Sharon. When Elazar resigned following the recommendations of the Agranat Commission, Menahem Begin proposed Sharon for the position of the Chief of Staff. The government, however, headed by the Labor Alignment, selected Mordechai Gur for this position. Sometime after Rabin was elected Prime Minister, Sharon again attempted to return to the IDF. Sharon hoped that the good relations he had maintained with Rabin and the political support he had given Rabin during his struggle to be Prime Minister, would enable him to fulfill his goal. Sharon hoped that his return to the IDF would again put him among the contenders for the office of Chief of Staff. Rabin indeed tried to find a suitable role for Sharon in the army, but Gur and Defense Minister Shimon Peres vehemently rejected these attempts. Gur claimed that after the Yom Kippur War and the recommendations of the Agranat Commission, the former high command had been replaced by younger officers who were now free of the disgraces of the war. Sharon's return, argued Gur, would put an end to this positive trend by adding an element of unwanted contentiousness.

Gur's refusal was further confirmed following a conversation he had with Sharon, in which he posed questions about Sharon's actions during the war. Gur questioned Sharon why he had attacked the high command for its failure to predict the onset of the war, while Sharon himself, as head of the Southern Command, had shared these same evaluations. Gur asked why Sharon had delayed after crossing the canal on the western bank and had not proceeded south as ordered by Bar Lev and Elazar. Or, on the other hand, why, after deciding to turn north, he had then failed to advance in his march toward Ismailiya. The new Chief of Staff was not persuaded by Sharon's explanations and remained adamant in his opposition to Sharon's reinstatement.

In July, 1974, there was a turning point in the attitude of both Gur and Peres. They both realized that in order to fulfill their plan to rehabilitate the IDF and enlarge its framework, they must be assisted by veteran senior officers. Sharon's expressed willingness to return to uniform could serve this purpose. As a first step in his attempted return, Sharon consented, together with Shmuel Gonen, to the cancellation of their respective complaints against each other. When Gur nevertheless made it clear that he would not approve Sharon's return, the discussions focused on finding a formula which would enable Sharon to be appointed to a senior position as a reserve officer. Sharon accompanied this pressure with a public campaign intended to push Gur and Peres to find him a suitable role. He refuted the arguments against him that his return would upset the harmony of the army by stating that "this is a rusty old weapon that has been used against me in the past" and "that it is hard to believe that a person who has always been called upon to perform the most difficult missions, and moreover has done so successfully, will now destroy the harmony." Sharon responded defiantly that "the army is not a harmony club. The army is for fighting!"

By December the road was paved for Sharon's return to the army. The government had decided that any Knesset member with the rank of colonel or higher would not be permitted to hold an active commission in the IDF. Sharon had to choose between his membership in the Knesset or his return to active duty as a corps commander in the Southern Command. Sharon opted for the second alternative, explaining to the Likud leadership that the "arbitrary and anti-democratic decision of the government compels him to retire from the Knesset."

Sharon was motivated by mixed considerations. He undoubtedly had a genuine concern for Israel's security and the quality of the IDF. To his mind the military leadership, with Mordechai Gur and Shimon Peres, was inadequate to contend with the military and security challenges that now faced the country after the war. Other motives, however, also played a role in his decision. Sharon saw a new opportunity to compete for the position of Chief of Staff after Gur's retirement. He was disgusted with the political work of an opposition member of parliament. Sharon craved for action. Sharon was a failure in his first political experience, unable to find his place in the parliament. He tried, without success, to impose his personal authority on the political system, as he had grown accustomed to doing in the army. He aroused his own party members against him when he revealed his clear eagerness to compromise with the government. He also failed in his attempt to eliminate the constituent parties in the Likud.

Shortly after Sharon returned to the army, his subordinates discovered that he had not changed. In his new role, Sharon prepared a new plan for the deployment of the IDF along the lines established by the cease-fire agreement. Sharon presented his plan to his superior officer, Major-General Yekutiel Adam, Commander of the Southern Sector, who approved them. Some time later, the Chief of Staff, Mordechai Gur, came to the southern command to examine the plan. Before Sharon could present his ideas to the Chief of Staff, Adam made it clear that he had already examined the suggested deployment and had approved it. Gur thought otherwise. The plan did not satisfy him and he rejected it. Instead, he produced a different plan of deployment from his files prepared in the General Staff, presented it to Adam and to Sharon and told them to implement it. There was an argument about the nature of both plans but the Chief of Staff insisted and finally ordered Adam and Sharon to deploy their forces according to the plan he had brought with him from Tel Aviv.

The next day, Sharon met with the three division commanders of his corps to brief them on their deployment in the Sinai. A map indicating their deployment hung on the wall. Sharon pointed to it and declared, "Do you see the plan of the General Staff? Only an idiot could produce such a plan!" He removed the map from the wall and replaced it with one that showed his own plans for the deployment of his corps and began briefing the division commanders according to his plan. During the break following Sharon's briefing, the staff officers of the corps remained together. Yehuda Reshef, the chief operations officer of the corps, approached Sharon and in the presence of his colleagues said, "This you must not do. You cannot call the Chief of Staff an idiot in front of his soldiers. If that's the way you feel, present your case to the Prime Minister and convince him that your plan is better. You do not have the right to talk that way to officers serving under the Chief of Staff who may find themselves called upon by him to fight in a war. Your behavior will only lead to demoralization." Reshef declared that

he will not be reconciled to this type of behavior and that he felt
compelled to report it. Indeed, Adam, Chief of the Southern
Sector, soon after received a report that said that "Sharon was
preparing a meal" that Adam would have to pay for. That night,
however, Adam ordered Sharon to stop his briefings and return
to the General Staff. A couple of weeks later, when the briefing
was resumed, it was done according to the plan of the Chief of
Staff.

In June, 1975 Sharon took a further step toward being
appointed Chief of the General Staff: he was appointed special
advisor to the Prime Minister, Yitzhak Rabin. Sharon and Rabin
had conducted a series of secret meetings during which they had
discussed the possibility of Sharon's rejoining the regular army
and of Rabin's ability to help him. Rabin's motives were
complex. His relationship with Defense Minister Shimon Peres
had so deteriorated that he chose to create within the Prime
Ministry a separate defense team to monitor and balance the
actions of the defense establishment under Peres' leadership.
Rabin also apparently felt that by including Sharon on his staff
he would be severing him from his connections to the Likud and
would, therefore, tone down the opposition's criticism of the
government's policies. For years Rabin had viewed Sharon as a
very competent man of action who, however, required a
controlling hand to tame his rampancy. Rabin contended that by
including Sharon among his inner circle of advisors, it would be
easier for him to reach an interim agreement with the Egyptians
without exposing himself to the harsh and unbridled criticism of
the opposition.

Sharon explained his own willingness to cross party lines by
referring to the severe defense situation and the dangers which
the country faced. In practice, however, Sharon's only
motivation was his personal ambition to become Chief of the
General Staff. He estimated that in his position as advisor to the
Prime Minister, he would be involved in all of the most pressing
defense issues currently facing the General Staff and the
government. Sharon had long since become tired with his
political activity in the Likud and he faced no particular
ideological or moral problems in supporting and contributing to

a government that he had so vociferously opposed until recently. Indeed, from the moment he received his appointment, he stopped all criticism of the government's handling of the negotiations for interim settlements with both the Egyptians and the Syrians under the aegis of the United States. Much later, he would explain his reticence by declaring that it would have been inappropriate to criticize the government at the very time in which he was serving as an adviser to the Prime Minister.

Peres and Gur were completely surprised by Rabin's appointment of Sharon as his national security adviser. The two formed a united front to pressure Rabin into declaring that despite previous indications, Sharon would not take part in meetings of the General Staff and, in fact, would not even hold the title of national security advisor. Sharon would have to be content with the title of advisor only. Gur carefully prevented Sharon from participating in any activities of the general staff and in one instance even refused to call such a meeting because Rabin had requested that Sharon participate. In another case, Gur refused to attend a tour of the Mitla and Giddi passes in the Sinai, subjects of the diplomatic negotiations then going on, because he had been informed that Rabin intended to participate accompanied by Sharon. Sharon's involvement in any real defense work was, therefore, limited. From the start there were serious doubts as to how deeply Rabin expected his new appointee to be involved in such questions. Rabin's primary motivation had been to address internal Labor Party problems. Sharon confined his activity to expressing his opinion on the pressing security issues of the day. In one case he advised that Israel attack the Syrian forces that had entered Lebanon and advanced to the city of Jezin. The government under Rabin's leadership had been willing to reconcile itself to Syrian advances in Lebanon, but declared that it drew a line beyond which any Syrian advance would be considered an act of war. Jezin was on this line. Gur opposed Sharon's recommendation as unnecessarily belligerent and contended that the Syrians would withdraw from Jezin without a battle. The government accepted Gur's proposal and informed the Syrians through the United States that unless its forces were removed from Jezin, Israel would consider military action against them. The United States contacted the Syrians, and the Syrians began a gradual pullout from the city until finally all that was left was an empty tent with a Syrian flag waving in proud defiance. Gur was clearly proud that these results had justified his own moderation and declared that it served to prove that Sharon's aggressive proposals must be considered very carefully before being accepted.

Sharon's impact on the government and the country during his tenure as advisor to the Prime Minister was weak at best. He did, however, enjoy a few successful initiatives. He forced the Ministry of Defense to improve its budgeting and he intermediated in a dispute with a group of settlers who attempted to establish a new settlement in Sebastia, by getting the government to agree to a compromise whereby the settlers would be allowed to establish their new community on an army base not far from their original site. He proposed a far-reaching change in the electoral system in Israel designed to strengthen the government by direct election of the Prime Minister. According to Sharon's proposal, the Prime Minister would in turn select his own limited cabinet.

Sharon's ideas on a new form of centralized government did not arouse much debate. His idea had been presented not only in view of the obvious weakness of the Rabin government, but also because it represented his entire conception of the proper governance of Israel. Much as he had been bored by the slow processes of Israeli democracy as manifested in the parliamentary debates, so too was he impatient with compromises and checks imposed upon the government in the formulation of Israeli national policy. His proposal was for a highly centralized regime to be ruled by a popularly elected Prime Minister. His ideas reflected his own conception of how the country should be ruled.

Sharon held this position for only eight months. He resigned when it became apparent to him that his hopes for personal advance were premature and that Rabin was unwilling to confront Peres and Gur in order to secure a senior appointment for Sharon in the regular army. He also became aware that his position in the Prime Minister's office was in fact an empty one, devoid of any power or influence. As the days passed, even Rabin's attempts to have Sharon included in the important security meetings waned. The final straw, however, had been when Sharon discovered that he had been relegated to a secondary status in Rabin's circle of advisors, as evidenced by the arrangements made for Rabin's visit to the United States in January, 1976. Sharon, on the other hand, recounted later that he resigned as soon as he had become aware of the querulous relationship between Rabin and Peres. The two had been in a constant state of suspicion and personal rivalry that did, indeed, seem unappeasable; however, Sharon resigned as soon as it became apparent that Rabin was unwilling to fight Peres for Sharon's right to return to the regular army as a career officer.

In March, 1976, following eight relatively quiet months during which Sharon played little role in the arena of public policy, he now came full face with his first failure in politics. He had severed his connections with the Knesset; he had virtually stopped all political activity within the framework of the Liberal party or the Likud; and his limited attempt to advance by serving as advisor to the Prime Minister had also proved of very little value. Sharon continued to claim that the vicissitudes of his career were the result of his overriding concern for the security of the country and his forecasts of another war and of his own unused abilities and willingness to contribute to the benefit of the country. Within his own party, however, people began to view these claims as empty boastings. People began asking whether Sharon was only making venal, personal use of the problems of the country both by exaggerating them and then by promoting himself as the savior who could free the country from its troubles. After resigning as advisor to the Prime Minister, Sharon began to test out the Liberal Party to see if he could return, but this time he faced a steadfast refusal. His supporters remained faithful, but the party leadership opposed his return. At a meeting of the Liberal Party leadership, Simha Ehrlich addressed the forum, "We have tended a certain man for years and have tried to convince him to join our party. What haven't we done? Has anyone insulted him? Has anyone failed to treat him with respect? He slammed the door in the face of the army,

joined our party and formed the Likud. And then he left.
Without consulting, he simply informed us. We fed him with
mother's milk and in return received nothing but a kick.'' The
party leadership won and Sharon was barred from the key
committees of the Liberal Party.

Although at the time of his resignation as advisor to Rabin,
Sharon had declared that he was to enter a hiatus from political
life and continually referred to his wish to settle down on his
farm, he did everything possible to remain in the public
consciousness. He often told reporters that he would have
preferred to raise sheep and ride his horse, but the pressing
needs of the country did not allow a man of his ability to remain
dormant for long. He started on a long list of news conferences
and speaking engagements. He presented a potpourri of truths
and demagoguery designed to promote both reasonable ideas
and his oversimplistic solutions to the problems of the country.
His strategy was consistent. He portrayed the country as being
under imminent threat of annihilation by a host of political and
defense problems and then presented himself as the savior. His
positions and his targets, however, were opportune and
manifested no clear consistency. He began by attacking the
Labor Alignment, but soon shifted to the Likud.

He accused the Rabin government of hiding the truth from the
people and warned that the very existence of the country was by
no means assured. He saw the root cause of the ailments of the
country in its internal weakness. He wrote that the country was
living a life of lies, dictated by thirty men who formed the
leadership of the country and by some thousand civil servants
who determined how people should live their lives. He called
upon the Jews of the Diaspora to stop donating money unless
they could assure themselves of the right to supervise its use. He
warned of the plot of the United States to shift its support to the
Arabs and termed Henry Kissinger, the American Secretary of
State, Israel's greatest enemy. He promoted the new settlements
on the West Bank and raised them to the level of the primary
national goal. He called for a reassessment of the Soviet Union's
support for the Arabs and opposed any concessions on the
grounds that they would not accomplish anything, since the goal

of the Arabs had steadfastly remained the destruction of the State of Israel. He reiterated his position that talks be opened with the Palestinians, including the PLO, on the reconstitution of Jordan as a homeland for them. He recommended severe cuts in government activity, including the return of most Israeli personnel stationed overseas. And finally, he declared that only men of no political persuasion could "change Israel from a provincial country to the center of world Jewry."

Sharon was also amazingly adaptive. When the government began to criticize the new immigrants from the Soviet Union for dropping out and moving to the United States instead of Israel, he in turn attacked the government for its lack of compassion. During a meeting with potential Jewish immigrants in America, he declared his intention of establishing an independent organization to assist them as an alternative to the current establishment. Although the idea naturally captured the headlines, there was no follow-up on Sharon's part. After a brief meeting with President Carter in Washington, granted essentially as a courtesy, Sharon declared that he was returning with a major diplomatic concession on the part of the United States in the form of Carter's declared commitment to support Israel's essential interests. Sharon's adroitness at converting random meetings and passing associations to occasions for pompous announcements of major policy importance was amply displayed during this time. Aided by the press, he studiously nurtured an image of a major statesman capable of handling the entire breadth of problems facing the country. At his public appearances he continued to emphasize that his involvement in politics had nothing to do with personal ambition, but was a function of the needs of the country. He told reporters that he never lost his self confidence, that he had often faced difficulties but had always won out in the end and that although he frequently found himself isolated, ultimately he had always been vindicated. He boasted that "he was engraved in the hearts of the people as someone who has contributed to the nation in its most difficult hours."

Sharon's appearance on the political scene after his resignation from the Rabin government was a result of a mixture of careful calculation as well as a reflection of his own personality and sentiments. He made the most of the limited information at his disposal, exaggerating the dangers and the blunders, using facts with complete disregard for their accuracy or source, adapting his positions to the vagaries of the country's mood and announcing far-reaching solutions which he had no intention of implementing. Beyond this very skillful public relations, his own very powerful beliefs and motives rose to the surface. His belief in his own abilities to save the country was no charade. His continued reiteration of his proposal to change the form of the regime in Israel and create a strong central government with extensive powers in the hands of the Prime Minister who would be elected directly by the people was not accidental.

In November, 1976, Sharon turned his attention to attacking the Likud. Having failed in his renewed efforts to eliminate the constituent parties in the Likud and hold new internal elections for the leader of the reconstituted party, he now directed his barbs at the leadership of the Likud. Simha Ehrlich and Yigael Horwitz, the leaders of two of the Likud's parties, wrote to Sharon in reply that the parties of the Likud firmly supported the candidacy of Menahem Begin as leader of the Likud. "The blocs within the Likud are unwilling to agree to what is implied in your demands, that you lead the Likud parliamentary list for the Knesset." The two of them also accused Sharon of addressing the Likud in terms of ultimatums and ignoring the fundamental democratic procedures of party politics. Sharon denied these accusations, claiming only to be in favor of free elections within the party. But within the party, as well as in the press, Sharon's actions were interpreted as a call for the usurpation of Begin's leadership. Sharon's relationship with the Likud had reached its final impasse.

For a number of months, Sharon had contemplated the establishment of a new political party. The deterioration in his relations with the Likud only served to accelerate this process. He assembled a group of political associates, most of whom had been acquaintances from his earlier days in the army, and began to review the prospects for a new party. Under Sharon's leadership, they became convinced that the current political parties had atrophied and the country was now ripe for a new political organization. At these meetings the outlines of a political platform was also developed. It focused on defense and foreign affairs: the Palestinian problem could be solved by removing the artificial kingdom ruling in Jordan; the Jewish homeland should stretch from the Meditteranean to the Jordan River; in order to solve the Palestinian problem within the context of Jordan, discussions should be held with Palestinian representatives; and the unique connection of the people of Israel to the land should be nurtured.

The willingness of many of the most prominent people in the country (for example Ezra Zohar, Yeshayahu Bareket, Shmuel Presburger, Rafi Eitan, Moshe Tomarkin, Bezalel Gever and Benny Kalter, Meshulam Riklis's son-in-law) to join in his endeavor to establish a new political party reinforced his belief in himself and in the need of the people for a strong, confident leader. He noted that many people, professional and salaried workers, rich and middle class, were willing to forego their everyday activities in order to contribute to the success of this political exercise. He captivated and motivated them. The group that now coalesced around him was no longer dominated by his former soldiers and associates in the army, but by people who were genuinely moved by the arguments for a new form of leadership. Their actions could no longer be explained by virtue of their personal commitment to Sharon. The political situation in the country and the disappointment with the Labor Party had created an atmosphere of longing for change and a willingness for civic activity to institute this change.

With his announcement of the creation of a new political party, Sharon immediately set about to attack the Likud. At a press conference in Tel Aviv, Sharon declared, "the alternative (i.e. the Likud) is no better than the ruling party!" Sharon informed the journalists present that in his mind the Likud was not ruled democratically and that no form of primary elections were held. He added that, for him, a political party was only a means and not an end in itself. Sharon stated that he could not believe in a political framework that has lost its basic content. If good ideas cannot be fulfilled within a given framework, it was perfectly appropriate to seek an alternative means. He declared that if he were elected as Prime Minister, he would work for the change in the electoral system. He assured those present that he would under no circumstances return to the Likud, even if his own political attempts failed. "Even if our success is minimal and the number of Knesset members elected from our list is limited, I will continue," Sharon assured his audience. "I have never abandoned a military unit in the field of battle and I will not do so now." When asked about the territories captured in the Six Day War, he confirmed that his opinion had not changed. But, he added, "there is no advantage to the person who steadfastly maintains the same position over the years just for the sake of consistency. Changing circumstances require changing opinions. The security of Israel is my overriding concern on these issues. The current borders are not secure borders." Sharon added that he could not envision any circumstances under which Israel would cede Judea and Samaria (the West Bank); however, he would not reject any formal proposals out-of-hand.

Sharon's moderate political tone was intended to provide his party with a patina of love of peace and a willingness to make concessions in order to achieve it. His goal was clear: to pave the way for cooperation with other parties with similar views. Sharon wanted to face the voter with a strong and respected team behind him and he, therefore, negotiated with a variety of political figures, demonstrating a remarkable willingness to compromise and reformulate his political positions. He even contacted Yossi Sarid, a very well-known left-wing politician and asked for a meeting. When Sarid arrived at Sharon's Tel Aviv office, Lilly received him and led him to her husband's room. With no sign of surprise, Sarid listened to Sharon's offer to join Shlomzion with a guarantee of being given the second position on the party's list of candidates.

Sarid wondered out loud, "How do you think we can appear on the same list while our outlooks are so different?"

Sharon responded that he was convinced that the public was less concerned with foreign policy and the Arab conflict than it was with domestic economic and social issues. Sharon added confidently that on social issues, their views were quite similar.

"What are your social views?" Sarid asked.

"We both seek the well-being of the people of Israel. What can be the big difference between us?" Sharon told the incredulous Sarid. Sarid responded by saying that he thought such cooperation would not be likely, but that he would not object to continuing their talks. This was, however, the last of the contacts between them.

Three weeks after the formation of Shlomzion another new party was formed under the leadership of the late Professor Yigael Yadin: The Democratic Movement for Change (DMC). It was immediately apparent that the DMC would focus on the same voters to whom Shlomzion had addressed itself and that by absorbing the Shinui group, the DMC enjoyed the advantage of having a party organization in place. The DMC quickly attracted a number of the most prominent people from all walks of life in Israel, both independents as well as defectors from the other major political groupings. Sharon decided to approach Yadin and offer a merger of the two parties. Yadin's attests to Sharon's willingness to forego any question of principle that might stand in the way of a merger, to the point of accepting the DMC's platform on new settlements which called for "the establishment of military bases in areas critical to the defense of the country." The opposition to Sharon within the DMC proved, however, to be unassuageable and Yadin was forced to inform Sharon that his offer had been rejected. As he left the DMC headquarters, Sharon told his associates bitterly, "we'll screw then too!"

Sharon also tried to court Meir Amit, a long-time army rival, but was no more successful than he had been with the DMC. In fact, Amit, who defected from the Labor Party, eventually joined the DMC. Sharon's courtship of the small Independent Liberal party lasted somewhat longer. Although well-known for its dovish positions on questions of policy, it provided the advantage of being an older party, with a lot of experience and a strong organization. Moshe Kol, the leader of the Independent Liberals, although somewhat skeptical, asked Sharon who he would send to negotiate. Sharon answered, "Wait and see."

To everyone's surprise, Amos Kenan, a famous journalist known for his extreme dovish position and advocacy of full recognition of the rights of the Palestinians, appeared as Sharon's representative. When asked how he could possibly reconcile his support for Sharon with anything he believed in, he answered that they were good friends and he was convinced that Sharon could make a major impact for the good in bringing about the changes necessary for the country.

Amos Kenan's role as Sharon's liaison did not end here. Kenan was instructed by Sharon to try to arrange a meeting between Sharon and Yasser Arafat or one of his deputies. Kenan arranged such a meeting with Isam Sartawi, who later would be murdered by Palestinian dissidents because of his contacts with Israelis, but Sharon rejected the opportunity. He would meet only with Arafat himself or, at worst, with one of his senior deputies. A meeting was tentatively scheduled to take place in Paris, but at the last minute, the PLO leadership turned down this chance.

In discussions with Kenan, Sharon agreed to the transfer of the entire West Bank to Palestinian sovereignty on condition that all security arrangements be left in the hands of Israel. Sharon's dovish positions went so far that even Uri Avneri, the champion of a free and independent Palestinian state, was prompted to discuss his possible connection to Shlomzion.

The negotiations between Shlomzion and the Independent Liberals reached an advanced stage in which a platform for the combined party was, in great part, agreed upon. This was the easier part, as Sharon did not fight for any of the key policies he had so strongly advocated at the founding of the party. Eventually, however, the leaders of the Independent Liberals came to the conclusion that they had little to gain from this association and that Sharon's previous declarations presented too great a risk for this old and respected party. Kol informed Sharon of the party's decision. Sharon protested that he would convince the leadership otherwise, but Kol made it clear that the merger was a hopeless case.

The early stages of Shlomzion's development mirrored Sharon's strength as well as his weakness. His imposing leadership, his charisma and his ability to challenge people with the need to contribute to the solution of the most pressing problems of the day had all served to build the initial momentum with which the party set out. Sharon's timing seemed uncanny as well. There was at the time a genuine concern for the well-being of the country and a sense of the need for a new political force. The parliamentary crisis that had brought on the early elections was the culminating point in the long decline of the stature of the ruling Labor Party. Although it had been the dominant party in the country since independence, the public was rapidly becoming disaffected with the unbridled fractiousness of the Labor Party's leaders and the now-frequent revelations of corruption among its most prominent members. There was a yearning for an alternative to both the ruling Labor Party as well as the Likud, the major opposition party which was accompanied by a sense of urgency that this was the time for a change.

As an independent party, Shlomzion appealed across a wide range of political opinions. The Democratic Movement for Change was created and flourished for much the same reason and represented Shlomzion's major competitor for the votes of the disaffected. Under the banner of Sharon's charisma the party seemed destined to alter the entire political make-up of the country; however, during the ensuing few months until the elections, the Shlomzion party lost its allure, especially in comparison to the DMC. Whereas Yadin and the other leaders of the DMC had succeeded in preserving the momentum of their party and the credibility of their promise to bring about the necessary changes in the political life of Israel, Shlomzion's appeal waned. Disillusioned by the opportunistic and fickle platform and disenchanted by the less well-known side of Sharon's personality, most of Shlomzion's early enthusiasts defected.

Sharon managed the party as a guru ruling a cult, expecting and demanding total allegiance. He refused to consider opposing opinions and failed at creating an election team. Sharon's wife Lilly served the party as lady of the manor and clearly dominated the back office of the party. Staffers who did not find favor with Lilly soon found themselves dismissed by Sharon. The party workers quickly discovered that toadying to Lilly was a concomitant to succeeding with their party's leader.

Shlomzion staffers have described the atmosphere at party headquarters as one of suspicion and irritation that continued to deteriorate as circumstances did. In contrast to his expectations, based on the pledges of his early supporters, Sharon faced a depleted party treasury that further hampered his activity. These frustrations exacerbated his paranoia and his mistrust of even his closest associates. The feeble attempts to regenerate the enthusiasm that had marked the party's first steps now took on the form of 'remember how we got out of that jam...'

When his attempts to lure key political blocs and personalities from the left and center of the political spectrum failed, Sharon shifted course. He now portrayed himself as guardian of the extreme right wing, forever faithful to the tenets of nationalism. He preached the need to expand the Jewish settlements on the West Bank and solemnly warned of the impending war, certain to start "in the coming summer or fall." He met with the key proponents of the idea of "Greater Israel." The campaign message was Sharon, the man, the personality, focusing on his war record and his ability to instill confidence in the face of a sinister world. The centerpiece of the Shlomzion campaign featured the now-famous picture of Sharon in uniform during the Yom Kippur War with the blood-stained bandage around his forehead.

Two months prior to the elections it was clear that Shlomzion had little chance of achieving anything beyond nominal representation in the Knesset and Sharon began taking steps to assure his own political future by reopening his talks with the Likud. Of necessity, this was done with the knowledge and approval of only a handful of close party members without bringing the question before the full party leadership. Party slogans called for the creation of a national "front of those faithful to the Land of Israel," emphasizing the commonality of purpose between Shlomzion and the Likud. The party convention was scheduled on the rise of Maale Adumim, southeast of Jerusalem, a controversial new settlement. The site had been carefully selected in order to emphasize his loyalty to the idea of maintaining control of the West Bank and to remove the stigma of his brief flirt with the left wing and his announced willingness to pursue a peaceful solution to the Palestinian problem through major political and territorial concessions.

The key item on the agenda of the party convention was the selection of the party list to be presented to the electorate. The debate was a vigorous one. The rank and file and the popular leadership demanded that the issue be decided by a vote of the full convention. Sharon argued that the list should be determined in a vote of the leadership council of the party dominated by him. The proponents of the convention alternative contended that this would be the only democratic way of electing the party's candidates, while Sharon countered that this populism would result in an excessively homogenous list. Success in the forthcoming elections mandated the presentation of a varied list of candidates capable of appealing to a broad cross-section of the electorate. The compromise finally arrived at called for the convention to elect the 35 candidates on the list while the order of their placement would be determined by the party council. Sharon at this time was in the midst of his efforts to rejoin the Likud and it is clear that a major concern was to prevent the formation of a list that would hinder these efforts at a merger.

Sharon's platform was a mixture of populist rhetoric and ominous warnings about the future, designed to persuade the Likud as much as to court the voters. It called for the establishment of an emergency government, a drastic cut in government budgets, the prohibition of strikes and the elimination of the artificial pomp that had entrapped the current national leaders. His goals were clear. Although he had been well known for the time he devoted to planning his meals even in the middle of a battle, he was now trying to position himself as the champion of the common man, modest and willing to settle for only the bare necessities; capable of adapting to the exigencies of the time.

Begin, who always had a liking for Sharon, was in the hospital for treatment of a minor heart ailment and was unable to champion Sharon's initiative with the forcefulness it required. Simha Ehrlich, the leader of the Liberal Party within the Likud, adamantly opposed the inclusion of Shlomzion in the Likud list of candidates for the Knesset. The discussions nominally revolved around the exact positioning of the Shlomzion candidates on the Likud list; however, the real problem was the steadfast opposition of the Liberal Party. Sharon tried presenting an ultimatum: if by April 12, 1977 at 2:00 p.m., one day prior to the closing of registration, the Likud had not responded affirmatively, Shlomzion would present its own independent list in the elections. Concurrently, Sharon protested to Begin that it was Ehrlich's obstinacy that was obstructing a compromise. Begin intervened, but to no avail. When it became apparent to Sharon that the Likud was going to submit its original list without Shlomzion, he conceded to the Likud's demands. Sharon would receive the sixth position on the new Likud list and the other Shlomzion candidates would be relegated to unrealistic positions between the 47th and 51st candidates. It was obvious that although he was being granted an attractive position on the Likud list, the compromise meant that he must foresake his associates and friends in Shlomzion.

Sharon phoned Yitzhak Shamir, campaign manager of the Likud to inform him of his decision but couldn't reach him. Time was running out. He phoned Likud party headquarters, but succeeded only in reaching Yigael Horwitz who advised him to contact either Shamir or Ehrlich. Ehrlich, however, was ultimately successful in torpedoing Sharon's efforts and the Likud list was registered without Shlomzion.

Sharon sat at Shlomzion party headquarters with a handful of party leaders waiting for the official response of the Likud leadership. Begin finally called and informed him that he was unsuccessful in persuading his friends to accept Sharon and his party in the Likud. Visibly disappointed, Sharon responded, "Minor league party operatives have destroyed the chance to create a broad front. They preferred narrow, personal interests. After the events of the day, I am more than ever convinced of the wisdom of my move to leave the Likud. Anyone who saw the ugly maneuverings of the Likud knows why it is impossible to join forces with such a party." In all his tirades against the Likud leadership, Sharon carefully excepted Begin, whom he viewed as sincere in his wish to join forces. In Sharon's words, Begin "understood the greatness of the hour and the national implications of cooperation between the two parties."

During the two months of campaigning, Sharon manifested a tireless perseverence and a capability for endless work that impressed all those who worked with him. Not only did he personify the Shlomzion party, he was also its campaign manager, funds collector and overall organizer. He disliked the work, the fawning before wealthy donors, the vapid street walking and baby patting and the courting of anonymous party staffers throughout the country. The campaign coffers were empty and the professional workers were demanding pay. Twice he went to the United States to raise funds for his party, the activity he loathed more than any other. In one case he made a special flight to Los Angeles to meet a wealthy potential contributor. The meeting had lots of backslapping and bright smiles and Sharon left with a sealed envelope and a satisfied smile. When he returned to his hotel he opened the envelope and found a check for $25.00.

Towards the end of the campaign, Sharon focused exclusively on questions of defense and security, positioning himself as a recognized authority on such matters. He warned of the threats to the country and demanded the right to present his analysis before the Defense and Foreign Affairs Committee of the Knesset. He warned of the continued cease-fire violations on the part of Egypt, of the serious deterioration of the situation in Lebanon and of the preparations for a renewed blockade of the Red Sea. He toured the northern border and visited Major Saad Hadad, leader of the Israeli-backed forces in southern Lebanon, declaring that Lebanon's war was Israel's war.

Parallel to these efforts to sow fear and then present himself as the savior, he began to court Gush Emunim, a zealous group advocating massive settlement of broad areas of the West Bank. He reminded them of his crucial assistance in the settlement at Eilon Moreh and of his support and defense of Rabbi Kook. But Gush Emunim refused to support him officially. In anger Sharon declared that he no longer wanted to see or hear from "those whores."

Sharon now resumed his attacks on Ehrlich in earnest. He spread rumors that Ehrlich had planned to overthrow Begin as leader of the Likud. He stated that it would be easier to negotiate with Arafat than it would be with Ehrlich. They were the final efforts of a politician whose organization was crumbling about him. New public opinion polls began showing that Shlomzion was in serious trouble and in fact was in danger of failing to get even one candidate elected. Preliminary polls had indicated that Shlomzion would get enough votes to elect eight to twelve candidates. What had happened? He clearly lacked the funds to finance a major political campaign and was often disappointed by the failure of his supporters to provide the money that had been promised. But, more than anything else, Shlomzion lacked a viable organization. It was a one-man party. Despite Sharon's indomitable spirit and his untiring work, it could not but fail. Sharon had succeeded in alienating most of the key party people at some stage or other during the short history of the campaign and seemed to prefer surrounding himself with devoted admirers rather than the more independent professionals or broad based, popular, local organizations.

Sharon spent election night at the home of his advisor, Benny Kalter. At 5:00 a.m., when it became clear that the Likud had won its first election, Sharon phoned Begin to congratulate him.

"Your place is with us," Begin responded.

Sharon paused for a moment and then asked, "But how can that be done?"

"You must write a letter of conciliation to Ehrlich," Begin answered decisively.

Sharon immediately sat down to write the letter and sent it off to Ehrlich that same morning. It was a cautious letter that refrained from begging. Sharon recognized the significance of the Likud's victory (43 mandates in a Knesset of 120 members) and expressed the willingness of Shlomzion (two mandates) to join the Likud. With Begin's intervention, Ehrlich acceded. Shlomzion would be absorbed into the Herut Party within the Likud.

Sharon's acquiescence and his failure to demand that Shlomzion be allowed to preserve its fundamental independence as a party within the framework of the Likud generated some disagreements within Shlomzion. Although most recognized that Shlomzion had failed to become the swing party between the two large political blocs, they nevertheless reminded Sharon that he was betraying the very principles on which the party had been formed. He himself had argued that the current political organizations in the country had become atrophied and had lost their relevance. How could he now join them? Even if joining the Likud was a political expediency dictated by the results of the election, they could at least preserve their basic independence by retaining their party structure. If the absorption of Shlomzion into Herut was to be done on an individual basis with no trace of their former political identity, then it could have been done with no recourse to Shlomzion to begin with.

Sharon reacted angrily. "Joining Herut as an independent organization is a recipe for disruption. I will not form a seperate faction within the Likud because in my opinion it is imperative that the Likud eliminate its current factions. We must join Herut on an individual basis. My natural place is in the Likud. I must join the Likud."

Most of those present smiled ironically as they recalled Sharon's comments about Begin. He had often attacked Begin as an old-fashioned demagogue, a prattling fool who should not be taken too seriously. Those who had joined Shlomzion as a political organization in the hope of establishing a new political party capable of change were disappointed. The warnings of those who had reported that Sharon would use people for his own personal interest and then discard them should have been heeded. They understood that the leadership of the Likud would remain within Herut and given the tenuous state of Begin's health, Sharon was preparing for the battle of succession. But there was no stopping Sharon. With the same energy and determination that he had invested in establishing the party a mere six months ago, he now set about dismantling it. Sharon's loyalists within Shlomzion followed him into Herut.

Even before negotiations to form a government could be completed, Sharon threw himself into the fray and joined Herut in its campaign for the Histadrut, the National Labor Federation, the umbrella organization for all the unions in the country. He harped upon the most emotional social and racial questions of the day, inflaming emotions and reducing much of the campaigning to name calling. He successfully skirted a very sensitive personal problem. Sharon is a wealthy man, the owner of a huge farm in a country in which there is virtually no private ownership of farmland. He appeared before crowds of workers, urging them to vote for the Likud, the real party of the workers and not to vote for the Labor Alignment, the real party of the wealthy.

On June 17, 1977, the Herut caucus met to select its representatives to the government. With Begin's support, the caucus elected Sharon among its four candidates for the cabinet. Sharon was intended by Begin to serve as his Minister of Agriculture after it became obvious that the Liberals would oppose Begin's original intention of making Sharon responsible for handling terrorist and intelligence activity. Begin would also assign two other key functions to Sharon: chairman of the cabinet committee on new settlements and a member of the cabinet committee on security.

Sharon appreciated that if he was to succeeded in presenting a viable alternative for the leadership of Herut following Begin's retirement, he would have to become completely assimilated into Herut. He therefore began assiduously courting Herut staffers and creating the impression of being the most avid supporter of Herut's ideology.

CHAPTER *13*

On Sunday, November 20, 1977, the cabinet met to hear a unique report from Prime Minister Menahem Begin. Begin had called the meeting to review a subject of unprecedented importance: his talks with Egyptian President Anwar Sadat. Sadat had arrived in Israel on his landmark visit the previous evening and everyone anxiously awaited the results of the first meeting between the leaders of these two countries. Begin had worked secretly and carefully for five months to arrange for this meeting. Foreign Minister Moshe Dayan had been the only party to these delicate and crucial arrangements. Sadat's visit came as a surprise to all the other members of the government and they now waited impatiently to hear of the preliminary results. Begin disappointed many of the ministers by the paucity of information that he was willing to share with them. He reported simply that in his opinion Sadat was sincere in his desire for peace as evidenced by his very visit to Jerusalem. Begin also proudly reported that Sadat had emphasized his faith in the peace process, in particular with the Begin government.

Three months earlier, Dayan had met with Hasan El-Thuhami, the Egyptian Deputy Prime Minister for Presidential Affairs, in a secret meeting in Fez, Morroco. They had investigated the possibility of a meeting between Sadat and Begin during which, it was hinted, Israel would agree to the return of the entire Sinai Penninsula to Egypt. No one in the cabinet was aware of the long negotiations and diplomatic maneuvering to arrange such a meeting, carried out secretly through President Nicolai Ceaucescu of Rumania and President Jimmy Carter of the United States. These highest-level diplomatic channels were used to impress upon the Egyptian President the sincerity of the Israeli government's willingness to make far-reaching concessions in exchange for peace.

As they sat waiting for Begin to begin his report, they were all visibly excited, still under the influence of the highly emotional experience of meeting the president of one of Israel's most intractable enemies at the airport the previous evening. Their discussion revolved around what they could do to compensate Sadat for his willingness to break through the cordon of hatred with which the Arabs had surrounded Israel.

Agriculture Minister Ariel Sharon proposed a dramatic show of friendship toward Egypt by opening up the border at the northern Sinai town of El Arish to any Egyptian wishing to visit Israel. Another minister, Meir Amit, offered to allow Egyptian ships to use Israeli port facilities. In the midst of these attempts to find some show of appreciation to the Egyptian president, Dayan dulled their enthusiasm. He explained that in his meeting with the Egyptian Minister of State for Foreign Affairs, Butrus Ghalli, it was made clear that Sadat would be embarassed by any special show of gratitude on the part of Israel. Egypt, it was explained, did not want to appear to negotiate independently with Israel and, therefore, did not want to appear to get anything in return. Egypt did indeed anticipate some gesture on the part of Israel, but this would have to be to the entire Arab nation.

Throughout the 14 tense months of negotiations, Sharon's behavior was mercurial and, at times, even capricious. It ranged from spontaneous enthusiasm such as that displayed at the first meeting to the most obstinate opposition on petty issues. On the whole, however, he supported the peace process at the most critical junctures in the negotiations, exposing himself to further criticism that his positions on policy had nothing to do with principle but were determined by his own self interest at any given moment in time.

As the details of the proposed settlement became clear, a number of key people began voicing their opposition to the far-reaching concessions being made by Israel. Sharon and Chief of Staff Mordechai Gur were among the leading opponents to the complete withdrawal from Sinai. The country would be indefensible without this buffer between it and the largest of its neighbors. The entire process of withdrawal must extend over a considerably longer period of time in order to assure them of the sincerity of Egypt's desire for peace. Begin, together with Dayan, successfully convinced the cabinet that Egypt would not consider even the most minor border adjustments. Sharon finally concluded, "I have fought in the Sinai three times, but I am willing to withdraw completely in exchange for peace." Gur remained alone in his opposition.

The question of granting autonomy to the West Bank also evoked a heated debate, with Sharon and Burg raising the questions of the status of the new settlements and the danger of such a step leading to the creation of an independent Palestinain state at Israel's doorstep. Begin, however, convinced the entire cabinet with an impassioned speech in which he outlined his expectations. He conceded that the situation would be fluid and less than clear, but this was the very point of the compromise. It skirted the whole question of sovereignty. In the meantime, Israeli settlements would continue to be formed, and the security of the West Bank would be solely in the hands of Israel, while the local Arab population would be granted the alternative of two different passports: Israeli and Jordanian. "This program will create a new reality that may lead to changes in the fundamental positions of the Arabs of Israel and their attitudes toward the State of Israel. The problem is complicated; however, if we do not agree to this proposal we will lose our moral standing in the world and forfeit any chance for peace." Sharon was persuaded by Begin.

The prospects for peace had trapped Sharon much as they had the other members of the cabinet. Could they now relinquish the chance for peace with the largest and most important of the Arab nations, the goal of the country since its very inception?

Alternatively, how could they accept the risks inherent in a peace accord with Sadat that called for the withdrawal from Sinai and the establishment of a new order on the West Bank and Gaza Strip? Sharon, as a military man, faced a special dilemma. He had since his youth learned to see the Arabs through the sight of his gun. How could a real peace be possible? Even as he supported the peace process he remained skeptical of Egypt's ultimate purpose and he never stopped seeing the Sinai as the site of some future military engagement.

Overall, Sharon's reactions to the peace proposals were a function of his involvement in the setting of policy. He had finally become a partner in the highest circles of the country, and as a cabinet member and a member of the cabinet committee on security could now play a key role in determining the future of Israel. Yet, he nevertheless remained restless, seeking new outlets for his energy. He developed a reputation for being unruly and rebellious at cabinet meetings and, in general, his hunger for power and influence was insatiable. He was irritated by the fact that he was not among the small group that actually conducted the negotiations: Begin, Dayan and, later, Defense Minister Ezer Weizman. His attitude to peace was not only determined by his evaluation of the costs and benfits of such a move, but also, and probably mainly, by the extent of his involvement in the process of establishing policy. His behavior, therefore, often seemed fickle and unpredictable, at times enthusiastic and at others despondent and bitterly critical.

Sharon's tool for disrupting the peace process was his control over the establishment of new settlements on the West Bank. As Agricultural Minister and chairman of the cabinet committee on settlement, he had the authority to devise and implement the government's policy for the settlement of the occupied territories (the West Bank, the Gaza Strip and the Golan Heights). Forty days following his appointment, he announced his master program, "The Sharon Plan," for the creation of new Jewish settlements throughout the West Bank. The plan envisioned the creation of a new population corridor cutting across the West Bank, consisting of urban centers and their satellite communities. The successful implementation of this plan would preclude any possibility of withdrawal because it would be impossible to extricate the Jewish communities from the indigenous Arab population regardless of how ingeniously a border could be drawn. In addition, Jerusalem was to be surrounded by a circle of suburban centers and towns, insulating it from the threats of the local population. To implement this plan, Sharon initiated the establishment of as many new settlements as possible. Although most consisted of only a small handful of settlers, he saw them as the nucleus for their future development. Sharon understood that his control of the sensitive issue of the new settlements in the occupied territories provided him with a potent tool to intervene in all aspects of government policy, and he made calculated use of this power.

Shortly after entering office, in September, 1977, Sharon surprised everyone by announcing that the government had been secretly establishing new settlements on the West Bank. The announcement had been timed to coincide with Dayan's visit to the United States to discuss a possible reconvening of the Geneva convention to promote a peace settlement between Israel and her Arab neighbors. The declaration created an uproar in Israel and embarassed and angered the American government. It was never clear whether the timing was the result of naivete or the blunder of a headline seeker or a calculated attempt to disjoint Dayan's talks with Carter.

One month later, as the Democratic Movement for Change joined the Begin government, it was discovered that an additional 12 settlements had recently been authorized. When questioned by what authority they had been approved, Sharon reported that it had been the decision of the cabinet committee on settlement. Meir Amit of the DMC queried Dayan about this claim, but Dayan denied any knowledge of such a decision although he himself was a member of the committee. When confronted with this evidence, Sharon smugly produced the protocol of the meeting at which the decision had been made. Dayan continued to insist, however, that there never had been such a meeting. Further investigation eventually proved that there never had been a meeting. Sharon had polled enough members of the committee by telephone to assure a majority and then had written up the protocol to indicate that an official meeting had taken place. Amit protested this high-handed method of making decisions, but this protest had little impact on the actual outcome.

Throughout the long negotiations between Israel and Egypt, Sharon made very careful and calculated use of the settlement policy of the government. To his close associates and supporters, both within the Agriculture Ministry and without, he appeared as the clearest champion of the Zionist tradition of resettling the land. He was viewed as a far-sighted statesman, vigilant and dedicated to the key patriotic test of the time: the settlement of the barren lands captured during the Six Day War. He told his associates that he was fighting a lonely battle. The other members of the government, in his opinion, were merely paying lip service to the idea of settling the West Bank and, had it not been for him, nothing would have actually been done to implement this policy. He was critical of all the cabinet members, with the possible exception of Dayan, accusing them of indifference. Although apparently granting Dayan's sincerity, Sharon accused him of evading clear-cut answers, diplomatically avoiding any situation that would jeopardize the peace process. The others, including Prime Minister Begin, however, earned nothing but his contempt.

Those outside of his inner circle of associates, on the other hand, perceived Sharon's activities in a very different light. To them Sharon was a guileful activist who was using the government's settlement policy as ammunition for his own personal political advancement. Settlements were being established with no thought for their future viability and with no connection to any broad Zionist vision, but solely to enhance Sharon's own political reputation and to provide him with a means to intervene in the decisionmaking process regarding the peace talks with Egypt. Far from being the only sincere proponent of the government's declared policy, Sharon's actions were interpreted as a clear inversion of the government's intention. Sharon had taken advantage of the often vague and ambiguous language of governmental decisions to formulate his own policy and then claim to be its only unequivocal supporter. These conflicting perceptions had their most salient expression in January, 1978.

Since the formation of the Begin government, Sharon had become increasingly impatient with the delays in implementing the Likud platform calling for the expansion of Jewish settlements in the West Bank and in northern Sinai. The delays were at first the result of the imminent Geneva conference on the Middle East problem and then as a result of the delicate peace negotiations between Israel and Egypt. Sharon had often demanded that the government discuss the question in detail, but his demands were ignored. It could not gainsay its own platform, yet, at the same time, it was wary of the diplomatic price such a policy would demand if implemented in its full. Sharon finally succeeded in forcing the issue. At a cabinet meeting on the new settlements, Sharon proposed that three additional settlements on the West Bank be created and, more critically, that existing settlements in northern Sinai be expanded. None of the ministers present dared to oppose such a proposition.

Sharon had prepared for the meeting by holding preliminary discussions with Dayan during which he had convinced him that the expansion of the settlements would be a critical test of Egyptian intentions and sincerity in the entire peace process. It would clearly indicate Israel's determination to maintain control over the settlements in Sinai regardless of the nature of any final treaty between the countries. Sharon gave the impression that he was referring to a minor expansion of the fields currently being farmed by settlements already existing and to the drilling of a few more water wells. If the Egyptians accepted such a move, an important principle would have been established; if not, Israel would have a better understanding of what to expect from the Egyptians on this central issue. Dayan agreed and secured Begin's approval as well. Defense Minister Ezer Weizman, who had not been a party to the decision, was the only minister to oppose the decision openly.

Dayan, Weizman and Sharon were given the task of drawing the specific boundaries for the expansion of the fields around the existing settlements. They met at Dayan's home, where, kneeling over a detailed map of the region, they marked off these boundaries and then signed the map. Weizman, who continued to believe that such a move represented an unnecessary provocation of the Egyptians at a particularly delicate juncture in the negotiations, said bitterly, "from my point of view you can plow the entire Sinai."

A few days before the Egyptian-Israeli political committee was to meet in Jerusalem on the weekend of January 6, 1978 to define the subjects to be included in any peace treaty, the press began reporting that extensive settlement activity was taking place in the eastern Sinai. Begin was very concerned by the implications of these reports. The Egyptians would naturally interpret these actions as an attempt to establish facts in the field that no amount of negotiations could retract. This action stood in direct contradiction to the very draft submitted by Israel to Egypt, calling for continued Israeli control of the settlements already existing. The Egyptians would see the current Israeli expansion of the settlements as a cunning attempt to expand its sphere of control. Begin phoned the government's press secretary and ordered that the government's decision be published in its entirety: "The government has approved the development of lands for farming in the Rafiah salient. This action is designed to strengthen existing settlements in the region." Begin hoped that such a move would dispel the negative implications of the earlier press coverage by making it clear that the government had no intention of creating new settlements. The move was ineffective and the initial impression remained.

The entire affair exposed the weaknesses in the government and its means of making decisions. Sharon contended that he had been authorized by the government to set up a number of new settlements in the region of Rafiah in eastern Sinai. He complained that as soon as the political implications of the decision became apparent, he was abandoned by all the ministers who had initailly approved the decision. Sharon's opponents, on the other hand, argued that he had intentionally mislead them by presenting a case for very limited expansion of the existing settlements to improve their economic viability. This limited approval had been used by Sharon for the creation of new settlements in an insidious, self-serving move. Sharon had only himself to blame for the attacks of the press. He had leaked the news and had even encouraged the exaggerated interpretations of Israeli intentions for the very purpose of disrupting the peace talks with Egypt.

In March, 1978, Sharon once again used his control of the new settlements to upset the peace talks with Egypt. With these talks at an impasse, Defense Minister Weizman went to the United States in an attempt to get the process moving again. While still in the United States, Weizman was astounded by the news that Sharon had commissioned bulldozers to prepare the land for new settlements in the Samaria region, the northeastern portion of the West Bank. Weizman phoned Begin and threatened to resign immediately if the bulldozers were not removed at once. Ehrlich, leader of the Liberal wing of the Likud, indicated to Begin that Weizman would not be the only one to resign if Sharon's initiative were not stopped. Sharon was incensed, but Begin valued the integrity of his government over the risk inherent in Sharon's ire. In April, 1978 Begin made a fundamental change in the decisionmaking process of his government. From now on, the cabinet committee on defense would approve the establishment of new settlements instead of the committee on settlement.

Sharon, nevertheless, successfully continued to force the government into a corner over its policy toward new settlements. Whenever the peace negotiations seemed to reach a dead end, he went on the initiative in forming new settlements. He forced the government into decisions against its better judgement; he skillfully took advantage of Gush Emunim, a group of zealous advocates of Jewish settlement throughout the West Bank and northern Sinai; and he stealthily formed new settlements without government approval by establishing satellites to existing settlements and presenting them as mere expansions of existing ones.

Despite these attempts to sabotage the peace talks, Sharon would play a key role at a critical moment in the Camp David talks. On September 5, 1978, President Carter, Prime Minister Begin and President Sadat led their respective missions in a marathon meeting to break the deadlock in the nine-month-old negotiations between Egypt and Israel. They met at the U.S. President's vacation home in Camp David, Maryland. During the 13 days of talks, over 23 different drafts were reviewed. Sharon played his part on the twelfth day, in convincing Begin to make the crucial concession of foregoing the settlements in the northern Sinai.

Sharon had wanted to be a part of the Israeli mission to these talks, but pressure from many of the bloc leaders in the Likud forced Begin to leave him off the list of participants. Begin, understanding Sharon's ability to undermine these talks, maintained close contact with Sharon, phoning him regularly to brief him on the progress to date. On the twelfth day of negotiations, with virtually all issues of importance solved, one key dispute remained: the future of the Israeli settlements in northern Sinai. Sadat refused to consider any treaty that did not include Israeli assurances of a complete withdrawal from "every inch of the Sinai." It was a very difficult concession for Begin to make after he had assured the settlers in the region just prior to his departure for Camp David that under no circumstances would he foresake them.

Defense Minister Ezer Weizman and his military attache, Avraham Tamir, firmly believed that a real peace treaty was preferrable to any settlement. In their estimate, Sharon could play a valuable role in swinging Begin over to their position. Tamir, a former comrade-in-arms of Sharon who had assumed the role of a liaison between Weizman and Sharon, phoned Sharon. He briefed Sharon in detail, telling him that all issues of any importance had been decided with the exception of the future of the Israeli settlements. Tamir asked Sharon to intervene on behalf of peace and encourage Begin to make this last concession. Sharon paused, thinking, and finally told Tamir that he could tell Begin on his behalf that he, Sharon, was in favor of making this concession if all other issues had been solved. He could say that the Minister of Agriculture preferred peace to the settlements in northern Sinai. Tamir did not let up.

He asked Sharon to phone Begin and tell him so personally. Sharon relented.

A few hours later, as the Israeli mission met for a review of their position, Begin informed those present that he had just spoken to his Minister of Agriculture and that Sharon had recommended that making the concession was preferable to ending the talks at an impasse over the fate of the settlements.

Sharon's advocacy on this issue was very important in prompting Begin to show the flexibility required to reach a peace accord with Egypt; however, it was not decisive. Begin convinced himself by means of a procedural suggestion made by members of the Israeli mission. The Israeli negotiators at Camp David would not make the concession. It would be left to the Knesset to make the final decision. There is no doubt, however, that Sharon's phone call to Begin eased the way considerably and in retrospect surprised many. How could Sharon reconcile this action with his persistent declaration of support for the establishment of new settlements and his frequent criticism of the peace process with Egypt?

There is no clear-cut explanation for this anomaly. Some contend that, from the time of Sadat's surprise visit to Jerusalem, Sharon had joined the group of political leaders favoring the peace process. According to this view, Sharon's disruptions of the process, mainly through the inopportune creation of new settlements, had been a tactical maneuver designed to improve Israel's bargaining position. His willingness to intervene at this critical juncture and encourage Begin to make the necessary concessions was evidence of his deep-seated support for peace with Egypt.

Others interpreted Sharon's activities during the long months of negotiation as representing his true belief in the supremacy of the settlements, for both Zionist as well as security reasons, to any peace accord. His willingness to intervene at a critical moment was the result of cold calculation. Sharon understood from his conversation that the decision to yield on the question of the settlements had in fact been made in principle. As he had done many times in the past, when faced with defeat, he himself yielded and compromised. With no chance of stopping the peace process, it would be better to appear to support it than to remain in the minority.

There is yet another interpretation of Sharon's surprising behavior. Although he remained somewhat skeptical of the possibility of peace with Egypt, his support and opposition to the peace process at various points in its progress had been dictated by the extent of his involvement. When called upon to participate, he contributed to its success; however, when left out of the decision making process, he did everything possible to sabotage the talks. Sharon's support of the settlements, and in particular of extreme fanatical groups such as Gush Emunim, was opportunistic in nature. His willingness to limit all new settlements to a mere military presence on the West Bank in his talks with Yigael Yadin in 1977 and his avid support of the new settlements since the formation of the Begin government were both the product of his reading of the political map of the time. The ease and alacrity with which Sharon had turned around and spoken to Begin on behalf of peace was evidence of the fact that his position on the settlements had not been based on either emotional or on ideological grounds.

There is evidence to support the latter view that Sharon's own personal involvement was the determining factor in dictating his position regarding both the peace process and the settlements. On March 1, 1979, Begin appealed to his cabinet to approve a number of articles in the peace treaty that had remained unresolved until then. He was calling from the United States where he had been visiting President Carter. In the face of the opposition of a small group of ministers who opposed Begin's proposition, Sharon swung the government behind its Prime Minister and Sharon's proposal was accepted. Ten days later during Carter's visit to Jerusalem, Sharon played a key role in easing the tension between Carter and Begin. Sharon had been a member of a small group of ministers assigned to find solutions to the issues discussed at this meeting. Despite this support for the Prime Minister and the peace treaty, Sharon was one of only two ministers to vote against the treaty. He explained his vote as a protest against Begin's failure to bring the question of the nature of the autonomy of the West Bank and the Gaza Strip before the government for examination prior to the signing of the treaty. His opposition to the treaty on this seemingly minor issue was so strong that he refused to join the Israeli mission invited to participate in the signing ceremonies in Washington. This opposition, however, did not prevent him from voting in favor of the treaty when it was brought before the Knesset for ratification, much to the chagrin of his supporters on the far right and in Gush Emunim.

The peace negotiations between Israel and Egypt were the dominant subject of the first two years of the Likud government, overshadowing everything else. It provided Sharon with an explanation for his neglect of the daily management of his ministry, Agriculture. Sharon had a difficult time adjusting to the routine of the civilian work in his ministry. He seemed to expect to find a military-style hierarchy that would be at his disposal 24 hours a day. In the face of these disappointed expectations, Sharon designed an alternative means of operation that would allow him to contend with the civilian bureaucracy. He surrounded himself with a small cadre of advisors and assistants, selected from among the young loyalists in his Shlomzion party. To them he delegated most of the work of managing the department. Among his appointments was one professional only: Avraham Ben Meir, Director-General of the Ministry.

Sharon rarely confered with the senior civil servants in his department and totally ignored the highly respected planning authority. His decisions were based on the advise of this small coterie of associates and were implemented through them as well. His relationship with these advisors was a complex one. He treated them in much the same manner as he had treated his staff in the army. He expected complete loyalty and dedication and demanded unswerving support from them on all his positions. He was suspicious of all of them, frequently changing his preferences among them or forcing aside an advisor who had fallen out of favor. He generated an atmosphere of competition among his aides as they competed to fulfill his every wish. The clearest indication that an advisor was counted among the inner circle was an invitation to participate in the Friday afternoon political conferences. These were unofficial meetings at which political strategy and tactics were discussed. Beyond the reporting and planning relevant to the Ministry of Agriculture, they would discuss the key political issues of the day or the relations between the Prime Minister and one of his ministers or, in more general terms, how Sharon's personal interests could be advanced given the political environment of the week. Sharon consulted this group on how to compete with Ezer Weizman, what positions to take on the peace talks and how to use the settlements to advance his aims.

Sharon's wife, Lilly, would also attend some of these meetings. His close associates quickly understood that she was a woman of considerable power whose influence over her husband was considerable. She was involved in all political decisions and her advice was greatly valued by her husband. She apparently was the only person whom Sharon trusted fully. She provided him with the confidence he needed in his own skills and actions. She praised his public appearances and encouraged him. When an advisor or friend left this inner circle, whether voluntarily or not, Lilly would sever all social connections as well. She had a reputation as being a wife who was so dedicated to her husband that any political opponent became a personal enemy as well.

Sharon had created this small group of diehard supporters just as he had done while in the army. To them he could do no wrong. They admired and respected him, and often described his friendly, warm nature and his sense of humor. They told stories of his trips through the countryside to admire the scenery. They believed his accounts of his yearning to take a vacation from the exigencies of political life, to shepherd a flock of sheep in the Judean Hills with nothing more than pita bread, olives and a wedge of cheese. They were impressed with his knowledge of the smallest alleys and lanes throughout the country and they particularly enjoyed the relaxed atmosphere and conviviality during these outings. These close associates were overwhelmed by Sharon. His changing moods marked them and they were unable to find release from the almost hypnotic effect he had upon them. If he were in a good mood, they returned home happy and content; if, however, he were in a foul mood, irritable or angry, they would return home angry with their families or depressed and silent, unable to control their own reactions. They learned to warn each other about what to expect in terms of Sharon's moods, but even this preparation failed to insulate.

Even his closest associates disliked Lilly. They saw her as domineering, seeking to be involved in all political issues. She frequented his office and took an active interest in everything going on. She queried the workers to find out their real feelings toward her husband and then would express her opinion to him about their loyalty or their abilities. These comments often served to dictate Sharon's own attitude toward the workers. But the real similarity between Sharon and his wife was their overbearing suspicion of everyone. Despite the obvious adulation that his close associates showed him, Sharon never ceased to suspect them of betrayal. He was overheard cautioning one advisor never to trust the others. He strove to control the office staff by inciting them against each other. If someone had been well received by Sharon one day and completely rejected the next, it was only natural to assume that someone had instigated this change of opinion.

Despite the uncomfortable changes of mood and the overall dictatorial atmosphere of the office, these associates were enthralled by Sharon's personality and charm. They admired the statesman he so much wanted to be and had complete faith in him when he said that his real concern was the good of the country. They fully identified with his political views and accepted his pronouncements that the settlement of the West Bank was indeed the battle for the future of the country. In this respect they fully agreed with Sharon's strategy as well. The best way of promoting the settlement of the West Bank was to establish the very fact of settlement: another settlement here and another there; an expansion of an existing one; a paramilitary one someplace else. They accepted the obvious contradictions as well: the passage of a cabinet resolution freezing all settlements in northern Sinai while at the same time expanding existing ones; or Sharon's support of the peace process at the critical point in the talks at Camp David while at the same time providing covert support to the movement to stop the withdrawal from Sinai.

Sharon never attempted to hide his fondness for Gush Emunim, even when it took positions counter to expressed government policy. Beyond the fact that they served his own political ambitions, he saw these religious settlers as the true pioneers of the 1970's and '80's. He appreciated their hierarchical organization and their complete submissiveness toward their rabbi leaders. The aura of pride that radiated from him when he was encircled by the singing and dancing settlers could not be mistaken. These were expressions of loyalty and adulation that he had not even experienced in the army. Gush Emunim, on its part, saw Sharon as a political ally and in many respects as the last bastion in their battle against the defeatism of the other members of the government, including Begin. When Sharon's duplicity in his dealings with them became apparent and after Sharon voted in favor of the withdrawal from Sinai in the vote of the Knesset, they became a little wary of their relationship to him; however, they never rejected him as a political partner.

The members of Sharon's staff took his approach to the press for granted. He looked upon most journalists as enemies with, moreover, a personal grudge for him. He generally referred to them as "slime" and "traitors." Sharon nevertheless made careful use of the press, manipulating it to his own advantage by leaking information and providing his own assessment of events. He used his own staff to leak sensational news that would serve his own personal interests. He shared his disdain and contempt for the other members of government with the journalists, referring to Begin as the "corpse" and using his rich vocabulary of epithets when referring to the other ministers. In his opinion the other members of the government were a bunch of cowardly, dense, unskilled incompetents who had fallen under the charm of Sadat and the Egyptians and were now totally uncapable of thinking for themselves.

Sharon developed the reputation of a Minister of Agriculture who took little interest in his work and who ignored the needs of both the country as well as his ministry. He devoted himself solely to the question of the new settlements. Although personally not oblivious to the needs of the farmers, he saw his position as the avenue for his involvement in public policy in general rather than a professional activity in which he strove to distinguish himself. His ministry, as well as even his chairmanship of the committee on new settlements, were the agency through which he would expand his own personal influence by using the considerable impact he had over this key economic sector. During his tenure in office, Sharon made two important decisions in the field of agriculture proper: to increase the resources devoted to the growing of flowers and the expansion of the poultry industry. Both proved catastrophic and resulted in the bankruptcy or near collapse of many a farm. Sharon's failure was a result of his ignoring the advice of experts in the field as well as his desire to impress everyone with the grand scale of his actions. When he made the decision to expand these two branches of agriculture, he did so on a massive scale, resulting in a quickly saturated market. Sharon took an active part in one other decision, nominally within the realm of his department. He worked for the "preservation of the integrity of the land," a cruel euphemism for the eviction of Bedouin tribes from land they had developed and lived on for years.

The Ministry of Agriculture also enabled Sharon to enjoy his petty revenge against the regional agricultural organizations and national marketing groups. In his childhood he had believed that these organizations had stifled the farming spirit and had served blatantly political functions; however, in time he learned that these organizations were indispensible to the agricultural industry in Israel and his attempts to undermine them quickly declined. Many who knew Sharon noted during his visits to the farms in the country that for a man who could be so cruel and impatient with other people, he was remarkably kind to animals. He could be seen kneeling in a barn to pet a lamb or a foal, oblivious to the dirt around him and the startled looks on the faces of his hosts. Although he never fully overcame his opposition to the kibbutzim because of their association with the rival labor parties, he nevertheless enjoyed visiting them and seeing them flourish. His confrontations with the kibbutzim focused on institutional and personal political interests. He never took more than the most superficial action, however, to change this situation, despite his public posturing about the reforms he was going to institute. He did follow through in consistently giving his office an air of asceticism by serving his guests water only and by setting up a small kitchenette and bedroom to save money on hotel expenses.

In managing the personnel of his office, Sharon was impatient and temperamental and his staff learned to be wary of his changing moods. They witnessed his vicious attack on his longtime driver, Meir Aknin, when he informed his boss that he was resigning because his newly-wed wife insisted that he seek a better profession. Aknin was fully devoted to Sharon and was willing to do absolutely anything for him, but he was shattered by Sharon's response: "You're good for nothing. Get out of here. Go home and do the laundry for your wife." Aknin broke down and cried.

This was not Sharon's only outburst. Key personnel were constantly changing. Some were fired by Sharon and others left in indignation or disappointment. Three senior aides, two office managers and a number of key officials in his office left during his term of office. Finally, Avraham Ben Meir, the Director-General of the Ministry of Agriculture also resigned. Ben Meir was careful to emphasize that his departure had nothing to do with his personal relations with Sharon; however, from his few public comments it became clear that he was extremely disappointed in the government's approach to agriculture and his Ministry's role in determining that policy. He was not alone in this opinion. Many senior officials in the Ministry of Agriculture felt that agriculture was suffering under the Likud government because of the minister's neglect and because of Sharon's inability to get along with the other ministers in promoting his office's policies. Although Ben Meir did everything possible to underscore his personal respect for Sharon, he was nevertheless subject to an insulting attack by Lilly Sharon.

Sharon's behavior during the first Begin administration was apparent in all areas. He was irritable and offensive and became an almost constant focal point for the ugly and strident personal political infighting that plagued the government. Twenty-five years after the establishment of the 101st Unit, Sharon still exhibited the same patterns of behavior. He was aggressive and at times even cruel to those around him; his attitude toward the other ministers, including Begin, was one of condescension; but he assiduously nurtured a small coterie of devoted followers that seemed always to hover about him. He harbored the same ambitions for higher positions and more responsibility, and belittled anyone who presumed to be competent enough to fill the roles to which he aimed. His overriding interest remained within the defense establishment. The major difference was in the response which his behavior engendered. As a young army officer, his comments and actions would have an impact on a relatively small group of people. Now, however, as a prominent member of the government, his frustrations, his conceits and his deepest desires had become a part of the public domain. His style of behavior and attitude toward others were affecting the entire country.

Defense Minister Ezer Weizman suffered the brunt of Sharon's ire. Jealous of the fact that Weizman had been chosen above him for the position he coveted, Sharon engaged in unbridled attacks against Weizman on both a personal level and a professional one. He made particularly effective use of the press by leaking information about cabinet discussions, using the journalists whom he had courted as his unwitting dupes in his campaign to portray Weizman as unwilling to fight for the country's most important interests. Sharon orchestrated an attack of pernicious innuendos and rumors, implying that Weizman was either trying to depose Begin or was about to defect to the opposition Labor Party. These attacks peaked during the long negotiations with the Egyptians, as Sharon criticized Weizman for his excessive indulgence in appeasing the Egyptians. His perceived rivalry with Weizman was so extreme that it could be said that the timing behind his settlement initiatives was planned mainly to embarass and confound Weizman at critical junctures in the peace negotiations rather than to promote Israeli settlements on the West Bank.

The main issue in Sharon's attacks was Israeli policy on the West Bank, both in terms of the autonomy granted the Arab residents in the peace treaty signed with Egypt and in terms of the establishment of new settlements. He accused those who opposed the settlements because they jeopardized the delicate peace with Egypt of foresaking the ideals of the country; while he accused those who in principle supported the expanded settlement policy of failing to fight forcefully enough against the attempt to isolate Sharon. Sharon had argued within the cabinet to bring the question of the nature of the autonomy to a full and detailed discussion, but he had been overuled by Begin, who felt that an open discussion of such a subtle and sensitive question would only cause trouble. At a cabinet meeting in March, 1979, Sharon's frustrations on this issue burst out and he charged Begin with paying only lip service to the idea of Israel sovereignity over Judea and Samaria (the West Bank).

Begin responded angrily, "Don't preach morality to me on questions of patriotism."

Sharon pouted and complained sulkily, "Once again there's no need for me."

Sharon also criticized the alacrity with which his colleagues rushed off to Egypt at every chance. He attempted to cloak his criticism in terms of national interest by pointing out the paucity of return visits to Israel by prominent Egyptian political leaders. His key concern, however, was the fact that he had not yet been invited himself, for as soon as he received his first invitation, he too sped off to Cairo.

Throughout his tenure in office, Sharon's attitude toward the government was the same as it had been 25 years ago when he was a major in the army. It was as if his membership in the political elite of the country served as proof of his contempt for all politicians. As a cabinet minister he learned the weak points of the democratic system and took ample advantage of them all. Intolerant and pusillanimous, he was continually embroiled in petty disputes with virtually all members of the political establishment. The political arena was a mere substitute for the battlefield and every means was allowable. He pounced on every opportunity and used his entire armamentarium of wiles and stratagems.

One of Sharon's favorite devices was his use of maps. Taking advantage of the limited experience and lack of knowledge among his colleagues in the government, Sharon often used maps to present his proposals or to analyze a particular situation. What could be more objective? On October 22, 1979, during a ministerial-level meeting to discuss Sharon's proposal to expand a number of existing settlements in Samaria, a bitter argument broke out when Dayan intervened. Sharon had presented a little map prepared in order to illustrate how the settlements would be expanded. Dayan did not trust Sharon and from his experience in the army he knew that Sharon had to be given clear and complete instructions or else he would interpret them to suit his own purposes. Dayan demanded to be given the map and the outline for the proposed expansions. Later it became clear that Dayan was justified in his suspicions. Sharon had instructed his assistants to prepare the maps in such a way that they would enable him to get approval for his proposals without the other ministers having been aware of what exactly they were reviewing. The maps had been prepared with new settlements indicated by colors identical with the background color of the map, making them literally indistinguishable.

Dayan's investigation showed that the proposed expansions were indeed new settlements disguised by the fact that they were given identical names to existing, adjacent settlements. Dayan added that if an existing settlement wished to expand and add a new neighborhood, there was no need to bring the subject before a cabinet-level meeting. Through Begin's intervention, a meeting was arranged between Sharon and Weizman to determine which new settlements would be founded and which existing ones would be expanded.

As the Sharon-Weizman decision was brought before a plenary session of the government, Yadin objected that Sharon had not operated in accordance with the government's decisions and that no mention was made of the new settlements in the protocols of the meetings. The specific new settlements in question had not been mentioned in the minutes of any government meeting; however, there had been a reference to a

review of "eight issues" between Sharon and Weizman. Yadin
objected that this could not serve as the basis of the
government's decisionmaking process. Sharon broke out in a
rage: "Mr. Deputy Prime Minister (Yigael Yadin). I'll strip you
bare and naked on the table of this meeting. These are not the
Dead Sea Scrolls, but the minutes of government meetings."

Begin ordered that Sharon's comments be struck from the
record and Sharon burst out again, this time attacking Begin.
"Your decision means nothing. I'll knock this government down
yet."

This was not Sharon's only attack on Begin. Throughout the
last year or so of Begin's first administration, Sharon would
repeatedly assail Begin, often in the most vicious manner. Other
ministers would at times intervene with comments such as that of
the Minister of Commerce and Industry, Gideon Patt, "No
minister in this cabinet will stand for such talk (against the Prime
Minister)." But none of them did anything, preferring to
reconcile themselves to Sharon's obscenities and disrespect for
the Prime Minister. If anything, Sharon's attacks became even
more vicious as first Dayan and then Weizman resigned from the
government. Sharon now had his opportunity of grabbing the
post of Minister of Defense and he set about that task with brute
force. This was a critical, tactical mistake on his part, for had he
been more subtle and restrained in his pursuit of the position, he
would have had a far better chance of succeeding.

With Prime Minister Begin acting in the interim as Minister of
Defense, Sharon read out a prepared statement at a cabinet
meeting reviewing the dire circumstances which the country
faced: concentrations of Soviet tanks in Lybia and the Persian
Gulf; Iraq's imminent development of a nuclear capability; and
the continued agitation and terrorism among the Palestinians,
especially on the West Bank. He summarized his comments by
pointing out that if the Prime Minister was fully aware of the
seriousness of the defense situation he most certainly would not
consider using the nomination of the minister as "payment of a
prostitute's fee" in political terms. A new Minister of Defense
must be chosen from among those most qualified. He must be
"someone whose very appointment would serve as a deterrent to

the Arabs."

Begin, offended by Sharon's use of the term "a prostitute's fee," retorted, "In many democracies the law forbids the appointment of former senior officers to the position of Minister of Defense."

Sharon was quick to respond. "Only a charlatan would claim to be able to solve all of the security problems of the country alone. We must prefer the most competent man for the position." Begin interrupted him and asked, "At least tell us who spoke that way." "You did!" Sharon answered sarcastically, "at the recent convention of the Herut Party. I would add, however, that only a charlatan would not do everything in his power for the security of the nation and to combat terror. National security is above the constitution." Unable to control himself, Yadin yelled out, "Never!"

At this point Sharon left the meeting for about an hour and a half and when he returned Begin asked him ironically if he had had enough time to leak the contents of the meeting. Sharon spat out, "That's petty vengefulness. If anyone thinks they can harm me they are wrong."

Begin reprimanded him, cautioning him not to raise his voice. Sharon half apologized, "You intentionally provoked me. Unlike our former Minister of Defense, I will not capitulate when under attack. I will fight back whenever I believe it necessary."

That same week, Begin publically declared that he would not appoint Sharon as Minister of Defense, adding facetiously that he was afraid that as Minister of Defense, Sharon's first act would be to surround the government buildings with tanks.

Sharon did not give up. He continued his pressure on Begin, threatening to resign from the government if he were not appointed Minister of Defense. He granted frequent interviews to the press in which he descried the sorry state of affairs and the imperative of appointing a full-time Minister of Defense. Despite these warnings, Sharon did not resign. He truly proved to be, as he stated in an interview, "the only general in the government not to be broken by the politicians."

Although his closest associates in the Ministry of Agriculture described him as a methodical and careful planner, it is difficult to reconcile this characterization with his brutal and violent outbursts during government meetings. Could these have been planned as well, designed to provoke his rivals or create a certain image? It is far more likely that these were spontaneous outbursts, expressions of his frustration and anger at the ability of others to thwart his strongest ambitions. His behavior in the Ministry of Agriculture, moreover, was a reenactment of his actions and demeanor throughout his military career. He seemed condemned to be in conflict with his environment. His ability for elaborate and thorough planning contrasted with his moodiness and his loss of control whenever he became angry. Sharon was easily baited and, when roused, reacted violently, as those who served near him discovered. In the army he had discharged many of his aides, often for the pettiest of reasons and he did likewise in Shlomzion and the Ministry of Agriculture. This was not the result of a cautious, well-planned campaign. The real Sharon, the one exposed to only small groups of people prior to then, was now in clear view of the entire country. He was violent and irritable, eternally suspicious of everyone. He was power hungry and refused to put up with any delays or obstructions in his pursuit of this power. It is true, undoubtedly, that some of these outbursts were tactically planned; however, when surprised he invariably responded with a Krakatoa of vilifications.

The reticence of his fellow ministers can be explained both by their failure to understand the implications of his behavior and that their public silence would be interpreted as condoning or, at least, accepting this new norm of political debate. But beyond this, they were undoubtedly cowed by Sharon's violence. Politicians learned to tread cautiously in his presence, for Sharon seemed to find enemies in the most unlikely of places.

In mid-1980, Uri Dan, a journalist and later Sharon's official spokesman, reported that a band of terrorists had been caught in the vicinity of Sharon's farm in the Negev desert. It was alleged by Sharon that this band had operated with detailed information regarding the security arrangements at the farm gleaned from the excessive publicity generated by his opponents as his request for the allocation of very large sums of money was reviewed in the Knesset Finance Committee. Sharon interpreted this as clear evidence of the attempts being made to attack him.

Sharon's farm, one of the largest privately-owned farms in the country, was the focal point of another political debate. The ownership and control of such a farm would be in conflict with any cabinet minister; however, when the owner was also the Minister of Agriculture, the conflict of interest became unconscionable. As a result of the public uproar, an ad hoc judicial committee was formed to review the situation. It was their unanimous decision that Sharon's ownership of the farm stood in direct violation of the principles of democratic government. They rejected out of hand Sharon's attempts to appoint a comanager of the farm, declaring that this step was a mere charade, for Sharon's wife Lilly continued, in fact, to manage the farm. Sharon finally found a solution. He leased the farm to a close friend and disassociated himself and his family from the economic activities on the farm. The public furor did not subside, but the judicial committee that had reviewed the legal and ethical aspects of the problem declared that as long as the responsible manager was not a relative, the solution proposed by Sharon met the criteria set down by the Knesset. To eliminate some of the lingering sense of conflict, the committee proposed that Sharon commit himself to transferring any ministerial decisions likely to affect his farm to an independent commission for review.

Sharon's political role afforded an opportunity of viewing a hitherto hidden facet of his life on his farm. Essentially a very private individual, he now bore the burden of social as well as ministerial responsibilities. On his farm in the Negev he appeared relaxed and comfortable, far from the political fights and contests and within the warm and supportive environment of his family. He was a perfect host who charmed his guests with reminiscences and stories of his past exploits in the army. As he sat with his guests after a good meal, smoking his cigar, one could not but be impressed with his warm, good humor. Sharon never enjoyed the large receptions that typified public life where he seemed lost and uncomfortable. Lilly too was exposed to the public in this manner. Sharon's guests discovered a woman who enjoyed art and music and who loved flowers and plants; but they also perceived a woman who jealously guarded her prerogatives as a minister's wife.

This family environment surprised his guests. Could it be that the violent and aggressive nature they had come to know was merely a thorny exterior on a soft and warm-hearted man? Was the picture of the nasty irascible politician possibly the result of journalistic hyperbole? Or was the warmth of the home and family a carefully guarded sanctuary, a refuge from the tribulations of the political arena? The very support he received at home may have been what enabled him to quarrel with everyone else.

Sharon concluded his tenure as Minister of Agriculture together with the rest of Begin's government six months prior to the scheduled elections. A coalition crisis had forced Begin to call for early elections. Now, as elections approached, Sharon began to understand that the elusive goal of Minister of Defense was now within reach and he devoted himself to the Likud election campaign. Sharon encouraged Begin to convince the cabinet to approve the bombing of the nuclear reactor in Iraq, an act which later public opinion polls would show was a decisive factor in determining the Likud victory in the elections. He organized tours of the new settlements, portraying the Likud government as one of action and not just words. And he wholeheartedly supported the cynical economic policies of the new Minister of the Treasury, Yoram Aridor, which strove to rapidly raise the standard of living of individuals even if this was at the expense of the long-term economic health of the country. Sharon was a central figure in the election campaign, aided in large part by his ability to point to the accomplishments of his ministry in founding new settlements on the West Bank and the Gaza Strip. A key contributing factor to the centrality of Sharon in the Likud campaign was Begin's attitude to him.

Throughout his tenure in office, Begin was captivated by Sharon. Begin had long striven to surround himself with the powerful and the famous, and in the formation of his first government he selected five key generals to serve in his cabinet:

Dayan, Weizman, Amit, Yadin and Sharon. As he sought reelection, four of these men had already dropped out, worn down by politics, disappointed by the unfulfilled promises of the new government or simply fed up with the Likud. The sole survivor was Sharon. Although Sharon had been a minor figure in the key accomplishment of Begin's first administration, the peace treaty with Egypt, he now rose up as a dominant personality largely because of his survivability. Begin had come to be dependent on Sharon. This was particularly obvious when the settlements in Yamit, in northern Sinai, were evacuated as part of the withdrawal agreement. Begin believed that Sharon alone could forestall the violence and bloodshed that at one point seemed inevitable.

There is no question that Sharon was an important electoral attraction appealing to the masses both thorugh his military record as well as through his blustering image of action. Few endeavored to examine this record closely. His support, however, was equally as strong within the party. In the Likud primary elections to select the candidates for the party list, Sharon came in second to Begin only, passing all the traditional leaders of the Likud. This was not only the result of his having packed the Likud caucuses with 61 of his followers from Shlomzion four years earlier. Sharon clearly enjoyed the popular support of the masses in the party as well.

A clear policy of appeasement existed between Begin and Sharon during the election campaign. Sharon came to realize that at this point his career would be best served with Begin on his side. Begin, for his part, needed Sharon. The people of the country could not have been expected to have shown any greater sensitivity or responsibility than Begin himself had. Begin, who was viewed as something of a father figure in the country, an indomnitable leader who was merciful with the Jews and forceful with the Arab enemies. Sharon, by association, was now enjoying the status of being second only to Begin, the declared candidate for the second most important position in the government: Minister of Defense.

For Sharon it was an opportunity to set the future of the country. He would form the basis for the ongoing security of the country and put an end, once and for all, to the Palestinian problem. He would joggle the IDF out of the torpor into which it had fallen. The results of the elections in June, 1981, reinforced Sharon's perception of his power. He was convinced of his critical role in the narrow Likud victory and of Begin's dependence on him. His stubborness and aggressiveness were paying off. Not only did his conflicts and fights with Begin and the other members of the Likud not affect his standing as the heir apparent, but they may even have helped. He was determined that the position of Minister of Defense should become the most important position in the government.

Shortly before the elections, in the heat of the campaign on April 30th, Sharon also voiced his opinion about the policy of the government toward Lebanon. In a newspaper interview he stated that "Lebanon, in large part, has effectively been annexed by Syria; the world remains silent in the face of the massacre of the Lebanese Christians by the Muslims; and a large part of the country is ruled by terrorists who have converted it into the world center for terrorism operated by the Soviets."

As Minister of Defense, Sharon would indeed alter the situation in Lebanon and fulfill his prophecy of making the Minister of Defense the most important position in the government.

CHAPTER *14*

Just two months after taking office as Minister of Defense, Arik Sharon instructed the General Staff to work out detailed plans for "Operation Big Pines," keeping the following objectives in mind:

– to remove Israeli settlements in the northern Galilee from the range of terrorist shelling;

– to crush the terrorists in Beirut, militarily and politically;

– to set up a legitimate government in Lebanon which would sign a peace treaty with Israel;

– to insure the evacuation of Syrian troops from the Beirut area.

The plans were completed by January 1982.

The timetable attached to the operational orders stipulated that the IDF would reach Beirut and complete the occupation of the city within ninety-six hours of the beginning of the operation.

The operational orders were not drawn up fortuitously. They were part of a larger plan of attack on the PLO in Lebanon which had been made at the behest of the Chief of Staff, Rafael Eitan, a year earlier, when Menahem Begin was still filling in as Minister of Defense. Sharon's first reconnaissance junket as Minister of Defense, four days after taking office, was along the northern border. A few days earlier, the cabinet had ordered the air force to bomb PLO headquarters in the heart of Beirut – an air raid which resulted in dozens of casualties among the civilian population. At the end of October 1981, the army discussed a plan to attack Lebanon from the north (by landing amphibious troops), and from the south (by moving divisions across the Israeli border), in a pincer movement designed to destroy the Syrian army in Lebanon. This plan differed from a previous conception based on deep penetration of the western sector up to Beirut while freezing the situation on the eastern sector (where the Syrian army was concentrated). On December 20, 1981, the cabinet was convened to hear a report from the Prime Minister on a conversation between him and the American Ambassador, Samuel Lewis. Lewis had protested to Begin against the decision of the government (and the Knesset) to annex the Golan Heights. In response to Lewis's critical remarks, the Prime Minister launched into a tirade. At the meeting of the cabinet Begin reconstructed his response to Lewis and ordered the government secretariat to release it to the media. His mood was stormy. Begin had arrived at the decision to initiate the annexation of the Golan Heights while he was suffering from severe pain as a result of a fracture of the thighbone. He was in the same state when he made his angry retort to Lewis. His irate mood and his determination to publicize his verbal tiff with Lewis ("Israel is not a vassal state of the United States") worried some of his ministers. But nobody dared oppose him. This was not the case, however, when the Chief of Staff and his aides-de-camp presented their plan for a military operation in Lebanon and the Golan Heights. Their basic assumption was that the Syrians would take military action in response to the annexation of the Golan Heights. Begin supported the idea and suggested that he be authorized, together with a select number of ministers, to decide when the plan be put into operation. Three ministers – Simha Ehrlich, Yosef Burg and Yitzhak Moda'i – expressed certain reservations about the plan. Their feeling was that the timing of the operation was not the decisive issue. The decisive issue was whether or not the Syrians would indeed take military action which would oblige

Israel to retaliate. Some of those who took part in the meeting later admitted that they were worried that the IDF might simply provoke the Syrians in order to provide an excuse for putting the Chief of Staff's plan into operation. When Begin realized that some of his ministers were hedging, he dropped his proposal.

In February 1982, just a few weeks after "Operation Big Pines" had been blueprinted, a terrorist unit crossed the border from Jordan into Mechula, in the Jordan Valley. It was discovered and captured before it managed to do anything. Eitan proposed to the cabinet that the army retaliate against the terrorists in Lebanon. He claimed that the PLO had undertaken to cease all activity against Israel in the wake of the cease-fire agreement mediated by the American emissary, Philip Habib, in July 1981. Since then, the border with Lebanon had been quiet. After the unit was captured, the military establishment made a number of moves designed to escalate tension between Israel and the PLO: the Chief of Staff called a press conference at which he described circumstances leading to the capture and stressed the ties of the unit to the terrorist command in Beirut; a number of leading Israelis came out with statements threatening the PLO for reneging on the cease-fire agreement; a large military force was moved up to the Lebanese border.

The cabinet, convened to discuss the matter, was given contradictory evidence as to where the unit had originated: IDF representatives subordinate to the Minister of Defense claimed that they had come from Lebanon; representatives of the General Security Services (the Shin Bet), directly responsible to the Prime Minister, contended that they had come from Amman. A majority of the cabinet were inclined to agree to the idea that the air force should bomb terrorist targets in Lebanon. It was clearly understood that this would lead the PLO to reprisal shelling of Israeli border settlements in the Galilee and, following this, that the overall plan for demolishing the PLO infrastructure in Lebanon would become operable.

With five members of the cabinet opposed the majority voted to go ahead with the bombings. A ministerial committee would decide exactly when. At a meeting of this committee the next day, the wisdom of the proposal was again questioned, with the

Minister of Interior, Yosef Burg, expressing severe doubts. The committee members began to reappraise the entire idea, spurred, in no small measure, by repeated warnings from the northern settlements themselves. Leaders from those same settlements bordering on Lebanon, which had been the main targets of terrorist attacks and for whose safety "Operation Big Pines" was ostensibly being put into effect, sounded the alarm. They drew public attention to the large concentration of troops on the border and warned against any extensive operation in Lebanon. They pointed to the fact that the agreement between Israel and the PLO had resulted in a quiet border and they saw no justification for breaching the agreement now. The American administration, aware of Israel's military preparations, added its voice to those opposed. Begin began to have doubts. His support for the bombings began to waver. The ministerial committee decided on a different tack: they would dispatch a high-ranking Israeli to the United States to meet with Secretary of State Alexander Haig and inform him of the seriousness with which Israel viewed PLO behavior and the incursion of terrorists from Jordan.

The prime minister proposed Army Intelligence Chief, Yehoshua Saguy, for the mission. Arik Sharon preferred the Director-General of the Foreign Ministry, David Kimche. Begin was adamant. Haig, he pointed out, was a retired general and would be more attentive to assessments made by a military expert than those made by a diplomat. Saguy left for Washington where Haig made it clear to him that the infiltration of terrorists into the Jordan Valley was no justification for a major military operation in Lebanon.

Begin understood that without American support, certainly without Haig's support, it would be better to hold fire. The idea of a large-scale attack on the terrorists in Lebanon was shelved for the time being. Yet a certain understanding had been reached, primarily with Haig, that should there be a more serious provocation, such an attack would be considered justified.

In March 1982, Philip Habib made an attempt to reinforce the cease-fire agreement between Israel and the PLO. A discussion ensued, meanwhile, between Washington and Jerusalem as to what, in fact, would constitute an intentional breach of the agreement and a justification for military action. During Habib's talks in Jerusalem, Arik Sharon's behavior toward the emissary was not particularly diplomatic. His tone was rash and he often raised his voice. He accused the Americans of ignoring PLO violations of the cease-fire and of actually promoting a PLO build-up. At the same time, he said, the Americans were cultivating the image of Israel as a trigger-happy country, prevented from attacking the terrorists only by American intervention.

On April 21, 1982, the cabinet ordered the air force to bomb three terrorist bases in Lebanon in retaliation for the planting of a mine in southern Lebanon, in the area under the command of Major Saad Haddad, the Israel-backed head of the south Lebanese militias. The mine had exploded under an Israeli army vehicle, killing an Israeli officer. The air raids did not provoke a military response from the PLO.

On Thursday, June 3, 1985, the Israeli Ambassador to the Court of St. James, Shlomo Argov, was shot by Palestinian terrorists in London.

On Friday, June 4, the cabinet was urgently – and secretly – convened. The ministers assumed that Israel's response to the attack on Argov would make up the agenda. The Minister of Defense, Ariel Sharon, did not attend the meeting. He was at the time on a visit with his family to Rumania, his wife's birthplace. Begin was in an aggressive mood. No sovereign nation, he asserted, could reconcile itself to such an attack. The terrorist bases and commands in Lebanon were, he insisted, responsible for the dastardly deed. Speaking with emotion, he maintained that the fact that the government persistently refrained from attacking PLO "breeding grounds" was an absurdity. It was time, he said, to put an end to their activity. After reviewing a number of proposals presented by the army, the cabinet decided to instruct the air force to bomb two targets in Beirut: a PLO ammunition dump in the sports stadium and a terrorist training camp. The air force was further authorized to bomb additional PLO targets in southern Lebanon. The army assured the ministers that there would be few civilian casualties from the bombings as the area around the stadium was sparsely populated. Most of those living there were, at any rate, members of the PLO.

Twice before, in December and in February, the army had proposed a massive operation against the PLO: it would begin with air raids which would be followed by PLO shelling of the north. This would create the proper atmosphere for a large-scale Israeli ground attack against the terrorists in Lebanon. Twice before the cabinet had rejected the plan. This time, on June 4, 1982, they paid close attention to the probable consequences of the proposed air strike.

Not all of the ministers were eager to approve of the whole plan despite the fact that they had agreed on the necessity of the air strike. They were told that it wasn't absolutely certain that the PLO would retaliate: it hadn't retaliated in April. If it held back this time too, the ground attack would not be put into operation. The cabinet gave the green light to preparations for the ground attack should there be an escalation after the Air Force bombings.

On that same day, Friday, June 4, 1982, the Air Force bombed the targets in the Beirut area. Because of weather conditions, some attacks on targets in the south were dispensed with. The Beirut bombings resulted in dozens of casualties. The terrorists retaliated by shelling settlements in the Galilee. Crossfire between the IDF and the PLO continued over the next day, Saturday, June 5.

On Saturday night, the cabinet met again. Precautions were taken to keep the meeting secret: ministers were invited to Begin's home and not to the government complex. Access to the house was blocked by the police. The military censor was instructed to prohibit any reference to the meeting in the media. This time Sharon took part in the meeting. He had returned post-haste from his Rumanian jaunt. The ministers were informed that not only had the PLO retaliated on Friday, but on Saturday it had taken the initiative and renewed the shelling. Furthermore, it had turned their artillery on civilian settlements although it could just as well have shelled military installations in the area. Begin made an impassioned speech in favor of a large-scale attack. Using his most persuasive rhetoric, he expatiated on the moral right of the cabinet to decide, once and for all, to smash the PLO in Lebanon because of its murderous attacks on the peaceful civilian population of Israel. Chief of Staff Eitan proposed that the cabinet authorize the army to wipe out terrorist concentrations in southern Lebanon. Begin enumerated the number of times the PLO had infringed the cease-fire agreement since July 1981. Most of the Likud ministers, among them all the members of Herut, came out in support of Begin's position. There were, however, a few who had reservations. The Minister of Interior, Yosef Burg, suggested another air strike instead of large-scale ground action. Yitzhak Berman of the Liberal Party remarked that the decision to use the air force on Friday entailed, as a matter of course, the subsequent ground attack. The cabinet was given to understand that the entire operation would not take more than forty-eight hours and that its purpose was to establish a forty-kilometer buffer zone north of the Israeli-Lebanese border, to destroy the PLO's military infrastructure in Lebanon and as many terrorists as possible. Asked if the army's intention was to reach Beirut, both the Minister of Defense and the Chief of Staff replied that the purpose of the operation was to push PLO artillery forty kilometers from the Israeli border. If in the course of the operation circumstances proved to be propitious, then the army would attempt to influence internal developments in Lebanon. Such a likelihood was mentioned as a contingency and not as a major goal. It certainly wasn't relevant to the practical stages of the operation being discussed by the cabinet, and the cabinet did not discuss it. The Chief of Staff and his aides, in their overall presentation, referred to the deployment of PLO fighters shielded by the Syrian army in the Bekaa Valley, that is, in the eastern sector of the operation. The ministers were told that the army would attempt to get the Syrians to evacuate the terrorists from their positions there voluntarily. If they refused, the army would deal with the matter. There was no discussion of this issue either.

In accordance with Begin's recommendations, the cabinet

formulated the goals of the war as follows: to remove Israeli settlements from the range of terrorist fire, terrorist commands and terrorist bases in Lebanon; to refrain from attacking the Syrian army unless first attacked; to seek a peace treaty with an independent Lebanon while maintaining the country's territorial integrity.

Three of the seventeen participants in the meeting dissented. Yosef Burg adhered to his suggestion that another air strike would suffice; Simha Ehrlich and Yitzhak Berman, both of the Liberal faction of the Likud, abstained.

The cabinet decision was, to be sure, of a general nature and it provided the army with a good deal of elbowroom. It went so far as to refer to PLO commands as possible targets and mentioned a peace treaty with an independent Lebanon as a desirable objective. Yet, despite all this, no one could have possibly imagined what the real goals of the war were or what its consequences would be. The ministers left the Prime Minister's home with the impression that the IDF would embark on a large-scale attack against the terrorists within a forty-kilometer area north of the Israeli border. As far as they were concerned, Begin's formulations regarding strikes against terrorist commands referred to operations within the forty-kilometer zone. With the exception of Arik Sharon and, apparently, Menahem Begin, none of the members of the cabinet was aware of the fact that while they were still discussing a plan ostensibly dependent for its execution upon their approval, irreversible steps had already been taken: during the day, the IDF had entered Lebanon with tank units, artillery, mortar and half-tracks. On Friday, even before the cabinet had reached any official decision, an amphibious unit had been alerted and readied for landing ten kilometers north of Sidon, close to the Awali River. This was far beyond forty kilometers from the Israeli border.

Begin, Sharon (who had demonstrably supported the Prime Minister at the cabinet meeting Saturday night), and Eitan joined forces to perpetrate a national deception the likes of which had never been seen in the State of Israel. In the following weeks, Begin himself would become a victim of a similar duplicity, perpetrated on him by his own Minister of Defense.

On Friday, June 4, the operational orders of "Big Pines" were whisked out of General Staff headquarters and delivered to commanders whose units had been mobilized and deployed along the Lebanese border. The orders were not a revelation either to the division or battalion commanders: for months now their men had been undergoing training in line with these orders. A not insignificant number of units had been given extensive training in house-to-house fighting in built-up areas in preparation for a possible entry into Beirut. On Saturday, according to "Big Pines" and before the cabinet had approved the plan, large amphibious forces were on their way to a point somewhere between Sidon and Beirut. The following day, at the weekly cabinet session, the prime minister gave "Big Pines" a new name. From now on it would be known as "Operation Peace for the Galilee."

At that same meeting, Begin prevailed on his cabinet to issue an announcement of the the official commencement of the operation and called in leaders of the main opposition, the Alignment, to inform them of what was about to happen. Shimon Peres, Yitzhak Rabin, Haim Bar Lev and Victor Shem Tov were briefed by Arik Sharon, who was present at the meeting along with Foreign Minister Yitzhak Shamir and Chairman of the Knesset Foreign Affairs Committee, Eliahu Ben Elissar. They were told that the operation would last anywhere from twelve to twenty-four hours and that it was designed to create a buffer zone at a depth of forty kilometers. The plan was no novelty to the Alignment leaders either. A month earlier, on May 16, they had heard from Begin that the cabinet was determined not to respond to every single PLO assault separately but, rather, to embark on a more comprehensive action – should the assaults continue – to drive the terrorists from the border region. Now, listening to Sharon's report that "Big Pines" was being put into operation, they were informed that the IDF intended to push the terrorists up to the line running from Sidon to the south of Lake Karoun. To Rabin's question if the operation included the occupation of

Sidon, Sharon played dumb. He left the room three times, purportedly to clarify the question. His telephone calls on the subject left the Alignment leaders with the impression that there was, indeed, some doubt as to whether the army would enter Sidon or stop on the outskirts. Meanwhile, during the first hours of the operation, IDF forces had landed some distance north of Sidon.

The Alignment leaders were, for the most, men with a rich military past. Shimon Peres had been a minister of defense; Rabin had been Chief of Staff and Prime Minister; both Bar Lev and Mordechai Gur had been Chiefs of Staff. From the benches of the opposition in the Knesset, they still maintained close contact with high army personnel and others in the know. They were, in fact, more knowledgeable than most of the members of the cabinet as to what the IDF was up to in Lebanon.

That same Sunday morning, the cabinet was informed that a letter had been received from the President of the United States, Ronald Reagan, demanding that Israel refrain from military escalation. The cabinet approved Begin's answer – that Israel had no intention whatsoever of attacking the Syrians. The possibility of Syrian intervention plagued the ministers and that evening, at a further cabinet session, they gave the go-ahead for the mobilization of additional reserve units to swell the number of troops on the Golan Heights. They had been given to understand that this was necessary in order to deter the Syrians from opening fire there in an attempt to deflect the IDF from its course of action in Lebanon. They did not know that during the first stages of the fighting, the Israeli air force had bombarded Syrian radar installations north of the Beirut-Damascus highway. Nor did they know that the IDF's original operational orders were to reach that highway.

On June 7, the Golani commando unit successfully occupied the Beaufort fortress from which Israeli settlements had been shelled over a long period of time. The Prime Minister announced that the heroic operation had been carried out without losses to the IDF. In fact, six soldiers had been killed in the battle. That same evening, the cabinet met to discuss the American reaction to the operation as presented by Philip

Habib, and Sharon's proposal to authorize the IDF to attack terrorist concentrations in the Bekaa Valley.

By this time, it had become clear to members of the cabinet that the maximum latitude of forty kilometers was a rather flexible notion. Assuming that the IDF would advance forty kilometers in the eastern sector and forty kilometers in the western sector, they were surprised to learn that by the evening of the first day, units in the western sector had reached the outskirts of Damour, on the Mediterranean coast, a distance of eighty kilometers from Israeli's border. In answer to the question just how this squared with a forty-kilometer buffer zone, Sharon and Eitan had a ready answer: forty kilometers in the western sector would create a security belt of only twenty kilometers in the eastern sector; in order to shield eastern Israeli settlements from possible shelling from the west, it was necessary to take control of areas up to eighty kilometers along the coast. A forty-kilometer buffer zone, they explained, would be created by controlling enough territory to insure that not a single Israeli settlement would be vulnerable to terrorist artillery.

On the night of the second day of the war, June 7, Arik asked for authorization to step up operations by attacking terrorist concentrations in the eastern sector, in the Bekaa Valley where the Syrians were deployed. A majority in the cabinet objected and proposed instead a political move: an appeal to Syrian President, Hafez el-Assad, through the good offices of Philip Habib (who was sticking close to the area), to evacuate the terrorists from the Bekaa and thus avoid the danger of a confrontation with the IDF. In order to "encourage" the Syrian ruler to agree, the IDF was authorized to conduct maneuvers in the Bekaa, in a show of brinkmanship which would fall short of actual engagement. The cabinet also approved a request by Sharon to open another axis of advance in the central sector in order to circumvent the Syrians stationed in the Lake Karoun area. Cabinet members were unaware of the fact that on Saturday night officers in the Northern Command had already been primed for a move along the central axis and that their instructions were to destroy Syrian forces in Lebanon.

The next morning Arik had another request to make of the cabinet: to allow the IDF to "improve its positions" by opening another line of advance to the west of the force on the central axis. The movement of this force had been impeded for the time being. He provided three reasons: it would allow the IDF more leeway, it would avoid concentrating too many troops on one axis in the central sector, and it would tighten encirclement of the Syrians in the Bekaa. The new line of advance would bring the IDF closer to the Beirut-Damascus highway – although he made it abundantly clear to the cabinet that the IDF had no intention of reaching the highway itself.

Yitzhak Berman wryly remarked that today Sharon was asking permission for the IDF to occupy more territory and tomorrow he would ask permission to expand the combat zone on the grounds that our forces were in danger. He caustically suggested to Sharon that he get his authorizations today for what he would need tomorrow. The Minister of Defense burst out laughing and complimented Berman on his sense of humor. Yet Berman, despite his perspicacity, supported Sharon's request for another axis. Yosef Burg was the only member of the cabinet to object. Not long after, Sharon wanted still another axis, this time between Damour and Ein Zehalta. Without it, he said, the IDF would find it difficult to put the previous decision into effect. The cabinet inclined to believe that the army was moving towards the Beirut-Damascus highway in order to outflank the Syrians and avoid having to engage them. They accepted Sharon's explanations that although the bypass severely exceeded the forty-kilometer limit, it would pressure the Syrians to evacuate the terrorists from the Bekaa. They didn't know that the encirclement of the Syrians from the Beirut-Damascus highway was not necessarily intended to prevent engagement. It was intended, rather, to improve the IDF's firing position vis-a-vis the Syrians and free part of the IDF's forces for the siege of Beirut.

On June 8, 1982, the Prime Minister, addressing the Knesset, declared: "I want to reiterate – we are not interested in war with Syria. From the floor of the Knesset, I appeal to President Assad: insure that the Syrian army refrains from attacking Israeli soldiers and we will not attack them. We are not interested in hurting anybody. We are interested in one thing only: that no one attack our settlements in the Galilee, that our citizens no longer suffocate in bomb shelters day and night, that they no longer stand in fear of sudden death from Katyusha missiles. That is all we want. We are not interested in a clash with the Syrian army. When we reach the forty-kilometer line north of our border – our job will be finished. All fighting will stop. I am appealing to the president of Syria. He knows how to honor agreements. He signed a cease-fire with us and honored it. He did not allow either Syrians or terrorists to breach it. If he is prepared to act in this spirit now, in Lebanon, not a single Syrian soldier will be hurt by our troops."

At that very moment, bitter fighting was taking place between the IDF and the Syrian army near Lake Karoun (in the eastern sector) and in the Jezzin area (in the central sector). Assad had every good reason to consider Begin's Knesset declaration a shameless hypocrisy. The Syrian army had been reporting provocative movements by the IDF since the first day of the war. They were thoroughly convinced that the IDF was intent on dragging them into the war. The Syrian command, in line with Assad's directives, ordered its troops to refrain from opening fire unless the IDF actually reached Syrian positions or fired on Syrian troops. The Syrians permitted the Israeli air force to operate in Lebanon despite the fact that they had sophisticated antiaircraft missiles at their disposal. They even reconciled themselves to the bombing of their radar stations during the early stages of the war.

On Wednesday, June 9, Arik Sharon asked the cabinet to allow him to complete the move he had started the day before: the destruction of the Syrian missile batteries in Lebanon, reinforced the night before. He warned the cabinet that failure to destroy them would leave IDF troops open to attack by Syrian planes and helicopters. He grimly cautioned them against overlooking any possible danger to the troops which could be averted. The cabinet, which had been trying throughout to ward off the danger of engagement with the Syrians and which was totally unaware of the scope and intensity of the fighting in the field, acquiesced. Most of them were simply ignorant of what was going on. Others believed that the destruction of the missile batteries would really prevent the Syrians from engaging the IDF on the ground. Still others believed that without the destruction of the missiles, IDF forces in the central sector would be wiped out.

In fact, the destruction of the missile sites had a twofold purpose. The first was to close Begin's long-standing account with Assad. The Prime Minister had long warned Assad that the placement of Syrian missiles on Lebanese soil contravened the agreement between Israel and Syria and that the day would come when the IDF would eliminate them. The second was Sharon's overhelming ambition to get the Syrians out of the Bekaa Valley. By weakening the Syrian position in Lebanon, Sharon was sure he would be able to effect a change in Lebanon's internal situation, and thus pave the way to stable relations with Israel. To this end, the IDF had to move its eastern forces forward and for this they needed an aerial umbrella. The move was intended as well to ease the position of troops on the central axis whose advance, as already noted, had been impeded. This was the force trying to reach the Beirut-Damascus highway. In the western sector, troops were getting closer to Beirut and opening fire on terrorist concentrations and Syrian positions just south of the Lebanese capital. Another force was approaching the capital from the east – from the same axis of advance allegedly required in order to bypass the Syrians in the Bekaa, as Sharon had so convincingly explained to the cabinet at the time.

On Wednesday, June 10, President Reagan stepped into the picture, demanding in no uncertain terms that Israel agree immediately to a cease-fire. The cabinet was convened on short order at four o'clock in the morning. Begin wanted to get his answer out by six. And now, of course, the cat was out of the bag: everyone understood that by acquiescing to Sharon's demands since Sunday not only had they been easing the difficulties of the army's advance as they arose; they had also been expediting the implementation of the grand design – to reach Beirut. A number of ministers were sharply critical of the scope of the operation. Others, and notably among them Yitzhak Berman, Mordechai Zippori and Zevulun Hammer, wanted a full-dress discussion of the aims of the Lebanon war. Their request was turned down on the grounds that the cabinet had urgently to address itself to an answer to the American President. The Prime Minister promised a full-dress discussion at some later date. (It was never to come to pass as there were always more urgent matters on the agenda.) Taking up criticism of the scope and nature of the operation, Sharon vigorously contended that every single move had been dictated by circumstances in the field. He cautioned against a precipitously positive answer to the President and proposed instead that the army be permitted to finish the job. He explained that now that they were in sight of Beirut and the Beirut-Damascus highway, the opportunity should be fully exploited to rid Beirut of the PLO once and for all. Furthermore, he went on, the Syrians would be pushed out of the Beirut area and conditions created which would be conducive to the holding of presidential elections in Lebanon. Bashir Gemayel would be elected president and sign a peace treaty with Israel.

Sharon's description sounded very tempting. The cabinet agreed to postpone the beginning of the cease-fire until noon the following day. The IDF would be allowed to continue its advance north. Alexander Haig was given to understand that it would be most propitious if he himself could reach the Middle East to handle the cease-fire. It would be, so to speak, a feather in his cap. Both Begin and Sharon were of the opinion that Haig's success augured well for Israel. At first, the Secretary of State's answer was positive, but a second message reached Jerusalem from the White House announcing that Haig would not arrive. The cease-fire was arranged for 12 noon on the following day.

Between June 10 at six in the morning and June 11 at midnight, the number of IDF casualties doubled. Forces fighting in the three sectors were ordered to advance as rapidly as possible in the direction of the Syrians. The orders were executed with great difficulty and delays were frequent. A number of commanders expressed skepticism with regard to the wisdom of the orders. They were unsure of their ability to carry them out and felt that they did not accord with the Prime Minister's official pronouncements. There were officers and men who voiced their lack of confidence in both their military and civilian superiors. Such reluctance was inevitable. It was the result of the system of deception perpetrated by the Minister of Defense in collusion with the Chief of Staff and, apparently, the Prime Minister, in pursuit of their real aims: the evacuation of the PLO and the Syrians from Beirut and the engineering of presidential elections in Lebanon. Just as the cabinet was fed with half-truths and partial information at various stages of the campaign, so too was the army. Throughout, commanders were given contradictory, abstruse and ambiguous orders.

At the beginning of the war, certain division commanders received orders designed to create field conditions appropriate to the original "Big Pines" conception. Others, particularly those stationed in the Golan Heights, were not let in on the secret. Commanders of smaller units, of regiments, battalions and platoons, received tactical marching orders every day without being briefed on the larger military aims. Certain officers were later to claim that the smoke screen in which GHQ wrapped the operation increased the number of accidents in the field: units advanced and retreated without having any comprehensive view of the battleground.

The deception lay not only in the fog through which all but the most senior commanders moved but in the tactical orders issued from time to time: they were simply self-contradictory. For example, because GHQ wanted to provoke the Syrians, units received orders to move in the direction of the Syrians, to refrain from fighting and to answer fire. What resulted, in fact, were some of the bloodiest and most extensive battles of the war.

When the cease-fire was announced at noon on Friday, June 11, troops at the front received the information. Nonetheless, in practice, heavy fire and artillery exchanges continued. After the cease-fire had come into effect, certain units received orders to reopen fire on the grounds that the Syrians and the terrorists had breached it in other sectors. When men from different units met later, it turned out that this too had been a trumped-up story: the cease-fire had been breached at the initiative of GHQ. Units at one part of the front were told that other units, out of their field of vision, were being fired on, and the ploy was used at regular intervals. The distrust that emerged in the field mirrored the spurious relations between the various levels of command in the Lebanon war and were a direct outcome of Sharon's efforts to mask the real aims of the war.

From the very beginning, there had been no national consensus on the war. For months preceding the invasion, all the party leaders knew, as did members of the settlements in the north, that a major operation was under consideration to eliminate the PLO in Lebanon. One reason for the scope of the operation given by the Chief of Staff at a cabinet meeting was to keep the army in trim. It was reasons like this which made the public so wary of the whole idea. The war began following an attack on the ambassador in London. From that point on, there was a concatenation of events which aroused suspicion that the government, or perhaps the army, under Sharon, had simply been waiting for an auspicious moment in which to launch their carefully worked-out attack on the PLO and Syrians in Lebanon. Among the general public which questioned the wisdom of the operation were reserve officers and men who were being called upon to put their lives on the line. The feelings of dissatisfaction with the government grew as the situation developed and changed. During the first few days, most people kept their reservations in check under the impact of the terrorist shelling of the Galilee and the rapid advance of the IDF up the Lebanese coast, forcing the PLO back. But once the momentum slackened and the fighting became more and more drawn out, criticism could be heard, and the criticism acquired a momentum of its own: both soldiers and civilians began to feel that they were being had, that official explanations and battle reports did not quite jibe with reality. Among the soldiers were people who were not ready to accept either the subterfuge or, for that matter, the purposes of the war which were becoming more and more evident as the first week of fighting drew to a close. They

didn't want to see the army – and through it the entire country –
dragged into the internal intrigues of Lebanese politics. They
didn't want to see the army involved in the election of Bashir
Gemayel as president.

That this was, indeed, the real purpose of the war became
clear to everyone two hours after the cease-fire came into effect
on June 11. Fighting was renewed and was especially fierce in
the Beirut area. On Friday night and Saturday, IDF armored
forces increased pressure on the southern outskirts of the capital
and advanced in the direction of the presidential palace in
Ba'abda. The Israel offensive continued on the following day,
Sunday, June 13, and ended with the cordoning off of the
palace. On the eastern front, the cease-fire had already been
more or less observed for two days. At the weekly meeting of
the cabinet that Sunday, Sharon was asked to explain the reason
for the continued fighting since Friday, after the cease-fire was
to have become effective. He replied that the reason was
continued fire on the part of the terrorists. He was also asked
why the air force was brought in to bomb targets in Beirut, to
which he replied that the exigencies of battle required it. The
Minister of Defense assured the ministers that the air force
aimed its strikes only at "terrorist concentrations" in the
Lebanese capital. Sharon's explanations were not quite accurate,
as the cabinet shortly learned. What he described as an IDF
response to terrorist breaches of the cease-fire was, in fact, the
final push to join up with Phalange units in the eastern part of
the city and surround the presidential palace. Again the cabinet
had been presented with a fait accompli: contrary to the
impression left on them by Sharon who had said more than once
that it was part of IDF tradition never to enter an Arab capital,
army units were then being directed to the eastern part of the
city.

On Tuesday, June 15, Prime Minister Menahem Begin left for
Washington for talks with President Reagan and Secretary of
State Haig on the situation in Lebanon. His place was taken by
his deputy, Simha Ehrlich, whose military erudition was even
more infinitesimal than Begin's. On Tuesday, June 22, after a
week of sporadic shooting, Sharon telephoned to Ehrlich from

the northern front and informed him that the terrorists and the Syrians were attacking IDF positions. He proposed that certain steps be taken to repulse the attack. Ehrlich, naturally, agreed. Army units were then given a series of orders, "in installments," so to speak, whose full measure could only be gauged in retrospect: the IDF took control of the Behamdoun-Aley stretch of the Beirut-Damascus highway. From the very first days of the war, the Minister of Defense and the Chief of Staff had intended the army to occupy this area, but because of the stiff resistance put up by the Syrians, they were not able to. Now, under the guise of responding to infractions of the cease-fire, Israeli troops were at last able to capture the position. Their advance was not easy, however, and the operation took until Friday, June 25. So, there was Begin in the United States assuring President Reagan that Israel was observing the cease-fire, and assuring the leaders of American Jewry that the only thing the government wanted was "to bring our boys home." (Of course, he added, they had to understand that as long as there was danger to our troops and to the northern settlements, we would remain in Lebanon.) And all the while, IDF units were pushing their way north to complete the occupation of the Behamdoun-Aley area. This operation had never been sanctioned by the cabinet.

During the four days of fighting for control of the Beirut-Damascus highway, cabinet ministers were not informed of the extent of Israeli losses. This had been true of previous stages in the war as well: Sharon had never provided more than partial information. Just as members of the government had no idea what the cost in life had been from Israeli bombings of the Lebanese coastal towns, they had no idea what the cost to the IDF had been in dead and wounded from the various "green lights" they had given to Sharon. The public was also being kept in the dark: three days after the beginning of the war, Menahem Begin announced in the Knesset that there had been 25 casualties, and that was that until June 14, a week later, when the Chief of Staff announced that so far there were 170 dead and 700 wounded. Three days later, lightening struck again: Gen. Moshe Nativ, head of Manpower at the General Staff, listed 214 dead and 1114 wounded. Between the announcements on June

14 and June 17, there had been relative quiet in Lebanon and it was difficult to attribute the casualty figure to those three days alone. Thus, even in this particularly sensitive area, furtive methods were employed. It was part of the overall deception which characterized the war from its very beginning.

The fighting in the Behamdoun-Aley area was directly responsible for the first outbreak of restiveness among the Israeli troops. Some of the soldiers began to feel that they were fighting an unnecessary war whose goals appeared neither clear nor logical. Since no one bothered to explain to them just what the strategic goal of their tactical forays was – tightening the cordon around Beirut by evicting the Syrians from the capital so that Bashir could be elected President – both soldiers and officers began to strain at the leash. Some of them expressed the view that they were being used by Sharon and Eitan. Their disaffection was compounded by the lies being spread by official spokesmen as to what they were doing on the Beirut-Damascus highway in the first place. They knew very well that they had not been "returning fire," but rather carrying out battle orders to shatter Syrian positions – despite the fact that the Syrians had been observing the cease-fire.

The dissatisfaction and frustration which pervaded some of the fighting units found its first outlet in a demonstration which took place on Saturday night, June 26, in Tel Aviv. Some ten thousand people, among them not a few reserve officers and men, protested the war in Lebanon and its conduct. For the first time in the history of the state of Israel, a severe cleavage in the body politic manifested itself while the cannons were still roaring.

Sharon and Eitan were convinced that in order to prevent the Syrians from giving any assistance to the PLO in Beirut, it was necessary to dispatch troops from the western axis to the Beirut-Damascus highway. Sharon had, at first, thought it unnecessary for the IDF to occupy the city as well. This could be left to the Christian Phalanges with an air and artillery assist from the IDF. But when the forces had joined up at Ba'abda, Bashir made it clear to Arik that he didn't see things that way. He had no intention of fulfilling Israel's expectations – not with regard to the Phalangists' occupation of the city nor with regard to a signed peace treaty. A frustrated Ariel Sharon then decided to impose his expectations on the situation: he would make Bashir the ruler of Lebanon and then create conditions which would wear down his resistance to signing a peace treaty with Israel. Cabinet ministers would later explain their submission to all of Sharon's requests by declaring that they were, in fact, in agreement with the conduct of the war in Lebanon as presented to them by Sharon, the Chief of Staff, and the Chief of Intelligence, Yehoshua Saguy. Even Yitzhak Hofi, head of the Mossad, hardly ever voiced any strong objections to the positions of the defense establishment (although a month before the war at a meeting at Begin's home, both Hofi and Saguy were opposed to the implementation of "Big Pines.")

After a week of relative quiet during which Philip Habib tried to reach an agreement with the PLO for their evacuation from Beirut, the IDF began to tighten its grip on western Beirut. Armored units moved towards the refugee camps located east and west of Beirut's international airport, making severe inroads into PLO positions there. The Hai el-Salum quarter was Israel's main target. Cabinet ministers would later claim that Sharon initiated this action without prior authorization. But even this is not the whole story. Sharon actually proposed to the cabinet that the IDF occupy the quarter which was largely Shi'ite. The Shi'ites, he said, were amenable to the idea and would not offer any opposition. When asked if there were terrorists in the quarter he answered in the negative. The Prime Minister supported Sharon's proposal but his deputy, David Levy, asked for a postponement of the vote pending a consultation with Saguy. Saguy appeared the next day in front of the cabinet and was questioned about Hai el-Salum. He pointed out that a PLO unit was guarding the quarter. Sharon appeared unconcerned and claimed that he had not been aware of the fact. Begin became flustered and announced that he was retracting the proposal. All the above notwithstanding, ministers learned a few days later that the IDF was, nonetheless, advancing on Hai el-Salum.

Up until July 22, there was a relative decline in the fighting as

Israel permitted Habib and his aide, Maurice Draper, to continue their efforts to bring about the evacuation of the PLO from Beirut. The cease-fire was sporadically breached in the eastern sector and in the Beirut area, where the IDF was continuing its siege of the western part of the city. Its declared aim was to get the PLO out. Hoping to maintain the cease-fire, the cabinet ordered the IDF to return Syrian and terrorist fire with low ground fire only. Nevertheless, this order was freely translated at the front lines to mean shelling of enemy positions with low artillery fire. The siege of Beirut aroused a good deal of opposition among the troops and among the public at large, much as the war itself did. Again there was a demonstration in the plaza of the Tel Aviv municipality, this time attracting some hundred thousand demonstrators. The Likud called a counter-demonstration and a similar number of supporters turned out.

Between July 22 and 29, the IDF resumed its heavy assault on Beirut: planes, tanks, mortar and artillery densely battered the western part of the city, causing untold destruction. The attack was explained as necessary in order to convince the PLO that Israel was serious about the evacuation of the city, that it would be wiser for them to leave of their own free will than for Israel to force them out, street by street. Just at that time, Bashir Gemayel announced his candidacy for president of Lebanon.

IDF units stationed around Beirut realized that they had not yet finished their work, that they were likely to be ordered to break into the city. There was good reason for this assessment: Arik Sharon was determined to conquer the city and destroy the PLO leadership which had fortified itself inside. The cabinet had rejected his proposals to penetrate western Beirut but he nonetheless continued to bruit them about. The restiveness of the IDF units stationed around the city was growing. It was a direct outcome of the government's original inability to create a firm national consensus. Beginning with the outbreak of war, disagreement became more and more pronounced as the original, declared aim of the war – a forty-kilometer buffer zone – receded into oblivion. And now that the rigged election of Bashir appeared to be taking precedence over the evacuation of the terrorists, this restiveness increased and was compounded by an almost palpable animosity to the government. The Lebanon war did not figure in the minds of the regular army – and certainly not in the minds of the reserves – as a necessary war, designed to protect and assure the wellbeing of the people of Israel. Slowly but surely, as the days wore on, the naked intentions of the military establishment became apparent to all: the forceful intervention in Lebanese politics for the sake, among other things, of a peace treaty with Israel. The cynical political use to which the army was being put, not to mention the lies which were being circulated by official spokesmen as a cover, exerted unbearable moral pressure on some of the soldiers. Two commanders from paratroop brigades which took part in the siege of Beirut and were destined to take part in the ground assault into the heart of the city gave vent to their feelings at a meeting with Sharon: the occupation of the city, they told him, would involve a most terrible bloodletting on both sides without producing any appreciable gain. The commander of an armored brigade, Col. Eli Geva, held a number of conversations with his commanding officer, with the Chief of Staff, with the Minister of Defense, and with the Prime Minister, all for the sake of convincing them to refrain from moving on the city. Geva contended – particularly in his talks with Sharon – that the cost in human life would be very heavy and political gains insignificant. One could not impose Christian rule on all of Lebanon, he believed, by merely occupying Beirut. It would be necessary to secure Christian supremacy over Zahla and Tripoli as well. Moreover, the president-designate, Bashir Gemayel, could be murdered like Abdullah of Jordan or Sadat of Egypt. And not only that, he further contended, in order to carry out Sharon's plan to the end, it would be necessary to get the Syrians out of Lebanon, which would involve us in a bloody war with them. His final assertion was that the occupation of Beirut would inflict tremendous damage on the civilian population of the city. Geva's views led him to refuse to lead his men in the ground assault on Beirut and resulted in the Chief of Staff discharging him from the army altogether. His request to remain in his unit as an ordinary soldier was turned down. Eli Geva was the son of Yosef Geva, one of Sharon's rivals in the fifties: in 1958 Geva had Sharon removed from his position as head of Infantry Training when he discovered that he had lied to him.

At the beginning of August, it seemed likely that the IDF's option of entering the city was about to be realized: armored forces and infantry began moving up from the south and in from the east to the outskirts of the city. This movement was accompanied by an artillery barrage and air raids on the western city. Life for the civilian population was becoming intolerable. The declared purpose of the renewed assault was to pressure the PLO to accede to American mediation and agree to the evacuation of the terrorists from the city. The cabinet was not informed of the renewed assault despite the fact that Begin had promised to convene them in order to determine precisely when such action would be initiated.

On August 10, the cabinet met to discuss Habib's latest proposals for the evacuation of the PLO from Beirut along with the stationing of a multi-national force (American-French-Italian) in the city. The cabinet decided to accept the proposal in principle. They were then under the impression that conditions were now ripe to end the war with a compromise and obviate the necessity of further bloodshed. But that was only their impression: on the same day, the Air Force was ordered to renew bombardment and another brigade of paratroopers was mobilized in preparation for storming the city. Begin would later claim that the order was given without his knowledge. In all events, the bombing continued the next day and on August 12 began again at six in the morning and continued unabated for eleven hours. Wave after wave of bombers darkened the sky all day, wreaking unprecendented destruction on the various quarters of western Beirut. In Jerusalem, the cabinet, utterly astounded by the attack, was frantically convened at noon. Menahem Begin was as angry as everyone else: he had not known about the plans for saturation bombing.

It was at this cabinet meeting that most of ministers gave vent to their anger over Sharon's deceitfulness. They told him point-blank that this was not the first time that they had been presented with a fait accompli. The Minister of Interior, Yosef

Burg, revealed that his son, a reserve paratrooper, had been called up two days earlier. Burg wanted to know who decided to mobilize another brigade and why. A sharp exchange took place between Begin and Sharon, during which Begin reminded his Minister of Defense that he was the government's representative before the army and not the army's spokesman before the government. Sharon was accused of exceeding his authority, of doing things behind Begin's back. Begin told him that he was not a privileged member of the cabinet, that his position was not superior to that of the others. Sharon replied that the the air force had been used only in order to protect Israeli troops. His reply angered some of the cabinet members who saw it as demagoguery: an attempt by Sharon to prove that his concern for the soldiers was greater than theirs.

Sharon explained the day-long bombardment as necessary for two reasons: to protect Israeli troops and to convince the PLO, once and for all, to accede to Habib's evacuation proposal. Among those same troops, however, there was a different assessment of the saturation bombing: it was a prelude to their entry into the besieged city, and was designed to torpedo Habib's efforts. Sharon preferred hand-to-hand fighting with the PLO and the liquidation of their leaders over a settlement which would permit them to evacuate the city. According to this assessment, Sharon attributed highest priority to the physical annihilation of as many terrorists as possible, and, most especially, of the leadership.

Sharon's attitude toward American mediation gave greater credence to the view that his conception was grounded, first and foremost, in exhausting all the military options available to him. From the moment that Philip Habib came into the picture, Sharon tried to thwart him at every turn. He warned that the Americans were preparing a trap just when Jerusalem was issuing statements intended to conciliate Habib. He gave the war its most violent turn just as fragile negotiations with the United States were getting underway. He had done this before. When Begin was in Washington between June 22 and June 24 for talks, the army had received orders to occupy the Behamdoun-Aley area, after which Alexander Haig was relieved of his post as

Secretary of State. Haig had been Israel's best friend in the Reagan administration and through him, Israel had received the go-ahead for its planned operation in Lebanon. Sharon again upset the applecart on July 7 when news about American willingness to dispatch Marines to assist in the PLO evacuation was leaked to the press. The leak was enough to put an end to that particular plan. Again at the beginning of August, when Israel's Foreign Minister, Yitzhak Shamir, was in Washington to meet George Shultz, the new Secretary of State, and get from him a promise to continue American-Israeli understanding over Lebanon, the IDF began to tighten its grip on Beirut. When Israel began its heavy artillery barrage of the city, President Reagan warned Begin that American-Israeli relations would deteriorate if the barrage didn't stop. And a few days before in his talks with Habib, Sharon had positively outraged the American diplomat. During the saturation bombing of Beirut on August 12, President Reagan contacted Begin by telephone twice to warn him of the adverse political effects it would have for Israel and, further, to inform him that because of the merciless air raids, Habib's talks in Beirut had to be stopped. Sharon so incensed members of the cabinet that they decided that the air force could no longer be sent into action without prior authorization by the government or the Prime Minister. At that same meeting, which was being held during the last stages of Habib's mediation efforts, Sharon proposed that the army begin its thrust into the western part of the city. With the exception of Yuval Ne'eman, the entire cabinet was opposed. From that day on, the cease-fire was observed and Habib was able to bring negotiations to a successful conclusion.

The acrimony generated by Sharon's behavior during the entire course of the war was not bottled up in army units or in meetings of the cabinet and the Knesset. It spilled out into the streets and over into the columns of the newspapers. Even regular army officers sent unsigned articles to the papers in which they ventilated their criticism of the conduct of the war and the deception being practiced on the public. The army establishment retaliated in its own way: it stopped delivery of the highly critical morning papers to the front and removed the sections containing opinion articles from the afternoon papers. Arik Sharon, who had invited the press to a front-row seat in his theater of the Yom Kippur War, on the grounds that the public was entitled to know everything, now labeled the press "poison."

But that was not all. Crack units of the IDF complained in writing, both to Sharon and to Begin, about the conduct of the former as Minister of Defense. Groups of reserve soldiers back from the front organized demonstrations, strikes and petitions against Sharon and against his policies. The mobilization of one crack veteran brigade of paratroopers was postponed after its commander came to the conclusion that his men wouldn't show up. The Israeli public generally believed that the war was conducted by Sharon and that he alone was responsible for everything that was happening. And there really was no getting away from the fact that Sharon's personal stamp was felt at every single stage, conceptually and operationally. He worked out strategy and tactics for all the sectors and even personally supervised a number of battles. (In one case, he interfered directly in the command of a battle in the central sector. The incensed commander complained that Sharon was disrupting accepted military procedure.) He was also centrally involved in all political negotiations relevant to the war and its related developments. Thus, despite the fact that he went to great lengths to get official approval from the Prime Minister or the cabinet as a whole for his various strategems, he emerged as the architect of the war, singularly responsible for its achievements and for its disasters. Soldiers and officers were able to distinguish between Arik and the Chief of Staff, Rafael Eitan, who collaborated with Sharon throughout (although there is some evidence that he opposed the idea of a ground assault into western Beirut as he did the attack on the Syrian missle batteries). But Sharon was conceived by the public as the animating force behind the war, its heart and soul. Eitan was merely his lieutenant.

On August 27, Bashir Gemayel was elected President of Lebanon. In this respect, Sharon achieved his original intent. In the days preceding the elections, the IDF guaranteed that they would be held: it provided protection for the members of parliament, kept the roads to the assembly hall open and transported members to their destination. There is no doubt whatsoever that the IDF made a decisive contribution to Bashir's victory.

Less than three weeks later, Bashir Gemayel was fatally injured in an explosion which wrecked Phalange headquarters in Beirut.

Bashir's murder was a severe blow to Arik Sharon and to the senior command: the whole war was based on the assumption that the Phalange leader would stay in power, and now everything had been jeopardized. Arik was well aware of the fact that his entire political future lay in the balance. He decided to try and recreate conditions which would yet reasonably assure the fulfillment of his original war aims. He got in touch with Begin and asked permission to order the IDF to take up positions on certain intersections, separating the two parts of Beirut. This would create a barrier between the warring Lebanese factions. In fact, what he wanted and what it meant was that the IDF would be going into Beirut. Although he later explained that his purpose was to protect the Palestinians from the outraged Phalangists, he was really intent on a show of Israeli strength that would influence the selection of Bashir's successor. The Americans were given misleading information in order to camouflage the extent of Israeli penetration: on Wednesday, September 15, they were told that Israel had taken up positions at a number of strategic points in the city in order to maintain public order. Only a day later did Sharon report to the Americans that the IDF had carried out a broad deployment of troops in the town in order to weed out 2000 terrorists who, according to his information, had remained in Beirut following the PLO's evacuation.

On the day following Bashir's assassination, Sharon gave permission to units of the Christian Phalange to enter the Palestinian refugee camps, Sabra and Shatilla. He did this on his own authority. The ostensible reason for allowing them in was a wipe-up operation against the remaining terrorists. This would save the IDF the trouble of doing it themselves. The Phalangists, rather than weeding out terrorists, embarked on a systematic massacre of the Palestinian refugees in the two camps. Not only were they interested in avenging the death of their beloved leader: they also wanted to rid Lebanon of the Palestinians. Phalange leaders were of the opinion that the massacre in the two camps would result in a mass exodus of Palestinians from all parts of Lebanon. This wishful thinking coincided, oddly enough, with certain ideas which Arik Sharon had frequently expressed, namely, that the Palestinians should be "encouraged" to move into Jordan where they could undermine the rule of King Hussein. The fall of the Hashemite monarch would, accordingly, engender a revolution in Jordan which would bring the Palestinians there to power. Jordan would become a Palestinian state and the Israeli-Palestinian conflict would be at an end.

It didn't work out quite that way. The Phalangists' massacre in Sabra and Shatilla did not herald a mass exodus of Palestinians. It did, however, herald the eruption of an international uproar which astounded Sharon, Begin and the Phalange leaders by its ferocity. During the first few days after the horror was discovered, official Israeli spokesmen ran for cover under a disclaimer: the IDF had no idea that Phalange units were going into the camps. They had apparently sneaked through the ring of Israeli soldiers encircling the camp. But, not long after, because of the pressure of public opinion, the government of Israel appointed a commission of inquiry, headed by Supreme Court President Yitzhak Kahan, whose conclusions were at variance with that version. The Phalange units entered the camps, the commission concluded, with the knowledge, agreement and cooperation of the IDF. Furthermore, Israeli soldiers were in close proximity to the camps while the slaughter was being carried out. The commission went on to say that not only did Sharon and Eitan fail to assess correctly the possible results of their decision to let the Phalangists into the camps, but they also failed to act with the necessary speed when the atrocities became known to them. The commission concluded that despite Sharon's allegations that no one in the defense establishment could have possibly imagined that the Phalangists would behave with such unbridled brutality, he was responsible – indirectly – for what happened. The Chief of Staff was similarly censured as were a number of other high officers. The commission exonerated the Prime Minister and the rest of the cabinet from any sort of involvement in the events.

Just how significant Arik's role was in the conduct of the war in general, including the army's responsibility for the Sabra and Shatilla tragedy, can be gauged from a meeting of senior army officers which took place in October that year. The meeting was organized by the General Staff at the behest of several officers who insisted on discussing the events that led to the massacre. A number of participants were severely critical of the army's conduct while the massacre was going on. Brig.-Gen. Ya'akov Even, the official IDF spokesman, claimed that he was unable to account for the army's conduct simply because he never had accurate information. As an example, he mentioned the fact that he had asked permission from the Chief of Staff to visit the camps, at which point he discovered that the Phalangists had entered from a different direction altogether than that indicated to him by Eitan. He added that this was not the only example. During the entire course of the war he found himself in situations in which the information he was given proved to be erroneous. A number of officers, among them division commanders, admitted that they were stunned by events and did not react quickly enough to stop them. The Chief Medical Officer, Brig.-Gen. Eran Dolev, was particularly bitter in the oral reckoning he made. He called the Minister of Defense a liar and said that you could expect very little from others when the Minister of Defense himself headed the list of liars. Other participants made the same accusation against Sharon.

Four days later the same people were called to another meeting, this time with the participation of Arik Sharon. Arik brought his friend, Gen. (Res.) Yisrael Tal, with him.

Arik opened the meeting by denouncing those who critized him in his absence. He had read their remarks in the minutes. He asked them to speak their hearts openly, but in a dignified manner, commensurate with their military rank. Not all of those present took up the glove. And among those who did, the tone was more conciliatory. But there were a few who didn't mince their words, mainly brigadier-generals. Those with the rank of general were more cautious, and avoided a confrontation with their Minister of Defense. Brig.-Gen. Dov Tamari declared that the massacre did untold harm to Israel and to the IDF and that the IDF had to bear full responsibility for what went on in the area, whether it was in possession of all the facts or not. And since the government was responsible for the army, he continued, both should draw the necessary conclusions. Brig.-Gen. Dolev repeated his accusations, although in more moderate language: in his estimation, Arik was not always truthful. Gen. Tal censured the officers for criticizing their political superiors. As long as they were serving in the army, they had to accept the authority of the government and its ministers. If there were commanders who wanted to voice their criticism, they had first to retire from the service.

Arik took up where Tal left off. He was of the opinion that officers were forbidden to demand the resignation of the Chief of Staff, the Minister of Defense or the government, which is what he understood the demand of Brig.-Gen. Tamari to be. At this point, he referred openly to the demand made for his resignation by Brig.-Gen. Amram Mitzna, commander of the IDF Staff College, in talks with the Chief of Staff and with the Prime Minister. He said: It is unthinkable that an officer demand the resignation of a minister. On the other hand, the reverse is eminently possible. I insist that Amram either withdraw his demand or leave the army.

The officers were rather impressed with Tal's and Sharon's performance. They saw before them a resolute Minister of Defense whose self-confidence had not been even slightly dented by adversity. They were also of the opinion that their army careers would remain in his hands for some time to come. But, beyond that, they accepted in principle the idea that the army must be subordinate to the political level. It was only later that some of them had second thoughts. Tal had chosen to defend Sharon precisely in an area in which Sharon himself had proved to be totally indifferent: in the Yom Kippur War Sharon had conducted negotiations with the Likud while still in uniform;

moreover, he was known to have loaded his talks with his soldiers with heavy political overtones.

The massacre in the refugee camps was the inevitable result of a war which had been conceived in cunning and executed by deceit. The psychological mechanism which had motivated Arik since childhood continued to operate with clockwork efficiency even at the age of fifty-four. Arik continued to manipulate his superior, his colleagues and his subordinates. The government had, ostensibly, been a partner to all of his moves during the war. Yet, in fact, he had fooled them, with regard both to its scope and its aims. He let them see the trees but never the forest. True, their ignorance and indifference proved useful. Even Begin who appeared to share fully Arik's basic aim of destroying the terrorists and their leadership often found himself faced with a fait accompli. This was the case with the mobilization of an additional brigade in anticipation of the breakthrough into Beirut; this was the case with the day-long saturation bombing of the city; this was the case with the entry of the Phalange into the refugee camps. Begin never knew about the plan to surround the presidential palace in Ba'abda with tanks nor was he informed about the extent of Israeli penetration into West Beirut after Bashir's assassination.

In the war in Lebanon, Arik employed the same strategems that he used in Kibia. Just as in 1953 he claimed to have been implementing the plan of the General Staff to cover for the totally unexpected outcome of the raid, so in 1982 he claimed that the government had given him the authority for the Phalangists' action in the camps. In June, the cabinet had decided that it would be desirable for the Phalange units to join in the war. It was to this decision that Sharon referred in September when explaining why he had not consulted with the cabinet about letting them into the camps. That the situation had changed beyond recognition after Bashir's assassination was of little import to him.

Arik's behavior in Lebanon was a repeat performance of his previous behavior – in Kibia, Kalkilyia, at the Mitla, at the northern border in the 1960's and during the Yom Kippur War. He again demonstrated his predilection for excessive violence and for destroying his own creations (militarily speaking). In 1982 Arik Sharon offered incontestable proof that he had neither matured nor mellowed over the years. All the patterns were still recognizable in his plans, his methods, his instincts and passions. They were the same patterns that emerged in every position he had held, from early manhood on. He was not able to control himself, he was not able to keep his passions in check, even as he attained the heights of national responsibility. The international uproar over the horrendous events in Sabra and Shatilla merely fed his paranoia: he was convinced that people had a grudge against him. According to Uri Dan, one of Arik's most loyal stalwarts and his official spokesman at the Ministry of Defense – it was his opinion that Arik's performance in Lebanon could be compared only to that of Judah Maccabee in the history of Israel – Arik really believed that the public outcry over the massacre was a conspiracy against him, born of jealousy.

Thus, in the autumn of 1982, Arik was exposed before the entire world as deceitful, crafty, uncouth, egotistic, and paranoid. It was evident to everyone that he had little use for democracy and its values: he saw the world as a bull ring. Previously, only a few people had been aware of his sick personality – those who had worked closely with him without falling prey to his charms. But now he had turned the whole Middle East into his own private playground. The entire Israeli army was at his disposal, not merely one small unit or one paratroop division. He had never known such power before. He didn't have to plead now with superior officers or prime ministers in order to put his ideas into practice. Now he was the big chief, the supreme commander, and he could maneuver the pieces to his heart's content. His underlying contempt for his fellow ministers and for any semblance of democratic procedure grew as the war wore on, and his success in hoodwinking everyone became more apparent. He could do with the army just as he saw fit. His insensitivity grew. As in the past, he was thoroughly convinced that absolute right resided with him alone and that he, more than anyone else, was able to provide the finest analyses of all situations and the finest solutions to all problems. His planning of tactical military moves was still original and brilliant and his military expertise impressed his government colleagues no end. But now, because of the sheer weight of the force concentrated in his hands, the entire world became privy to its effects. Arik in 1982 was being spurred on by those same impulses that spurred him on in 1952: the war in Lebanon was a raid of the 101st projected onto a giant screen.

At the age of fifty-four, Arik was still battling against the residue of his childhood complexes: he was still unable to come to terms with his environment and with his fellow men. His contact with others could only be mediated through a cabal of groupies. The world around was hostile and had to be treated with hostility. This went for the political scene in Israel as well as for the larger canvas – the Arab world. Both had to be treated roughly, in different degrees. It was the only way he could protect himself. But his defenses could never be airtight, and as he had been penalized in the past for his mistakes, so was he penalized now, and heavily: in the wake of the Kahan Commission, Arik was forced to resign as Minister of Defense. He fumed at the injustice being perpetrated against him. He and Lily were convinced that he was being made a scapegoat. Yet, a nagging thought keeps pushing itself to the surface: perhaps, after all, Arik was still punishing himself, according to a long-familiar but unconscious pattern. Perhaps, after all, Arik simply created circumstances which were sure, in the end, to result in his being hauled over the coals and punished.

The massacre at Sabra and Shatilla could never have taken place were it not for the callousness of the soldiers and officers stationed around the camps. Their callousness was a consequence of the kind of thinking inculcated into the top army brass by the Chief of Staff, Rafael Eitan, during his four years in office prior to the Lebanon war. According to his views, which he voiced frequently in army forums, "a good Arab is a dead Arab." A good soldier, then, is one who kills as many Arabs as possible during battle. Eitan's political outlook – of which he never made a secret – was that Israel must continue to keep the territories it occupied during the Six Day War. Attendant to this was the question of how to get the Arabs to move out of the West Bank and Gaza so that Israel need not concern itself with a worrisome demographic problem. It was a question that intrigued a number of Israelis and not only members of Gush Emunim. It was never discussed in any official forum but it did come up now and again informally. Thus, not long before the war, it came up at a meeting of senior officers in one of the northern divisions. The regional director of the Northern District in the Ministry of Interior, Israel Koenig, had been invited to lecture on current events. The discussion veered around to the practical possibilities of organizing the mass transportation of Arabs from the West Bank to Jordan. It was broken off only when the commander of the division at the time, Brig.-Gen. Amram Mitzna, insisted that the underlying presumption that Arabs could be moved from place to place had no validity. He reminded the assembled that the Camp David accords allowed for the possibility that the West Bank Arabs might take part in the establishment of autonomy there.

The Chief of Staff's conception of the Arab as either a target or a chattel that could be moved at will from one place to another seeped down into the ranks, brutalizing the men. As a result, it was possible for the Phalangists to carry out the massacre without interference. IDF Intelligence received word of the slaughter shortly after it started and passed the information along to the senior command. But neither the IDF nor the defense establishment took any of the necessary steps to halt the bloodbath. They had become callous.

Arik had two important partners in putting "Operation Big Pines" into effect. He had a chief of staff who believed that the maximum physical destruction of the terrorists and their leaders was the best and the only solution to the Palestinian problem as far as Israel was concerned, and he had a prime minster who shared this view. Under the protective custody of their joint acquiescence, Arik was able to manipulate the war as he saw fit. He was further assisted by Begin's military adjutant, an inexperienced lieutenant-colonel by the name of Azriel Nevo. Just a few months before the war, Begin's first military adjutant, Brig.-Gen. Efraim Poran, had resigned. Begin had inherited Poran from the previous Prime Minister, Yitzhak Rabin, and the two got along well together. Poran knew the army well and because of his excellent contacts was able to keep Begin well informed of what was going on. But a short time after Arik Sharon became Minister of Defense, Poran asked to be relieved of his job. It was his feeling that in view of Sharon's belligerent personality and overwhelming drive, there would be little room for him to act effectively in defense matters vis-a-vis the Prime Minister. When Sharon first took over, Poran went out of his way to see that Begin was properly informed. Cabinet members noticed that Begin often called in the Chief of Army Intelligence or the head of the Mossad to supplement Arik's reports. With Poran's resignation, Arik convinced Begin that he didn't need a senior officer as his new adjutant but could do with Poran's deputy, Nevo. Higher officers, he claimed, were needed at their posts. This fact was to cost Begin dearly during the war: his adjutant was ineffectual in Arik's shadow and was never able to shake Begin's belief in the absolute reliability of his defense minister's information. Begin and the rest of the cabinet became totally dependent on Sharon for their view of the situation and Sharon used his position accordingly.

From the very moment that he took over as Minister of Defense, Sharon was indefatigable in bringing "Big Pines" to fruition. From the minute the country's defense was given into his hands, he worked assiduously on the Lebanese issue, streamlining already exisiting plans to attack the PLO. He exhorted everyone in the country – the public, the army, the government – to take up the challenge against the terrorists in the north. In 1976, he had accused three politicians and a thousand bureaucrats of running the entire country. Now, six years later, he proved that one man alone could drag the country into events which would change its future. In 1974, he attended every memorial he could get to for soldiers who fell in the Yom Kippur War. Lily had convinced him that "if you take the boys to war you have to have the courage to face their bereaved parents afterwards." In 1982, he refused to attend the funerals or memorials for those who fell on Lebanese soil. In 1982, everything that Arik had said in years gone by came back to haunt him. In the wake of the Yom Kippur War, for example, he had formulated a "credo" with regard to carrying out "unreasonable" orders:

"When it comes to carrying out orders, a problem comes up: what are the priorities of your obligations? What is your first responsibility? As far I am concerned, my first responsibility is to my country, then to my soldiers, then to my superior officers. I'll say even more: even given that order of priorities, I sometimes debate with myself which comes first, my responsibility to my country or to my soldiers. I have no such problem when it comes to my superiors or my men. If I am given unreasonable orders which may endanger life, my first responsibility is to my men."

Thus Sharon at a press conference in 1974. In August 1985, he had Col. Eli Geva discharged from the army because he was of the opinion that his responsibility for the lives of his men took precedence over what appeared to him to be an unreasonable order (deploying his men for a ground attack into the heart of Beirut).

The war in Lebanon mirrored faithfully both Arik Sharon's personality and his *Weltanschauung*. It was his belief that Israel should use its military power to change the face of the Middle East, extending its "margin of security" to offset any possible negative change in the balance of power between Israel and its neighbors in the future. The destruction of the PLO infrastructure in Lebanon and the creation of a friendly government in Beirut were part of this margin. His appraisal of the situation in the Middle East and the interest of the superpowers in its affairs was shaped by his belief that force determined facts. In distinction to former ministers of defense who considered the IDF, first and foremost, a tool of defense, Arik considered it an instrument of war devised for the purpose of attaining political goals. And he considered himself an instrument of history: he had been endowed with the ability and the responsibility for extending and securing Israel's viability as a nation. To achieve this end, no means were taboo, certainly not misleading a bunch of ninnies who sat in the cabinet with him. Arik believed that the IDF could do anything: it could mortally wound the PLO; it could set up a government in Beirut which would sign a peace treaty with Israel; it could drive the

Syrians out of Lebanon and deter them from starting another war for long years to come; it could insure that Egypt did not interfere or, in case of a breach of the peace, dispatch troops to the Sinai; it could topple King Hussein and establish a Palestinian state in Jordan; and, finally, it could threaten the oilwells of Saudi Arabia should the Saudis decide to make an untoward move. In pursuit of this power fantasy around which Israel's security was to be welded, Arik was capable of doing anything – as he so demonstrably proved in Lebanon.

The war in Lebanon as orchestrated by Ariel Sharon resulted in a cleavage in the country and in the army whose results can not even now be gauged. He turned "Operation Peace for the Galilee" into a long and exhausting war of attrition. And though he succeeded in driving the PLO out of southern Lebanon and out of Beirut, and destroying their military infrastructure in the process, the total balance sheet for Israel was still negative.

The war cost Israel 666 dead and many thousands wounded, some crippled for life. It opened old social wounds and exacerbated ethnic frictions. It highlighted the lack of national consensus on the Palestinian question. It reduced an already shaky economy to shambles. It caused dissension in the higher ranks of the army and discord between the military and civilian authorities. It adversely affected freedom of expression and freedom of the press. It brought about a deterioration in Israel's relations both with the international community and with Diaspora Jewry. Finally, it even aggravated the security situation: both the reserves and the regular army were forced to carry a heavier security burden than before June 1982 and they became sitting targets in Lebanon. The PLO was hurt but not destroyed, and internal tensions in the organization produced a lack of stability and greater extremism in actions against Israel as PLO terrorists slowly filtered back into Lebanon. The danger of a flare-up with Syria increased, and unprecedented Soviet intervention in Syria made the possibility of a superpower confrontation in the Middle East more palpable.

Three years after, the absolute failure of the war was obvious, even from the vantage point of its architects. The IDF was forced to retreat from Lebanon under the pressure of local militias; the internal situation in that country became incontrovertibly worse than it had been; Israel's Christian allies lost their dominant position and were replaced by the Shi'ite Moslems; Syria acquired more clout in Lebanon than it ever had before; the anticipated peace treaty with Israel was shelved without further ado; Israel's deterrent power no longer seemed invincible to the Arabs; the PLO returned to Lebanon; the Shi'ites became Israel's sworn enemy; and Israel's northern border became more vulnerable than it was before the war when, thanks to Philip Habib's mediation, a cease-fire between Israel and the PLO prevailed. In 1982, Arik Sharon took a relatively peaceful country, whose northern border had been quiet for a full year, and plunged it into a maelstrom of death and destruction whose calamitous effects spread to every corner.

Arik wreaked havoc not only on the country but on his party as well. Because of the war in Lebanon, the Likud lost its dominant position in the Knesset after the July 1984 elections, when Shimon Peres of the Alignment became Prime Minister. Yet, the Lebanese fiasco notwithstanding, Arik Sharon once again proved that he is a survivor: he remained a member of the new national unity government set up by the Alignment and the Likud, and if he lost his post as Minister of Defense, he remained a member of the Ministerial Committee for National Security and a member of the inner cabinet. Today, in the second half of 1985, Arik is a major figure in the Herut Party and a rival for its top leadership position. With the situation in Israel as it is, he may yet become the undisputed leader of his party and, consequently, a serious contender for Prime Minister of Israel.

The war in Lebanon erupted a year after Arik took office as Minister of Defense and obliterated everything that he had done in the previous year.

The minute he took over, he set about changing everything that he found in the ministry – policy, methods of work, personnel. His aides were amazed at the singlemindedness with which he decided what he wanted to do and then set about getting it done. His admirers considered it a further demonstration of his unusual abilities; his detractors a futher demonstration of his proclivity for recklessness and oversimplification.

From the word go he was an indefatigable minister of defense. Within a few days of being sworn in, he called a press conference to present his new policy for the occupied territories. His aim, he said, was to create an atmosphere conducive to better relations between the army and the local inhabitants and between Jews and Arabs in general. He declared that there would be no more collective punishment, schools would no longer be combed by soldiers, soldiers and policemen at checkpoints would treat Arabs more humanely during security searches. The Minister of Defense wanted to make it possible to open a dialogue between moderate Arabs and Israelis in order to further the possibility of the establishment of autonomy rule as stipulated in the Camp David accords. He promised these leaders army protection in order to protect them from the threat of reprisals from PLO supporters.

In practice he did just the opposite. He increased arbitrary authority, thus generating ferment and protest. He dismissed the urban political leaders and tried to cultivate an alternate rural leadership. He established a civil administration under Prof. Menahem Milson, an orientalist from the Hebrew University who believed that were it not for the PLO, the large majority of the population of the territories would be prepared to accept a continued Israeli presence. Sharon failed. The rural leaders ready to cooperate with the civil administration were looked upon as quislings. The civil administration itself created political unrest and outbursts of violence. Tensions in the territories reached a new high. The IDF was forced to come down heavy on the local population to quash the protests. And that was the net result of Arik's declared conciliation policy. He armed members of the Milson-inspired Village Leagues who proved hostile to most of the other Palestinian inhabitants. In September 1982, following the massacre in Sabra and Shatilla and the government's initial refusal to appoint a commission of inquiry to investigate the extent of Israel's responsibility, Menahem Milson resigned his job. It was further proof of the hollow ring of Sharon's loudly trumpeted new policy.

In September 1981, a month after taking office, Sharon went on a visit to the United States with Menahem Begin. When he returned, he announced that Washington had agreed to formulate a strategic understanding with Jerusalem. Four months later, following extended discussions between the two countries, it appeared that Sharon's description of the understanding was somewhat unreal: more than it offered operative strategic cooperation between Israel and the United States, it gave Israel a role in America's global anti-Soviet policy. But even this limited agreement went up in smoke a few days after it was ratified: it was pigeonholed as a reaction to Israeli annexation of the Golan Heights. Just how seriously Arik Sharon took this solemn international understanding can be judged by the way he lashed out at the Americans towards the end of 1982, accusing them of trying to sabotage Israel's interests. This was during the negotiations for the evacuation of all outside forces from Lebanon.

While Minister of Agriculture, Arik had insisted that the defense budget could be trimmed and now, as Minister of Defense, he gave orders to cut it by 3 to 5 percent. In retrospect, this positive step proved to be less than a drop in the bucket: its effects were obliterated by the astronomical burden added to the ministry's budget by the war in Lebanon.

Sharon was also determined to reorganize the administrative structure of the Ministry of Defense and his efforts in this direction brought him into headlong collision with ministry employees. For the first time in the history of the state of Israel, employees of the Ministry of Defense went out on strike in protest against their minister's intermural policies. In the end, he was unable to put them into effect. He quarreled with numerous high officials, two of whom – Yosef Maayan, the Director-General of the ministry, and Gabriel Gidor, head of Israel Aircraft Industries resigned. Sharon also inaugurated new, and unofficial, methods of work. He attempted to take over certain responsibilities which in the past had been delegated to high officials. He was suspicious of his subordinates and tried to impress on them that it was up to him to decide everything. He initiated a variety of ventures, spelling them out noisily for the media, and acquired the image of a real go-getting minister of defense. But behind this public persona, he was making a lot of hasty decisions, creating a dither and annoying ministry personnel. He tried to put a friend of his – an Israeli-born American businessman by the name of Aryeh Genger – in charge of arms exports, making him responsible at the the same time for coordinating arms development with the the general staff. Genger was a confidant of Meshulam Riklis, the man who had helped Sharon acquire his hacienda. The appointment caused a storm at the ministry. Sharon was accused of pork-barrel politics, of trying to give Riklis Ministry of Defense business. It was further pointed out to him that one didn't entrust classified information to someone like Genger who didn't even live in Israel. Sharon bristled and denied everything. He wanted Genger in because the ministry needed a breath of fresh air. After an acrimonious fight, he had to retreat – but not before he threatened to "bring the army in" to work in place of the striking ministry employees.

Ariel Sharon was involved in Israel's attempts to renew relations with a number of African countries. He claimed to have been the power behind Zaire's readiness to reestablish diplomatic ties. He was later accused of exaggerating the scope of the business deals he made in Africa. The American administration denied his allegations that they were going to subsidize Israeli aid to Zaire. According to Sharon, Israel had been designated to serve as a bridge between the United States and a number of African countries as part of America's thrust against Soviet expansion on the black continent.

As Minister of Defense, Sharon was very vigorous in evacuating Jewish settlers from the Sinai town of Yamit when the area was returned to Egypt. But up until the day of the evacuation, April 21, 1982, he succeeded in persuading the government to show leniency towards the people who were entrenching themselves in the town in defiance of government orders. He repeatedly rejected attempts to pull them out by force. Sharon's idea was to keep the Egyptians guessing until the last minute: would the Israelis really pull out of Sinai? It was his contention that such conduct would assure Egyptian flexibility on other outstanding issues between the two countries. One of its immediate effects, however, was to delude the Yamit settlers themselves as to the government's intentions. The man who had called Begin at Camp David to congratulate him on his decision to evacuate all of Sinai was now instilling in these settlers the false hope that they might yet remain. Between April 22 and April 25, the IDF evacuated all of the settlers, using a maximum of restraint. Sharon was congratulated by his colleagues on the conduct of the whole episode. No one reminded him of what he had said on October 27, 1974 when asked how he would treat people who settled in places against government directives. He had said:

"The army has to carry out orders but I would never use the army against settlers, because the IDF is the army of the people, of us all."

Members of the cabinet who had privately enjoyed sending Arik out to that rather unpleasant confrontation were surprised when they learned that he had also ordered the total destruction of the city. This decision was in response to a request made to him by Gush Emunim: its purpose was to signify that no Jewish settlement would ever again be relinquished. The destruction of Yamit contradicted a cabinet decision, which Arik had supported, to hand over the city in its entirety to the Egyptians. Negotiations on the issue had been conducted with the Egyptian Foreign Office by two senior officers of the IDF, Gen. Abraham Tamir and Brig.-Gen. Dov Sion.

With his appointment as Minister of Defense, Ariel Sharon became the most prominent minister in the government. Because of his ambition, talent and push, he was soon in control both of Israel's security and its foreign affairs. He gradually appropriated policy areas which had traditionally been the province of the Foreign Minister. He became a key figure in Israel's relations with Egypt just as he had been in Israel's relations with the United States, and he became Begin's confidant. He would try out all of his ideas first on Begin, assuring himself of his support. Only then would he propose them in public or ask the cabinet to ratify them. The aging and ill Prime Minister, whose growing alienation from the conduct of the war had been pointed out by the Kahan Commission, was always impressed by Sharon's assumed deference in his presence. More than once, prior to the war, Sharon had appealed to Begin for assistance, claiming that without his advice he would be unable to solve certain problems. Begin was only too happy to help. He trusted Sharon. One wonders why. Was it because he found the burden of state too heavy and wanted to share it with someone like Arik? Or did he, perhaps, just want a forceful, confident person at his side? Maybe it was the other way around and Arik was, in fact, useful to Begin: in the face of Arik's usually extreme positions, Begin could appear moderate, conciliatory? Or maybe he liked giving him some of the dirty work to do – such as the evacuation of Yamit?

During Sharon's first two years as Minister of Defense, members of the cabinet reconciled themselves to his manipulations as they did to his growing control over various vital areas of public life. Personal weakness combined with a general disinclination to cross swords with Arik Sharon, and as a result they simply gave in to him on most issues. They reaped the bitter fruit of their passivity during the Lebanon war since there is no way that they will ever be able to shake off their collective responsibility for that national catastrophe. When they finally did join forces to compell Begin to cashier Sharon, in the light of the Kahan Commission's recommendations, it was too little, too late, and – as it turned out – too short-lived. Arik remained a member of the cabinet and, after the elections of July 1985, returned to the new cabinet, reinvigorated, as Minister of Commerce and Industry and a full member of all the inner councils of government.

The period following the release of the Kahan Commission's verdict was a difficult one for Arik. The media repeatedly fingered him as responsible for the war and all of its negative ramifications. In political circles he was viewed as dangerous, as a man who threatened democratic procedures, who refused to play according to the rules. Nonetheless, for large parts of the public, he remains an audacious and decisive leader. And within the complex social structure and deteriorating economic situation of Israel in the latter half of 1985, he is able to maintain his position in the front rank of national leaders. Within the Herut Party, he is one of the two or three major contenders for the mantle of leadership which would automatically make him the leader of the Likud as a whole. The Lebanon catastrophe has in no way lessened the possibility that in the foreseeable future he may be a most serious candidate for Prime Minister. Likud supporters, for the most, are ready to accept Sharon's explanation for the debacle: the defeatism of the opposition (the Labor Party and its allies) who "stuck a knife in our backs" (i.e., the backs of the government and the army) while the fighting was still going on; the capriciousness of the American administration; and the senseless military and political decisions which cabinet discipline forced on him, decisions which prevented him from "finishing the job."

His legal battle against the American magazine *Time* gave his public image another boost. In Israel, his failure to win the libel suit was blamed on certain unsurmountable legalistic formalities in the American judicial system and not on any shortcomings in the justice of his case. The renewal of terrorist attacks from Lebanese territory on northern settlements, following Israeli withdrawal, promised him even further popular support. In general, the severe economic crisis compounded by the weakness of the present government tends to make people hanker after "a strong man," someone who can "restore order." Arik Sharon is cut out for the job.

Ariel Sharon reached the summit of national leadership in Israel yet he was finally thwarted by the complex twists of his personality. His immense energy, his indefatigability and his stubborn zeal in seeking high office were always offset by his parallel drive towards destruction, even self-destruction. A planner of battles all his life, he was finally given the chance to design a full-fledged war. Thirty years after he blueprinted the raids of the 101st commando unit, he was able to blueprint Israel's large-scale invasion of Lebanon. And he failed. He failed precisely in his alleged area of competence: war. Over the years, this military architect lost his ability to lead his men in war, to urge them on in battle, to have them keep faith with him. Intoxicated by the enormous power given into his hands, he was unable to curb his passions or restrain his appetite for immediate and impressive results. In the Yom Kippur War, the first cracks showed: some of his officers failed to support his military initiatives. By the time of the Lebanon war, these cracks had broadened: the gap between commander and men had become more manifest. Soldiers in the field refused to follow their supreme commander, the Minister of Defense. Arik Sharon had ruined his own best talent.

Even so, his heart is still set on Israel's top political prize.